Basic Financial Accounting

M W E Glautier, B Underdown and A C Clark

Pitman

Pitman Publishing
128 Long Acre, London WC2E 9AN

A Division of Longman Group UK Limited

© Guardjust Ltd, B Underdown and A C Clark

First published in Great Britain 1985
Reprinted 1988, 1990

British Library Cataloguing in Publication Data
Glautier, M. W. E.
    Basic financial accounting.
    1. Accounting—Problems, exercises, etc.
    I. Title   II. Underdown, B.   III. Clark, A.C.
    657′.48′076   HF5661

ISBN 0–273–02293–8

Printed in England by Clays Ltd, St Ives plc

Contents

Acknowledgements

We express appreciation to C. Hitching, M. H. C. Lunt and R. W. Wallis for constructive comments on this work.

Our sincere thanks also go to the editors and staff of Pitman Publishing Ltd, in particular to Eric Dalton and David Carpenter.

1 The Nature, Scope and Objectives of Financial Accounting

> Traditionally, financial accounting has been concerned with the activities of business enterprises and with recording, classifying and summarising their transactions. The scope of the financial accounting process is limited to business activities finding their expression in monetary terms. The objectives of financial accounting may be said to consist in providing an efficient way of recording and classifying data, and making available to owners and managers information drawn from accounting records useful for making financial decisions. The most important of such decisions are to do with the profitability of business firms and their viability as economic entities.

The appearance of sophisticated methods of processing data has not altered the underlying techniques used by accountants, but rather has facilitated the routine processes applied to the recording of data in data processing systems. Equally, the advent of microcomputers and their use by business managers in a variety of management situations has not altered the principles of sound financial management, but rather has eased the access to data and the analysis of information. Modern technology has served to widen access to accounting data and information flowing through business organisations, making it necessary for many non-accounting specialists to have a sound knowledge of the nature and meaning of the accounting information which they are required to handle in making decisions.

The business enterprise

The study of financial accounting begins with an understanding of the way in which accountants see the business enterprise. As an economic unit, the business enterprise acquires, organises and transforms factors of production in the activity of producing goods and services. This reality may be portrayed as in Fig. 1.1, where it is seen that the input factors conform with the well-known economic classification—land, labour, materials, capital goods. The way in which these input factors are combined and transformed into an output flow of goods and services may be considered as a problem of maximising an output from a given input. In the case of a manufacturing firm, this would amount to an engineering problem. Figure 1.1 shows that

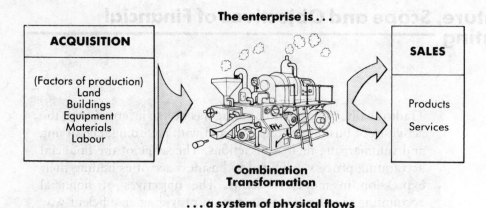

The enterprise is . . .

ACQUISITION

(Factors of production)
Land
Buildings
Equipment
Materials
Labour

SALES

Products

Services

**Combination
Transformation**

. . . a system of physical flows

Fig. 1.1

the input factors are acquired by the firm and lead to a physical output of goods and services.

The accounting interpretation of the business enterprise is an abstraction of the reality portrayed in Fig. 1.1. The business enterprise is viewed as a system of monetary flows, instead of a system of physical flows. In effect, when viewed as a system of monetary flows, it is noted that the output produced by the enterprise leads to an *inflow* of money and that the acquisition by the firm of the factors of production leads to an *outflow* of money. The way in which the enterprise functions as a process of combining and transforming factors of production into an output of goods and services is now seen in an entirely different perspective. The management of the enterprise is judged in terms of maximising the inflow of money from sales for a given outflow of expenditure. The criterion of managerial success ceases to be seen as purely an engineering problem, and is judged to be the size of the profit realised. This profit is the residue left to the firm from sales after the payment of expenses. Figure 1.2 shows that the accounting interpretation of the enterprise is the reverse of that of the engineer. It frequently brings the accountant in conflict with other managers in situations where the sales manager and the engineer may argue for the volume of sales and output and the accountant will be concerned with the profit obtained.

Business activities

Business activities consist of a varied and complex pattern of decisions affecting every sector and every department of the enterprise. They bring the firm into relationship with its business environment when factors of production are acquired and products and services are sold on the market. The accounting interpretation of business activities

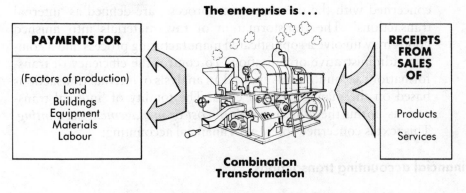

The enterprise is . . .

PAYMENTS FOR		RECEIPTS FROM SALES OF
(Factors of production) Land Buildings Equipment Materials Labour		Products Services

Combination
Transformation

. . . a system of monetary flows

Fig. 1.2

is an abstraction of the complex reality. In accounting, business activities are associated with transactions and, indeed, are limited to transactions. Thus, unless there is a transaction there is no observable business activity.

Accounting is transaction-based. A transaction occurs whenever the firm enters into a legal contract for the acquisition of means of production or the sale of goods and services. In accounting, all business activities are reduced to the perception of transactions as they occur. Business activities which do not lead to transactions remain unrecognised in accounting, and no evidence of such activities is susceptible of being recorded.

Transactions originate the monetary flows with which accounting is concerned. Transactions involving the acquisition of factors of production lead either to an outflow of money immediately, or an obligation to pay money at a later date. Transactions by which the firm sells goods or services lead to an inflow of money or the right to receive money at a future date.

The accounting interpretation of business activities consisting solely of transactions leads to further analysis of these transactions. First, transactions between the firm and its markets—both its supply markets and its selling markets—are defined as 'external transactions'. An external transaction occurs whenever the enterprise obtains any factor of production, be it land, labour, materials, services, and any legal right over corporeal and incorporeal property whatsoever. Equally, an external transaction occurs whenever the firm sells its products, whether as goods or services, or disposes of any legal right which it has previously acquired over any form of property whatsoever. The totality of 'external transactions' forms the subject matter of *financial accounting*. Second, transactions within the firm, consisting of the exchanges which occur between the various departments concerned with the transformation process, are defined as 'internal transactions'. The transformation of raw materials into finished goods may involve a sophisticated manufacturing process and a complex administrative organisation. To control the efficiency of transformation, accounting has evolved an analysis of internal transactions based on the management of costs. The totality of 'internal transactions' forms the subject matter of *cost or management accounting*. This text is concerned solely with financial accounting.

The analysis of financial accounting transactions

The accounting treatment of external transactions involves several phases. First, there must be evidence of a transaction. This occurs usually on the receipt or dispatch of an invoice, cheque or other commercial document instancing an external transaction. The appearance of such a document in the accounting department is the signal which triggers off the accounting process. Second, an inspection of the document yields the information required to be recorded, such as the parties, the monetary value, and the subject matter of the transaction. At this stage, an initial classification of the transaction occurs.

The Classification of Financial Accounting Transactions

1 Purchase Transactions
2 Sale Transactions — Transactions relating to the operating cycle of the business (Short-term analysis)
3 Financing Transactions
4 Investment Transactions — Transactions relating to the business structure (Long-term analysis)

Fig. 1.3

As shown in Fig. 1.3 financial accounting transactions fall into four broad categories. Transactions by which the firm acquires any factor of production which is committed directly to the operations themselves are treated as *purchase transactions*. Such transactions include the purchase of raw materials or goods for resale, the purchase of services, such as labour, insurance, electricity and the payment of rent, local taxes, etc. Transactions through which the firm disposes of its products in the course of trade—goods bought for resale in the case of a trading firm, goods manufactured out of raw materials in the case of an industrial firm, or services in the case of a service business, such as a transport company or a professional firm—are defined as *sale transactions*. It is important to note that the transactions treated in this analysis as purchase or sale transactions have a restricted meaning in accounting. They include only purchase or sale in the ordinary course of business: they do not include purchase or sale transactions relating to the firm's asset structure. Thus, where a company purchases a vehicle for use in the business, that purchase would be classified as an '*investment transaction*'. Equally, if the company decided to dispose of such a vehicle, the sale would not be classified as a sale transaction, but as realisation of an investment. It follows that whenever a firm acquires assets, such a transaction is classified as an '*investment transaction*'.

The accounting classification of expenditure, either as an acquisition of an asset or as a current expense, involves an accounting decision as to the end-use intended. If the thing that is purchased is to be resold or used in the ordinary course of business, it is called a revenue transaction. If not, it will be treated as an investment transaction. This classification hinges, therefore, on the decision underlying the transaction. If a motor dealing company purchases a vehicle, that transaction—on the face of it—may properly be treated as a revenue transaction. However, a purchase of a vehicle by a transport company would be treated as an investment transaction.

The last category of transactions is the 'financing transaction'. The enterprise requires finance in order to carry out its objectives. These objectives relate not only to the creation of an adequate business structure, but also to the carrying out of operations. Both have to be financed. Transactions by means of which a business acquires finance or funds are treated as '*financing transactions*'. They include transactions by which the firm obtains capital, loans or credit.

Bookkeeping: the record of financial accounting transactions

Once the evidence of transactions has been recognised and classified into the four broad categories mentioned above, the essential data is recorded in permanence in the bookkeeping system. As noted earlier, the essential data consists of the names of the persons or companies with whom the enterprise has transacted, the sum involved, the date of the transaction and the nature of the things transacted. When required to be used as information, the recorded data is consulted and an appropriate selection is made which will meet the needs of the user of that information.

Since the life of the firm is manifested in an on-going series of activities appearing as transactions, it is clear that the process of bookkeeping is an on-going accounting activity. One important responsibility of the accountant is to ensure that the books are properly kept. There is a legal obligation on companies and business firms to keep proper books of accounts. The books or accounts of an enterprise will involve, in some cases, complex operations, and a computerised technology. This will be true in the case of large companies operating in different countries.

The importance of the books or accounts lies not only in being the repository of the data relating to all the firm's transactions, but also as prima facie evidence of the rights and obligations incumbent on the enterprise. This means, for example, that if a sum is shown in the books as being owed to or owed by the enterprise, this information will be treated as correct unless it is subsequently proved untrue. Likewise, if property is recorded as having been acquired, it will be assumed that it has remained in the ownership and possession of the firm.

Whilst the books or accounts have an importance in themselves, it is as a source of data prepared as information for different classes of persons that their importance is of particular significance. In this connection, it is interesting to note that there are two different aspects of the study of financial accounting. First, there is the study of the technique of bookkeeping, which is the practice of accounting with regard to keeping accounting records. Second, there is the analysis of the problems of financial reporting, which is concerned with the way in which the data recorded in the books may be used to meet the information need of users.

The objectives of financial accounting

The accounting classification of transactions forms part of a fundamental objective of segregating business activities related to the long-term structure of the firm, as distinct from the short-term analysis of its operations. In effect, this classification reflects a concern with two major interests in financial accounting. The first is addressed to the analysis of the profitability of the business. To this end, it is a firmly established accounting concept to make periodic measurements of profit. This is effected normally on a yearly basis by comparing the sale and the purchase transactions and establishing the difference, which is either a profit or a loss for the year. A profit will be shown when sale transactions are greater than purchase transactions during the year: a loss will be shown in the reverse case.

In financial accounting, the operating cycle is conventionally treated as a period of one year. This suggests that the profit or loss is a short-term analysis of business activities. Figure 1.3 shows that not only do purchase and sale transactions fall into this time period analysis, but that there are also financing transactions which relate to the operating cycle. Those financing transactions leading to an obligation to repay within a period of twelve months are treated as current liabilities. Creditors for goods supplied constitute a significant proportion of short-term business financing.

Figure 1.3 also shows that investment transactions fall into the long-term accounting analysis of transactions. The accounting convention in this regard is to treat as long-term any transaction which will have an impact on the firm lasting more than one year.

The second major interest in financial accounting, therefore, is directed to the analysis of those transactions having a long-term impact on the firm. These transactions include, on the one hand, investment transactions by which the firm acquires assets of potential use for more than one *accounting period*, as the operating cycle is more usually known. They include, on the other hand, financing transactions by which the firm obtains funds for use for more than one year. Financial accounting brings together investment and financing transactions in a statement of the financial status, or structure, of the enterprise which is commonly known as the balance sheet.

Therefore, the classification of transactions into four broad categories, which are subsequently reclassified as between short-term and long-term, serves to meet two important financial accounting objectives. These are the measurement of profit, and the assessment of the financial status of the business. The former is effected by means of a yearly statement of profit or loss, known as the profit and loss account; the latter is portrayed in a description of the assets and liabilities of the business at the end of each accounting period (which coincides with the last day covered by the profit and loss account). The balance sheet, therefore, not only gives an indication of the financial status of the business in terms of the investment transactions resulting in the acquisition of assets, but also an explanation of how that particular business structure has been financed by a set of financing transactions.

Clearly, the profitability of a business will depend, partly at least, on the assets which it has at its disposal. Equally, its financial status will depend on the financial obligations which it has to bear and on its ability to meet such obligations. The broad classification of transactions used in financial accounting serves also to explain the interrelationship between the business structure and business operations. Figure 1.4 depicts the way transactions are related in this analysis.

The two most important financial accounting reports, namely the profit and loss account and the balance sheet, have always had the objective of providing information periodically to the owners of the business concerning its profitability and financial status, allowing the owners to take appropriate decisons in the light of these results. Of recent years, a wider group of persons is seen as having an interest

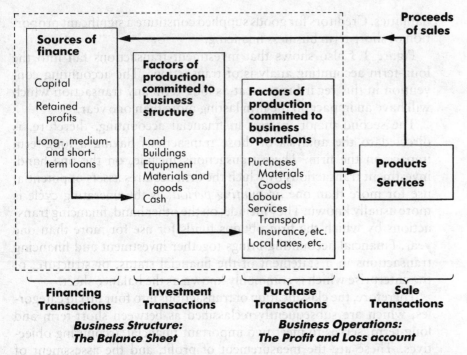

Fig. 1.4 The interrelationship of transactions: business structure and operations

in business enterprises, and the discussion of the objectives of financial accounting has been conducted in terms of the information needs of such users.

Users of accounting information and their needs

The list of persons defined as users of accounting information produced by the enterprise consists primarily of those persons involved directly or indirectly in its activities. Whereas the practice of accounting treats the owners as the most important persons, legislation and the practice of business itself has modified this situation. In effect, in addition to the owners (in the case of a company, the shareholders), creditors, management, employees, trade unions, the State, the clients and the local community in which enterprise activity is located are regarded as users and potential users of accounting information.

The problem of deciding what accounting information should be produced as compared to what is being produced leads to a discussion of what decisions are involved by the various parties mentioned above. These decisions relate to their special interests in the business, which may be defined as follows:

Persons	Interest in the business
Owners/Shareholders:	Value of the capital invested
	Income earned by the invested capital

Creditors/Lenders:	The duration of credit and the ability of the business to repay both the credit received and the interest thereon
Management:	Evaluation of previous management decisions Making management decisions for the future
Employees:	The ability of the firm to provide continuing employment The negotiation of improved wages and conditions
Trade unions:	Wage negotiations and improved conditions for members
State:	Tax to be paid on profits Output contribution to the economy Employment level
Clients:	The quality, price and conditions of supply Factors affecting future supplies
Local community:	The contributions made by the enterprise to community welfare, and the costs, if any, borne by the locality as a result of activities (pollution, etc.)

The list shown above is by no means exhaustive, but serves as a guide to the type of questions with which different groups of persons are concerned. In several instances, there is an evident conflict between the interests of these groups. For example, the income of the owners will be reduced by the sums paid out in taxes and in better wages. Management is interested in keeping all costs down, including wages, to secure higher profits, thereby showing better results.

In effect, accounting information reaches different groups in different ways and to a different extent. Management and the State have easier access than employees and shareholders to certain types of data. The concern of financial accounting, however, is to produce *general financial reports* periodically for use by all the persons listed above. In making generalised accounting information public in this way, the stock market, financial analysts and the public at large obtain knowledge about the activities of business firms operating as public companies. A large sector of total activity remains in the hands of private individuals, and little accounting information reaches the public from this sector.

The nature of financial reports

Financial accounting reports are based upon the data recorded in the bookkeeping system. They are produced periodically and, in the case of companies, such reports have to comply with the requirements of the Companies Acts. In this text, attention will be focused on the preparation and contents of the following three financial reports:

The profit and loss account.
The balance sheet.
The source and application of funds statement.

The profit and loss account has the purpose of establishing the profitability of the business during the period covered by this report. The balance sheet and the source and application of funds statement are reports concerned with the business structure and the manner in which it has been financed. In all three cases, these reports are historical in the sense that they relate to a period of activity which has ended. The balance sheet is drawn up at the last day of the period covered by the profit and loss account, and sets out the business structure taking into consideration the result of the activities of the period just ended. Nonetheless, the balance sheet reflects the evolution of the business structure and its financement over the entire period of time during which the business has existed. The source and application of funds statement is also a financial report concerned with explanations of the business structure and its financing. However, it deals only with the changes which have occurred during the accounting period. In this sense, it explains how the size and elements constituting the structure and its financement have changed between two points in time. These two points in time are the dates of two successive balances sheets. Figure 1.5 shows the relationship between the three financial reports. The Greek letter Δ indicates change.

Questions

1. Explain the abstractions which the accountant makes when interpreting the activities of the business enterprise.

2. What do you understand by the term 'financial accounting transactions'?

3. Discuss the manner in which the accounting classification of financial accounting transactions helps in providing accounting information to users.

4. Define the objectives of financial accounting.

5. Who are the users of financial accounting information? Do they need the same type of financial accounting information?

6. What is a balance sheet, a profit and loss account, and a source and application of funds statement? How are these financial accounting reports related to each other?

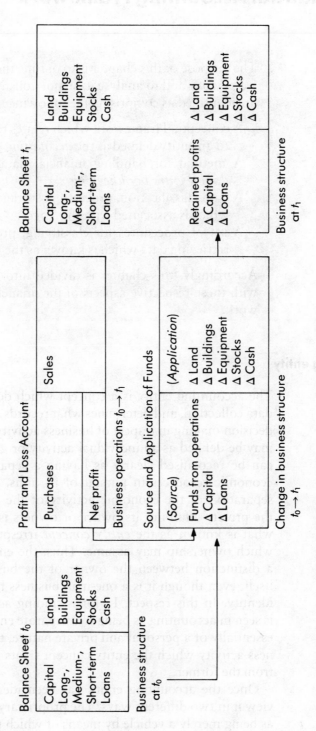

Fig. 1.5 Balance sheet, profit and loss account and source and application of funds

2 The Financial Accounting Framework ⎯⎯⎯⎯⎯⎯⎯

The purpose of this chapter is to outline the financial accounting framework and to analyse its major constituent elements. These are identified as comprising the following:

A conceptual framework which relates the accounting process to an entity defined as the *accounting entity*.

A method for handling financial data which is known as *double entry bookkeeping*.

A data classification, processing, storage and retrieval system which is associated with the *ledger*.

A set of procedures for classifying, processing, storing and retrieving data which is known as the *bookkeeping system*.

Accordingly, this chapter is divided into four sections dealing with these respective aspects of the financial accounting framework.

The accounting entity

The accounting entity is a concept which defines the boundaries of data collection, and determines what records are relevant to informed decision making in respect of business activity. The accounting entity may be defined as an individual activity or group of activities which can be recognised clearly as having a separate identity and using economic resources in pursuit of its aims. The recognition of the separation of the economic activity of the accounting entity from the private affairs of its owner or owners is an essential feature of what is known as the *entity concept* irrespective of the legal form which ownership may assume. Thus, the entity concept establishes a distinction between the owner of the business and the business itself, even though it is a one-man business having no separate legal identity. In this respect, L. Jones trading as L. Jones, Greengrocer is seen in accounting as being two separate entities—the former being essentially of a personal and private nature, the latter being the business activity which the entity concept treats as distinct and separate from the former.

Once the accounting entity has been identified, it is possible to view it in two different ways. The proprietary theory views the entity as being merely a vehicle by means of which the owner or proprietor derives income. By contrast, the entity theory views the entity as having its own objectives and interprets the status of the legal owners as similar to that of other external claimants. Due to its distinct legal status, the joint stock company appears to afford the most realistic example of a form of enterprise which reflects the entity theory. This chapter begins with an examination of the business activities of a sole trader, the typical small business which is usually both owned and managed by a single proprietor. Consequently, the approach adopted initially in this chapter will reflect the proprietary theory of the accounting entity.

Bookkeeping and the dual aspect

The double-entry bookkeeping system has been in existence for some 700 years and its survival has been due to its ability to fulfil certain functions. These functions include keeping an accurate record of indebtedness between the entity and other parties, providing an analysis of expenditure and measuring income. The first two of these functions are examined in this chapter. In this regard, the purpose of this analysis is to explain the manner in which accounting numbers are derived and aggregated as well as the bookkeeping techniques involved in the manipulation of these numbers.

Double-entry bookkeeping is associated with a standardised set of procedures for recording and explaining basic accounting data. The procedures make use of a specially designed form of stationery. Exhibit 1 below represents an 'account', which is a typical format used to record transactions and to provide at the same time the essential data which explain the circumstances surrounding such transactions.

Dr (1)								(2) Cr	
			Name of account						
Date	Details	Folio	£	p	Date	Details	Folio	£	p
	(3)	(4)							

EXHIBIT 1   *Traditional form of accounting stationery*

Notes

(1) *Dr* is notation for *debit*. By convention this indicates the left-hand side of an account.

(2) *Cr* is notation for *credit*. By convention this indicates the right-hand side of an account.

Both these terms are Latin in origin but the abbreviated forms of *Dr* and *Cr* are now merely notation. These terms are used as verbs, nouns and adjectives. Essentially, the term 'debit' indicates an inflow of money value *to* an account and the term 'credit' indicates an outflow of money value *from* an account. The meanings of these terms are different, therefore, from those associated with their use in everyday language.

(3) Each side of an account has space to provide details of the origin and destination of the flow of money value recorded. In the case of a debit entry, the details given would be the name of the account *from which* the flow of money value originated. In the case of a credit entry, the details given would be the name of the account *to which* the flow of money value has gone. The practice has now been abandoned of prefacing a debit entry by the word *To* and a credit entry by the word *By*.

(4) The reference or 'folio' column is used to indicate the corresponding accounting entry in the ledger.

The double-entry technique of recording financial transactions reflects a fundamental accounting principle which equates the resources held by an enterprise with the claims against an enterprise in respect of these resources. The nature of this basic accounting equation is explained in the following example.

Example 1

Varlberg commits his personal savings of £10,000 to starting his own business as a painter and decorator. He transfers this sum to the business's bank account. In accordance with the accounting entity convention, the financial position of the business may be expressed as follows (Exhibit 2):

Assets		Claims against the business
(Bank £10,000)	=	(Owner's claim £10,000)

EXHIBIT 2

The owner's claim against the business is more usually referred to as his *capital* whilst other external claims are referred to as *liabilities*. Exhibit 2 is really a balance sheet or position statement.

Suppose now that Varlberg purchases a van for £4,500 and equipment such as ladders, trestles, brushes, etc., for £750. The basic accounting equation would be redrafted (Exhibit 3) to read:

Assets		Claims against the business
(Van £4,500 + Equipment £750 + Bank £4,750)	=	(Capital £10,000)

EXHIBIT 3

It may be noted that the distribution of the assets has changed without disturbing the basic equation. The changes which have occurred are as follows (Exhibit 3A):

Van	Equipment	Bank
+£4,500	+£750	−£5,250

EXHIBIT 3A

If Varlberg now purchases from suppliers a quantity of paints and paper costing £500 which he intends to use as his stock-in-trade on terms which allow him to make payment for them at the end of the month following that of purchase, the basic equation before payment becomes (Exhibit 4):

Van	+	Equipment	+	Stock	+	Bank	=	Capital	+	Liabilities
£4,500	+	£750	+	£500	+	£4,750	=	£10,000	+	£500

EXHIBIT 4

It can be seen that the accounting equation is maintained by an addition to assets (+ stock) and an addition to liabilities (+ creditor) and that the subsequent payment will maintain the equation by a deduction from assets (minus bank) and a deduction from liabilities (minus creditor). The ultimate effects of transactions are summarised below in Exhibit 5:

Summary of Changes that Maintain the Accounting Equation

1. Additions and deductions of equal amounts to assets
2. Additions and deductions of equal amounts to capital or liabilities
3. Additions to assets and additions of equal amounts to capital or liabilities
4. Deductions from assets and deductions of equal amounts from capital or liabilities

EXHIBIT 5

Question 1

Fill in the missing figures for (a), (b) and (c) below.

Assets	=	Capital	+	Liabilities
£		£		£
4,500	=	(a)...	+	2,300
(b)...	=	6,514	+	8,342
24,375	=	16,397	+	(c)...

Question 2   A series of transactions from (a) to (l) is listed below. Place a tick in *one* of the columns 1, 2, 3 or 4 which are based on Exhibit 5 above. Thus, transaction (a) results in an addition of £5,000 to assets (+ bank £5,000) and an addition of £5,000 to capital (+ capital £5,000). A tick should be placed in column 3, and the net increase in the totals of the accounting equation is £5,000.

Note: The transactions are not necessarily connected in any way.

(a) Capital introduced in the form of cash £5,000.
(b) Purchase of vehicle for £2,600 on credit to be paid in full in two months' time.
(c) Paid £2,400 for a lathe for use in the business.
(d) Business obtains a bank loan of £12,000.
(e) Withdrawal of cash £1,000 by the owner for private use.
(f) Payment of bill from creditor for goods £175.
(g) Owner repays business loan out of his private bank account £3,000.
(h) Owner takes trading goods out of business for his own use £120.
(i) Business receives £1,000 from debtor who previously bought some goods on credit.
(j) Business receives £10,000 from insurance company in respect of warehouse burnt down.
(k) Business buys £392 worth of goods intended for resale on credit.
(l) Owner brings his own car valued at £2,300 into business for business use.

Transaction	1	2	3	4	Change in totals of accounting equation
a					Net increase £5,000
b					
c					
d					
e					
f					
g					
h					
i					
j					
k					
l					

The double-entry system of bookkeeping reflects changes in the accounting equation automatically through the procedures on which entries are made in accounts. For example, the data given in Exhibit 4 would be entered as follows:

Example 2

Bank account					Capital account	
£		£				£
(3) Capital 10,000		(1) Van	4,500		(3) Bank	10,000
		(1) Equipment	750			

Van account			Equipment account	
£			£	
(1) Bank	4,500		(1) Bank	750

Purchases account			Supplier account	
£				£
(3) Supplier	500		(3) Goods	500

Notes

(1) The number prefacing each entry categorises the nature of the changes to the accounting equation associated with each transaction. Thus, the purchase of the van for £4,500 is a class 1 transaction, for this transaction results in an addition of £4,500 to assets (+ Van account) and a deduction of £4,500 from assets (− Bank account).

(2) By convention, the term 'purchases' in bookkeeping is restricted to purchase transactions involving stock. It is not used to describe the acquisition of assets such as plant, equipment, motor vehicles, etc. which are capital transactions.

(3) The effect of analysing each transaction as consisting of a *debit* entry reflecting a flow of money value *to* an account as well as a *credit* entry reflecting a flow of money value *from* an account is to maintain the accounting equation. Example 2 shows the dual aspect of each transaction which consists of a flow of money value from one account to another account. It will be seen later that the double-entry bookkeeping system can handle more complex entries involving more than two accounts.

The foregoing examples illustrate the application of the accounting equation to such transactions as the introduction of capital and the acquisition of assets. These transactions create claims against the business in respect of the assets acquired. The accounting equation applies equally to the treatment of revenue and expenses.

Example 3

Consider now the transactions set out below for S. A. Nary who is just starting business as a fishmonger. All transactions relate to July.

July	1	Opened a business bank account and paid in £6,000.
	1	Paid rent for month of £100 by cheque.
	1	Purchased fittings for £1,200 by cheque.
	1	Paid for refrigerators £700 by cheque.
	2	Purchased motor van £2,000 paid by cheque.
	2	Paid for motor insurance £55 by cheque.
	2	Paid for licence for van £40 by cheque.
	3	Obtained £800 of fish and canned goods from J. Eulie on credit of seven days.
	4	Cash sales £643.
	5	Paid for cleaning—cash £3.
	6	Banked £600.

These transactions would be recorded as follows:

Bank account

	£		£
Capital	6,000	Rent	100
Cash	600	Fittings	1,200
		Refrigerator	700
		Motor	55
		Expenses	40
		Van	2,000
		Bal. c/d	2,505
	6,600		6,600
Bal. b/d	2,505		

Capital account

			£
		Bank	6,000

Fittings account

	£		
Bank	1,200		

Refrigerator account

	£		
Bank	700		

Rent account

	£		
Bank	100		

Motor Van account

	£		
Bank	2,000		

Motor Expenses account

	£		
Bank	55		
Bank	40		

Sales account

			£
		Cash	643

Purchases account

	£		
J. Eulie	800		

J. Eulie account

			£
		Purchases	800

Cash account

	£		£
Sales	643	Cleaning	3
		Bank	600
		Bal. c/d	40
	643		643
Bal. b/d	40		

Cleaning account

	£		
Cash	3		

Note: Individual transaction dates have been ignored but in practice these would be recorded as would the references for the opposite account of the double entry.

An important stage in the process of aggregating accounting numbers is to prepare a *trial balance*. This is merely a listing of the balances on *all* the accounts. Nothing is written in the various accounts during the process of extracting a trial balance.

The trial balance is a test of the accuracy of the bookkeeping process. It reflects the accounting equation and the principle that the sum of the debit entries should equal the sum of the credit entries. Accordingly, if the trial balance does not balance, this will be conclusive evidence of error in the bookkeeping process or in the associated arithmetic.

The following trial balance is dated 5 July and summarises the entries on the accounts of S. A. Nary up to that date.

Trial balance as at 5 July		
	Debit £	Credit £
Bank account	2,505	
Capital S. A. Nary		6,000
Fittings	1,200	
Refrigerator	700	
Rent	100	
Motor van	2,000	
Motor expenses	95	
Sales		643
Purchases	800	
J. Eulie		800
Cash	40	
Cleaning	3	
	7,443	7,443

Question 3

(a) The transactions for the second week of trading by S. A. Nary are given below. Using the balances on the various accounts shown in Example 3 above, complete these accounts for the second week of trading.

Transaction number

1	July	7	Purchased fish from market by cheque £185
2		7	Cash sales £210
3		8	Paid cash for petrol, etc., £8
4		8	Purchased fish from market; paid cash £150
5		8	Cash sales £192
6		9	Purchases made from market; paid cash £195
7		9	Paid J. Eulie by cheque £800
8		9	Cash sales £172
9		10	Paid cleaning £3 cash
10		10	Purchased fish from market; paid cash £200

11	10	Cash sales £274
12	10	Purchased selection of frozen foods from Hermos Ltd on credit—payable end of August £640
13	10	Paid for electricity by cheque £14
14	10	Paid salary for week £25
15	10	Banked £150 cash

(b) Prepare a trial balance after all the entries have been made. (The transactions have been numbered to aid identification in the bookkeeping process.)

The ledger

All these transactions can be recorded in one book, but owing to the large volume of transactions, certain accounts are kept in separate books of their own although remaining part of one notional ledger. An illustration of such a separation is set out in Fig. 2.1.

Fig. 2.1 Separation of types of accounts from general ledger into functional ledgers

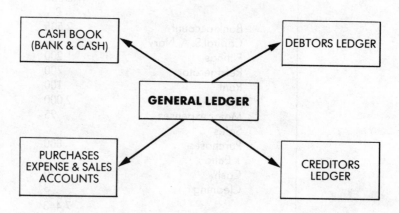

Question 4

(a) Write up the appropriate ledger accounts for the following entries which relate to the business of Sam Barker who owns a do-it-yourself store.

(1) Opening balance at bank £5,321.
(2) Sold goods to J. Green for £65, allowed one month to pay.
(3) Purchased goods from the Timber Supply Co. Ltd for £974 on usual trade terms (net monthly).
(4) Drew cash from bank £142 for wages.
(5) Sold goods for cash £74.
(6) Returned some goods to Timber Supply Co. Ltd as poor quality valued at £38.
(7) Sold goods on credit to Ace Hotel Co. Ltd £350.
(8) J. Green paid £25 on account—cash.
(9) Sold goods for cash £214.
(10) Paid cheque for repairs to shop £27.
(11) Sold goods for cash £118.

(12) Banked £250 cash.
(13) Paid cheque £2,000 for sawing equipment.
(14) Sold goods to SBS (Decorators) Ltd £110 on credit terms.
(15) Paid delivery expenses on goods to SBS (Decorators) Ltd cash £14.
(16) Drew cash from bank £158 for wages.

(*b*) After completing the entries, bring down the balances on all the accounts and draw up a trial balance. For this purpose, you are informed that the opening balance of assets amounted to £4,792. There were no outstanding liabilities at the beginning of the period.
(*c*) How much capital did Sam Barker have at the commencement of this period?
(*d*) How much does the business owe at the end of this period?
(*e*) How much is owed to the business at the end of the period?
(*f*) Indicate alongside the figure for each of the accounts in the trial balance which of the books would contain the account as suggested in Fig. 2.1.

The bookkeeping system

The outlines of the bookkeeping system and the relationship of the trial balance with this system is depicted in Figs 2.2–2.6 below. In practice, most accounting systems of varying degrees of complexity operate on the same principles.

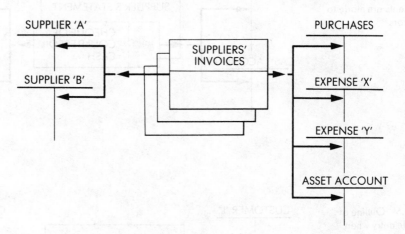

Fig. 2.2 Outline of double entry based on original source documents for goods and services purchased on credit

The figures used in systems such as those outlined in Figs 2.2–2.6 will be recorded observing the cost concept. This means that the actual transaction data is used which relies on the evidence of such documents as invoices, cash-till rolls, cheque-book stubs and cash receipts.

Fig. 2.3 Outline of double entry based on original documents for (a) sales made on credit and (b) cash sales

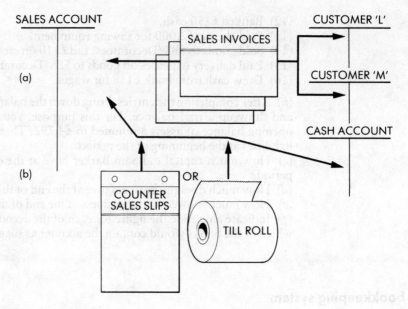

Fig. 2.4 Outline of double entry when payments are made to creditors

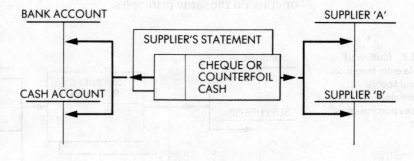

Fig. 2.5 Outline of double entry when debtors make payments to business

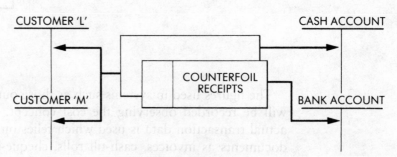

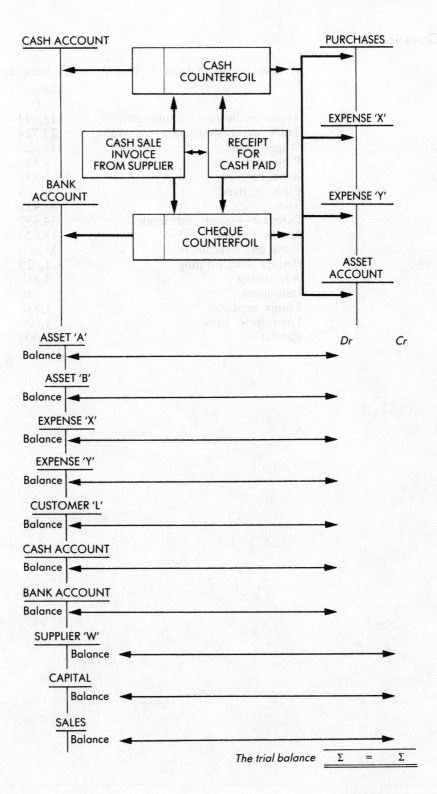

Fig. 2.6 Outline of double entry when payments are made immediately for goods, services and assets

Question 5

Prepare a trial balance from the list of balances shown below.

	Balance £	Dr £	Cr £
Trade creditors—accounts payable	13,642		
Trade debtors—accounts receivable	23,724		
Wages paid	14,625		
Rent and rates	6,520		
Bank balance	1,590		
Cash in hand	78		
Sales	87,428		
Purchases—goods for resale	34,697		
Motor vehicles	18,620		
Plant and machinery	15,000		
Postage and printing	1,720		
Advertising	3,450		
Insurances	210		
Motor expenses	1,836		
Loan from bank	5,000		
Capital	16,000		

3 Profit Measurement and the Final Accounts

Chapter 2 dealt with the routine procedures for recording financial data, and with establishing the conceptual basis of the financial accounting process. It is evident, however, that the purpose of financial accounting information is not simply to record data, but, of much more importance, to provide information which will be useful in making business decisions. Accordingly, the usefulness of the financial data stored in the bookkeeping system may be established by considering the objectives of business activities. At the outset, it should be stated that the nature of business objectives is the subject of some considerable debate. For the purpose of this chapter, the issues involved in this debate are simplified to the extent that business is assumed to be conducted solely with a view to profit-making. This assumption conforms with a traditionalist view of the nature of business organisation, and provides the rationale for conventional accounting practice.

> This chapter is concerned, therefore, with the nature of profit. It is divided into the following sections:
>
> The meaning of profit.
> Profit as a change in net worth.
> Profit measurement and the maintenance of capital.
> The profit and loss account.
> Preparing the profit and loss account.
> The trial balance and the preparation of the profit and loss acount and the balance sheet.
>
> These sections investigate progressively the various concepts and problems involved in the process of profit measurement.

The meaning of profit

The salary or wage which an employee obtains from his employer is usually called his 'income' and it is easily measured by reference to the payment which is made to him at periodic intervals. The income which a businessman derives from his business is usually referred to as his 'profit'. The measurement of business profit raises complex issues, some of which relate directly to the meaning of profit itself.

If a person had, say, £5,000 which was to be utilised in a venture which involved committing the whole sum to the purchase of certain goods and, after reselling them, the total cash recovered from customers amounted to £6,500, then the profit would be

£6,500 − £5,000 = £1,500. In such a simple situation, 'profit measurement', as the process is called, does not present any real difficulties. The conditions given in this example are, however, hardly likely to be found in the real business world. Nevertheless, it is important to note that profit is regarded as the excess recovered over and above the original amount invested.

Had the above example been posed in terms of the previous chapter, the amount available for purchasing goods for resale would have been termed 'capital'. Accordingly, profit could have been calculated by deducting the capital at the start of the venture from the capital at the end of the venture. This would accord with Hicks' definition of a man's income as the maximum value which he can consume during a period and still be as well off at the end of that period as he was at the beginning. The example given would state the situation in this way—£1,500 can be spent on personal satisfaction (i.e., non-business expenditure by the owner), leaving the business still worth £5,000.

Profit as a change in net worth

The use of the term 'well-off' creates difficulties for the accountant when determining business profit, for it immediately implies that valuation must take place when measuring profit. In effect, measuring profit as the difference in the net worth of a business at two different points in time raises a host of difficult questions about the manner in which the capital of a business should be valued. Nevertheless, it is accepted by accountants that one method of calculating profit is to compare the capital of the business at regular time intervals, as was illustrated in Chapter 1.

 Fig. 3.1

ASSETS − LIABILITIES = CAPITAL	ASSETS − LIABILITIES = CAPITAL	ASSETS − LIABILITIES = CAPITAL
Date t_0	Date t_1	Date t_2

Using Fig. 3.1 as a representation of this method of determining profit, the capital at date t_0 is deducted from the capital at date t_1 to reveal the profit of the intervening period. Similarly, the capital at date t_1 is deducted from the capital at date t_2 to reveal that intervening period's profit.

It was noted above that these are only initial figures. Any fresh capital introduced or any withdrawals by the proprietor would affect the size of the capital calculated. Consequently, the profit determined by this process would need to be adjusted in these respects. Not to do so would conflict with the definition of income advanced by Hicks, as the following example will show.

Example 1

For simplicity, assume that the initial capital of a business was £5,000, in cash and that this sum was wholly committed to the purchase of stock for resale. During the accounting period, further capital of £1,000 was introduced into the business and this sum was also committed to the purchase of additional stock. By the end of the accounting period, all the stock purchased had been sold for £8,000 cash.

On the basis of this information, the profit of the business could be calculated as follows:

	£
Capital at the end of the accounting period	8,000
Less: Capital at the beginning of the accounting period	5,000
	3,000
Less: Capital introduced during the accounting period	1,000
Profit of the accounting period	2,000

To ignore the extra capital introduced during the period would have resulted in the overstatement of profit by £1,000. Equally, to ignore any withdrawals by the owner would result in an understatement of profit.

Profit measurement and the maintenance of capital

The foregoing example illustrates clearly a principle which has long been accepted by accountants as being fundamental to the process of profit measurement. This principle stresses the importance of maintaining the value of capital intact in the process of identifying periodic profit. Example 1 shows the effect of the application of this principle. The total capital invested in the business is clearly £6,000. Profit is the difference between the capital at the end of the accounting period and £6,000, namely £2,000. The owner of the business may withdraw £2,000 and in so doing would maintain the value of the business intact. If he withdrew £3,000, however, the capital of the business would be reduced by £1,000. The additional £1,000 withdrawn would be classified as a repayment of capital.

Example 1 is stated in cash terms only. Hence, many of the problems of valuation are assumed away since that example did not contemplate the possibility that the business may hold a variety of assets and may have liabilities to parties other than the owner of the business. The process of measuring profit is much more complex than is suggested by Example 1.

A balance sheet showing all the assets owned by the business and all claims against the business could be drawn up at the beginning of the accounting period merely from the evidence adduced by appropriate documents and, where appropriate, by a physical check of the assets in the ownership of the firm. A similar balance sheet drawn up at the end of the accounting period would reveal the difference between the capital account at these two points in time. This difference would certainly be a measure of profit for that accounting period.

The drawbacks which accountants associate with this approach to profit measurement stem from the emphasis which it places on valuation and the failure to distinguish between realised gains stemming from correlated sales transactions and holding gains stemming from unrealised increases in value. Accountants are particularly anxious that profit should be an operational concept; that is, it should be addressed to the problem of business efficiency. Accordingly, the tradition in accounting has emphasised a transaction-based approach to profit.

The profit and loss account

The main criterion which accountants apply to the process of profit measurement is that the resulting numbers should be as objective as possible. The concept of objectivity has been given a restricted meaning in accounting and has been made synonymous with verifiability. From an accounting viewpoint, the advantage of a transaction-based approach to profit measurement is precisely that the accounting numbers derived from this approach are verifiable and hence satisfy the criterion of objectivity as understood in accounting. Nevertheless, valuation does enter into the process of profit measurement, particularly as regards such items as stocks of goods and raw materials unsold or unused at the end of the accounting period.

From a procedural viewpoint, the accounting approach to profit measurement relies on using the profit and loss account rather than the balance sheet. Figure 3.2 illustrates the relationship between a profit and loss account and a balance sheet.

Equity, as used in this illustration, is the term generally given to the net value of the ownership claim on the business. Here, it is the net asset value as shown by the balance sheet recorded under the cost concept.

The consequence of relying on the profit and loss account for the purpose of determining profit is to reduce the usefulness of the balance sheet in this respect. In effect, the balance sheet is by way of an appendix which collects the balances of the various accounts found in the bookkeeping system after the process of profit measurement

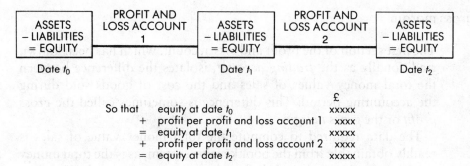

So that

		£
	equity at date t_0	xxxxx
+	profit per profit and loss account 1	xxxx
=	equity at date t_1	xxxxx
+	profit per profit and loss account 2	xxxx
=	equity at date t_2	xxxxx

Fig. 3.2

has been completed. Hence, rather than being in reality a statement of financial position based upon a process of valuation, it is more correctly described as a balance sheet which consists of the residual balances in the bookkeeping system.

In discussing the transaction-based approach to profit measurement, it is important to distinguish two different types of transactions which feature in the double-entry bookkeeping system. Profit results from *external transactions* in the course of which it is realised. The transactions are those which occur *between* the accounting entity and external parties. The process of measuring profit involves the aggregation and the modification of data associated with external transactions. The process requires a series of transfers and adjustments *within* the accounting system. These may be regarded as *internal transactions* and are usually undertaken during the process of profit measurement.

It should be noted that the basic accounting equation applies to both external and internal transactions. The application of the accounting equation to the treatment of external transactions was considered in Chapter 2. In this chapter, it will be observed that the accounting equation is of central importance to the set of procedures used for ensuring that all internal transactions are properly made. In effect, the aggregation of accounting numbers found in several accounts takes place by means of transfers involving *debit* and *credit* entries.

Preparing the profit and loss account

In this section, the profit and loss account will be considered as one account which has been divided into two sections. The first section calculates the *gross margin* and the second section measures the *net profit*.

Calculating the gross margin

The first section of the profit and loss account, which has been known traditionally as the *trading account*, isolates the difference between the total money values of sales and the cost of goods sold during the accounting period. This difference is sometimes called the *gross profit* or the *gross margin*.

The data required to compute the total money value of sales is readily obtainable from the bookkeeping system, as is the total money value of goods purchased during the accounting period. This data will be shown on the trial balance drawn up on the last day of that period. However, the cost of goods actually sold during the accounting period may be determined only after the value of the closing stock has been ascertained.

It is very important to note that the value of the closing stock cannot be ascertained directly from the double-entry bookkeeping system. Stock has to be physically counted and then valued before it can be integrated into the bookkeeping system.

Example 2

Quentin owns and runs a small business which has the sole agency to distribute a single size garden shed. During the year 19X7 he purchased from the manufacturer 140 of the sheds at a cost of £60 each. No sheds were on hand at the start of the year, 110 of the sheds at the agreed selling price of £85 each were sold during the year and the remainder were sold the following year.

The initial stage in the calculation of the gross margin involves transferring the balances on the purchases and the sales accounts to the trading section of the profit and loss account follows:

Purchase account				Sales account			
	£		£		£		£
Cash	8,400	Transfer to profit and loss a/c	8,400	Transfer to profit and loss a/c	9,350	Cash	9,350
	8,400		8,400		9,350		9,350

Profit and loss account			
	£		£
Purchases	8,400	Sales	9,350

The second stage in the process of calculating the gross margin is to determine the value which should be placed on the closing stock of sheds at the end of the year. It is known that 30 sheds out of

140 purchased were unsold. To calculate the gross margin as being the difference between purchase and sales (£9,350 − £8,400 = £950) would imply that the closing stock had no value. This assumption would only hold good if the 30 sheds had no marketable value whatsoever. Given that the 30 sheds will be sold during the next accounting period, it must be considered whether they should be valued at their cost value to the business or at their market value.

Stock valuation

No value attached to closing stock

The failure to attach any value to the closing stock results in a distortion of the profits of successive accounting periods. Thus, the gross margin of years 1 and 2 for the foregoing example, assuming that no further purchases were made in year 2 and that the 30 sheds were sold for £85 each, would be as follows:

Year 1: Sale £9,350 *minus* Purchases £8,400 = £950
Year 2: Sale £2,550 *minus* Purchases 0 = £2,550

The extent of the distortion will be appreciated when it is recalled that 110 sheds were sold in year 1 for £85 each, whereas only 30 sheds were sold in year 2 at that price.

Closing stock shown at market value

The consequence of valuing closing stock at market value is to anticipate the profit of the succeeding year, and to bring that profit forward into the year in which the goods were purchased. Thus, the gross margin of years 1 and 2 would be:

Year 1	£	£
Sales 110 sheds @ £85 each		9,350
Purchases 140 sheds @ £60 each	8,400	
less:		
Closing stock 30 @ £85 each	2,550	5,850
Gross margin		3,500
Year 2		
Sales 30 sheds @ £85 each		2,550
less:		
Value of stock brought forward from Year 1		2,550
Gross margin		—

It is clear, therefore, that this method of valuing closing stock also results in a distortion of the profits of successive accounting periods.

Closing stock shown at cost value

Accounting practice favours this method of valuing stock because it does prevent distortions of the profits over successive accounting periods as may be seen hereunder:

Year 1	£	£
Sales 110 sheds @ £85 each		9,350
Purcheses 140 sheds @ £60 each	8,500	
less:		
Closing stock 30 sheds @ £60 each	1,800	6,600
Gross margin		2,750

Year 2		
Sales 30 sheds @ £85 each		2,550
less:		
Value of stock brought forward from Year 1		1,800
Gross margin		750

The result of this method of valuing closing stock is to smooth the profits of successive accounting periods by attaching a uniform gross margin to each unit of product sold. The gross margin per unit is £25 (selling price £85 minus purchase price £60). Hence, the gross margin of year 1 is £25 × 110 units sold = £2,750 and the gross margin of year 2 is £25 × 30 units sold = £750.

Although the cost-based method of valuing closing stock overcomes the difficulties associated with the other methods of stock valuation referred to, controversy has been revived as regards this method owing to its inability to reflect the impact of inflation. For the remainder of this chapter, however, and for the purpose of the questions posed hereunder, it will be assumed that closing stock should be valued at cost.

Integrating closing stock in the bookkeeping system

Once the value of the closing stock has been determined by the method explained in the previous section, it must be integrated into the bookkeeping system itself before the process of calculating the gross margin may be completed. The procedure is to open a *stock account* and to debit that account with the value of the closing stock. The accounting equation is maintained by crediting the value of the closing stock to the profit and loss account.

Example 3

Assume that at the end of the year 19X0, which was the first year of trading, the closing stock was valued at £1,540. The integration of this stock into the bookkeeping system would be effected as follows:

Stock account

	£		
19X0 Profit and loss a/c	£1,540		

Profit and loss account for the year 19X0

		£
	Closing stock	1,540

It should be particularly noted that the purchases for the year are debited in total to the purchases account and that no adjustment is made to that account in respect of goods unsold at the end of the accounting year. The sole adjustment for closing stock is that described above. However, it is evident that the effect on the gross margin of crediting closing stock to the profit and loss account is the same as if the purchases account had been credited with closing stock.

The closing stock for the year 19X0 becomes the opening stock for the year 19X1. Accordingly, the entry in the stock account is reversed by the transfer of the stock for 19X0 to the profit and loss account for the year 19X1. In effect, the goods available for sale in the year 19X1 comprise the opening stock and the purchases of the year 19X1 less the closing stock at the end of the year 19X1.

Assume that the closing stock at the end of the year 19X1 was £1,893. The stock account and the profit and loss account for the year ended 19X1 would be as follows:

Stock account

	£		£
19X0 Profit and loss a/c	1,540	19X1 Profit and loss a/c	1,540
19X1 Profit and loss a/c	1,893		

Profit and loss account for the year 19X1

	£		£
Opening stock	1,540	Sales	xxxxx
Purchases	xxxxx	Closing stock	1,893
Gross margin c/d	xxxxx		
	xxxxx		xxxxx
		Gross margin b/d	xxxxx

The profit and loss account forms part of the double-entry bookkeeping system. Its essential purpose lies in the measurement of periodic profit. The object of this process is to communicate information about the efficiency of a business enterprise interpreted in terms of its profit-earning ability. For the sake of clarity, it is usual to present the profit and loss account in a vertical form as illustrated below:

Profit and loss account for the year 19X1

	£	£
Sales		xxxxx
Opening stock	1,540	
Purchases	xxxxx	
	xxxxx	
Closing stock	1,893	
Cost of sales		xxxxx
Gross margin		xxxxx

Calculating the net profit

Once the trading section of the profit and loss account has been prepared and the gross margin ascertained, the data required to complete the second section may be collected together and the net profit calculated.

The usual practice for preparing the profit and loss account is to use the trial balance as a working paper. It should be noted that the various balances shown on the trial balance reflect the different classes of accounts found in the bookkeeping system and fall into the following classes:

(1) Assets.
(2) Liabilities.
(3) Capital.
(4) Expenses (purchases, rent, etc.).
(5) Revenue (sales, fees, etc.).

Since the bookkeeping system reflects the accounting equation when handling both external and internal transactions, it follows that the five classes of accounts stated above may be arranged to reflect the accounting equation. Generally, the arrangement would be as follows:

(Capital ± Profit or Loss for the year) + Liabilities = Assets

It is clear, therefore, that the profit and loss account is a summary of all the changes which have occurred during the accounting period and which alter the value of the owner's equity in the business. Accordingly, the main procedural problem in computing the net profit is to identify those balances on the trial balance which are relevant to this purpose. Since the calculation of the gross margin has already taken care of purchases and sales, as well as the opening stock, it follows that the next stage is to transfer the remaining balances of the revenues and expenses accounts to the second section of the profit and loss account. The manner in which these balances are transferred is outlined in Figs 3.3(a) and 3.3(b) below.

Fig. 3.3(a) Formal presentation of the profit and loss account

Profit and Loss Account for the year ended 31 March 19X2	£	£
Sales		285
Cost of sales		
Opening stock	32	
Purchases	141	
Value of disposable goods	173	
Closing stock	37	
		136
Gross margin		149
Lighting and heating	10	
Rent and rates	16	
Advertising	20	
Wages	14	
Postages	12	
Repairs and renewals	8	
Delivery expenses	7	
		87
Net Profit transferred to Capital account		62

The trial balance and the preparation of the profit and loss account and the balance sheet

Figures 3.3(a) above and 3.3(b) illustrate the manner in which the net profit may be calculated. Figures 3.4(a) and 3.4(b) below show how the trial balance may be used to draw up both the profit and loss account and the balance sheet. It should be noted that the opening stock always appears on the initial trial balance prepared before any adjustments are effected. Once the closing stock has been valued, the trial balance is adjusted to include the closing stock as well as the opening stock. However, since the profit and loss account has not yet been prepared, the only way to maintain the accounting equation when introducing the closing stock into the trial balance is to enter it twice as shown on Fig. 3.4(a). The asterisks on Fig. 3.4(a) show that the closing stock appears both as a debit balance and as a credit balance, so as to maintain the accounting equation.

Note that in the balance sheet fixed and current assets are totalled separately. Fixed assets are long-term assets acquired for the purpose of creating the productive capacity of the firm. They are not intended

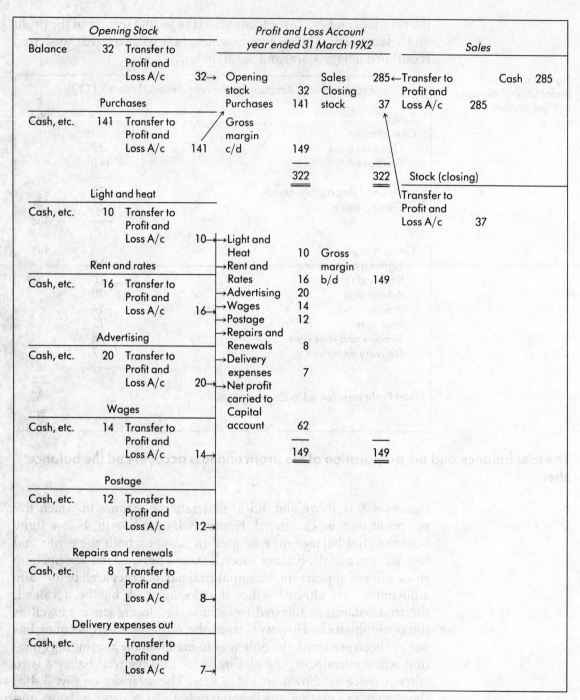

				Profit and Loss Account year ended 31 March 19X2						
Opening Stock									*Sales*	
Balance	32	Transfer to Profit and Loss A/c	32→	Opening stock	32	Sales Closing stock	285 37	←Transfer to Profit and Loss A/c	Cash	285
Purchases				Purchases	141			285		
Cash, etc.	141	Transfer to Profit and Loss A/c	141	Gross margin c/d	149					
					322		322	*Stock (closing)*		
Light and heat								Transfer to Profit and Loss A/c	37	
Cash, etc.	10	Transfer to Profit and Loss A/c	10→	→Light and Heat	10	Gross margin b/d	149			
Rent and rates				→Rent and Rates	16					
Cash, etc.	16	Transfer to Profit and Loss A/c	16→	→Advertising →Wages →Postage	20 14 12					
Advertising				→Repairs and Renewals	8					
Cash, etc.	20	Transfer to Profit and Loss A/c	20→	→Delivery expenses →Net profit carried to Capital account	7 62					
Wages										
Cash, etc.	14	Transfer to Profit and Loss A/c	14→		149		149			
Postage										
Cash, etc.	12	Transfer to Profit and Loss A/c	12→							
Repairs and renewals										
Cash, etc.	8	Transfer to Profit and Loss A/c	8→							
Delivery expenses out										
Cash, etc.	7	Transfer to Profit and Loss A/c	7→							

Fig. 3.3(b) Outline of bookkeeping involved in the preparation of the profit and loss account by the transfer of balances from the various accounts to the profit and loss account

	Trial balance		Profit and loss account		Balance sheet	
	Dr £	Cr £	Dr £	Cr £	Dr £	Cr £
Sales		36,422		36,422		
Purchases	20,100		20,100			
Opening stock	3,620		3,620			
Closing stock		4,701*		4,701		
Gross margin			17,403			
			41,123	41,123		
Gross margin				17,403		
Salaries	8,200		8,200			
Lighting and heating	910		910			
Printing and advertising	1,540		1,540			
Postages	320		320			
Rent and rates	2,060		2,060			
Repairs and renewals	624		624			
Net profit			3,749			
			17,403	17,403		
Owners equity – capital		2,761		3,749		6,510
Creditors and accounts payable		5,627				5,627
Fixtures and fittings	1,500				1,500	
Closing stock	*4,701				4,701	
Debtors and accounts receivable	4,210				4,210	
Bank account	1,690				1,690	
Cash in hand	36				36	
	49,511	49,511			12,137	12,137

Fig. 3.4(a) Working paper: final accounts for the year

for resale to customers in the course of business. Fixed assets include land, buildings, plant and machinery. Current assets are short-lived assets which are engaged in the operating cycle of the business. They are recycled into cash during the accounting period. Current assets include stocks, debtors and cash. Stocks are bought, then resold in the course of trade. Cash sales generate cash receipts immediately: credit sales create debtors, and impose a delay on the receipt of cash. Cash received either from cash sales or debtors is used to finance the purchase of stock, either by cash payments or through recycling creditor balances. In that sense, creditors grant the firm a delay for

Fig. 3.4(b) Formal presentation of profit and loss account and balance sheet

Profit and Loss Account for the year ended 31 December 19X6

	£	£
Sales		36,422
Cost of sales		
Opening stock	3,620	
Purchases	20,100	
	23,720	
Closing stock	4,701	
		19,019
Gross margin		17,403
Salaries	8,200	
Lighting and heating	910	
Printing and advertising	1,540	
Postages	320	
Rent and rates	2,060	
Repairs and renewals	624	
		13,654
Net profit transferred to Capital account		3,749

Balance Sheet as at 31 December 19X6

	£	£
Fixed assets		
Fixtures and fittings		1,500
Current assets		
Stocks	4,701	
Debtors	4,210	
Cash at bank	1,690	
Cash in hand	36	
	10,637	
Less: Current liabilities		
Creditors	5,627	
		5,010
		6,510
Capital		
Capital at 1 January 19X6		2,761
Profit for the year ended 31 December 19X6		3,749
		6,510

the payment of purchases constituting stock and the process of re-cycling creditor balances is linked with the process of replenishing stocks.

The assets of the enterprise, divided as they are into fixed and current assets, reflect one classification of assets. This classification shows the nature of individual fixed assets as having a permanence in identity. For example, a building defined as a fixed asset has a permanent identity in the accounting system—attached to a specific address. Current assets, by contrast, do not have a permanent existence but are recycled. For example, an individual debtor account will not have a constant value, or indeed a permanent existence. Current assets are defined in this classification as 'circulating assets'.

Another important classification is one which analyses the assets of the enterprise as between fixed assets and working capital. Working capital is defined as follows:

Working capital = Current assets − Current liabilities

Working capital represents the net current assets engaged in the operating cycle.

Balance sheets also tend to highlight the liquidity of the asset structure by ranking all assets in their relative order of liquidity. Importance is attached in financial analysis to the facility which the firm has of converting assets into cash. Cash is the ultimate form of liquidity. The most illiquid assets are fixed assets. Current assets have relative degrees of liquidity; for example, stocks have to be sold before they give rise to cash or rights to cash, debtors are more liquid than stock, since a demand for payment may be enforced in a court of law.

Questions

1. Complete the following profit and loss accounts by calculating the missing data

	A (£)	B (£)	C (£)	D (£)	E (£)
Sales	47,500	14,000	87,342	.....	143,564
Opening stock	7,430	.....	12,927	3,690	27,629
Purchases	30,100	8,490	.....	21,347	82,231
Goods available for sale	.....	.....	.....	.....	.....
Closing stock	8,910	710	14,250	2,190	.....
Costs of sales	.....	.....	.....	.....	.....
Gross margin	.....	5,600	11,565	6,140	58,004
	47,500	14,000	87,342	.....	143,564

2. John Marly trading as a grocer extracted the following trial balance from his accounting records on the 30 September 19X5 at the close of one year's trading. The value of the closing stock at that date was determined to be £9,743 at cost.

Required:
Prepare a profit and loss account for the year ended 30 September 19X5 and a balance sheet as at that date using the format illustrated in Figs 3.4(a) and 3.4(b).

Trial balance as at 30 September 19X5

	Dr £	Cr £
Purchases	78,326	
Sales		105,290
Opening stock	8,425	
Employees' salaries	12,640	
Insurance	118	
Rent and rates	3,750	
Repairs	874	
Hire of freezers	1,050	
Postages	362	
Printing and advertising	1,822	
Bank charges	86	
Motor expenses	1,736	
Telephone	210	
Electricity	864	
Capital at 1 October 19X5		13,668
Creditors and accounts payable		5,624
Delivery van	3,500	
Shop fittings	4,000	
Debtors and accounts receivable	2,896	
Cash at bank	3,737	
Cash in hand	186	
	124,582	124,582

3. Durant, a farmer, has asked for help in calculating his farming profit for the year ended 30 November 19X2. Owing to his preoccupation with farming operations, he claims to have been unable to maintain proper accounting records. Information obtained from Durant himself and from available records has enabled his accountant to prepare the following schedule of assets and liabilities at the beginning and close of the year.

Schedule of assets and liabilities

	1 December 19X1 £	30 November 19X2 £
Cash in hand	24	36
Cash at bank	3,427	5,622

	1 December 19X1	30 November 19X2
	£	£
Tractor	5,000	3,500
Land Rover	2,100	1,600
Farm implements (valuation)	3,620	4,291
Dairy equipment (valuation)	7,200	6,000
Livestock	3,600	6,700
Due from Milk Marketing Board	842	720
Seeds and growing crops	2,100	4,850
Subsidies due from the government	1,450	1,752
Due to creditors:		
Feed and corn	1,897	2,624
Motor expenses	84	320
Bank loan	5,000	4,000

The following additional information is also obtained:

(1) Cash drawing is estimated to amount to £25 per week.
(2) Mrs Durant has kept for her own use the proceeds from the sale of eggs, which are estimated to average £15 per week.

Required:
Calculate Durant's profit for the year ended 30 November 19X2.
Note: Cash drawings are a reduction of capital.

4. Benham is planning to start trading as a bookseller. He has approached various publishers and learnt that he will be able to acquire his initial stock of books on credit. He estimates his initial requirement in this respect to be as follows:

	£
From Beta Books Ltd	350
Alpha Books Ltd	375
Prime Editions Co. Ltd	1,700
Paperbacks Reprints Ltd	875
Tutorial Texts Ltd	2,400
Leisure Classics Ltd	1,200

He estimates also that sales for the first two months of trading will allow him to repay this initial volume of credit. In addition, shelving for the shop is estimated to cost £900. Benham's father has agreed to lend him £500 towards his initial cash requirement of £2,000.

Required:
Calculate how much capital is required to commence trading. (*Hint*: the accounting equation will be found useful for this purpose.)

5. The following trial balance was extracted from the accounting records of the Bidston Boutique at the close of business on 30 June 19X6. The closing stock at that date was calculated as £4,390 on a cost basis.

Required:
Prepare a profit and loss account for the year ended 30 June 19X6 and a balance sheet as at that date.

Trial balance as at 30 June 19X6

	Dr £	Cr £
Capital at 1 July 19X5		8,566
Freehold premises	15,500	
Fittings and display equipment	2,100	
Weldon Wholesale Clothing Ltd		840
Assistants' salaries	9,200	
Rates	785	
Monty's Model Gowns		190
Roscoe Denim Garments Ltd		1,243
Lighting and heating	674	
Purchases	35,319	
Opening stock 1 July 19X5	3,620	
Insurance	89	
Sundries and postages	146	
Telephone	103	
Sales		54,365
Cash in hand	48	
Cash at bank	2,620	
Loans S. Owens		5,000
	70,204	70,204

4   Periodic Profit Measurement: Some Further Adjustments

The purpose of Chapter 3 was to explain basic procedures involved in using the data recorded in the double-entry bookkeeping system in the process of profit measurement. Hence, the adjustments to the transactions already recorded are deliberately restricted to those essential to the determination of periodic profit, for example, the crucial adjustment for closing stock values.

The process of profit measurement is more complex than the simplified examples of Chapter 3 would imply, and the conceptual issues and practical problems involved remain the subject of considerable debate among accountants. Thus, our analysis of the problem of valuing closing stock was very much restricted to the elementary question of the need to make an adjustment and to pose some simple questions as to the appropriate basis for valuation.

In this chapter, we address ourselves to some further basic adjustments which must be made to the recorded data so that the process of profit measurement will reflect generally agreed and accepted principles relating to the nature of periodic profit. The adjustments which are now to be considered fall into three main categories. The first category relates to the timing of the recognition of revenues and expenses. The second category considers some accounting implications of credit trading, notably losses attributable to bad debts. The third category introduces depreciation, the process by which the cost of a fixed asset is charged as an expense in each of the accounting periods in which the asset is used by the firm. Although these adjustments do raise issues which are fundamental to the process of profit measurement, the analysis in this chapter will once again be restricted to the mechanics of the adjustments.

The chapter is divided into four main sections, as follows:

The accrual of revenues and expenses.
The treatment of bad and doubtful debts.
Depreciation.
Adjustments and the extended trial balance.

The accrual of revenue and expenses

The generalised use of credit trading as distinct from cash trading raises problems in the determination of periodic profit. Two alternatives are open to the accountant. First, it is possible to follow the most objective test and base the process of profit measurement solely on the cash receipts and cash disbursements of a particular accounting period, and this would result in a *cash flow statement of profit*. Second, it is possible to broaden the measurement base to recognise not just the cash receipts and cash disbursements of the period but also the *legal rights* to receive cash and the *legal obligations* to pay cash arising from the trading activities of that period. Conventional accounting profit is based on the second alternative, and is often referred to as *accrual accounting*. To retain the required degree of objectivity, the timing of the recognition of revenues and expenses must satisfy the criteria associated with the accruals convention.

The adjustments required to accommodate the accrual of revenue and expenses are the most frequently encountered adjustments to the data recorded in the accounts systems. Those relating to the accrual of expenses are more numerous and, therefore, will be considered first.

The accrual of expenses

Expenses paid in arrears

One of the most common consequences of periodic profit measurement is that expenses which are properly attributable to the operations of one accounting period are paid during the next accounting period. This arises either through the normal delay which occurs in the making of payments or because creditors delay in submitting their statements. Unpaid expenses must be accounted for in the particular period to which they relate, whether or not payment has actually been made. It is quite usual for accrual adjustments to be made in respect of unpaid telephone charges, rent, rates and electricity charges.

Example 1

At the close of the accounting year on 30 November 19X5, the electricity account of a business had been debited with the sum of £218 as follows:

Electricity account

	£	
Nov 20 Balance	218	

On closer examination, it is found that the payments going to make up the balance of £218 were by cheque against demands for payment made by the electricity board. The last recorded payment of £43 was made on 23 September for electricity metered up to 31 August. If the balance of £218 were transferred to the profit and loss account as an expense without any modification, it would understate the true cost of the electricity consumed by the omission of the electricity used in the last three months. Obviously, the true cost for these last months would not be known until the electricity board presented its bill, but this does not prevent an adjustment being made, and a reasonable estimate based on past experience can be used. Suppose that on this basis the cost of electricity consumed in the three months to 30 November were estimated to be £110. The adjustment to the electricity account would be as follows:

Electricity account

	£		£
Nov 30 Balance	218	Nov 30 Profit and loss a/c	328
Nov 30 Accrual c/d	110		
	328		328
		Dec 1 Accrual b/d	110

Note that this completes the double entry by a *debit* and a *credit* on the same account but with the *debit* in the first period and the *credit* in the second period. The account can now be transferred to the profit and loss account for the first period.

The sum of £328 is transferred to the profit and loss account as this is the cost of the electricity consumed (subject to the limits of accuracy of the estimate for the final three months) whether paid or not. The credit balance of £110 is included in the balance sheet as an accrued expense.

Two points should be noted:

(1) The accounting equation is maintained by the increase in external liabilities of £110 caused by the recognition of the debt owing to the electricity board and by the decrease of £110 in the net profit.

(2) If profit were calculated simply by measuring the changes in the capital between two dates, then the inclusion of this sum as a liability would obviously reduce the capital standing to the credit of the owner on the last date of the accounting period.

It will be appreciated that the accrual adjustment is made *solely* at the end of the accounting year in connection with the preparation of the annual profit and loss account. The question is—which accounts must be adjusted in practice? In fact, very few, since all suppliers will have invoiced the cost of purchases on a monthly basis. Hence, the only accounts requiring adjustment are those for which sufficient time has not elapsed for accurate invoicing. Generally, these accounts are of the nature of insurance, electricity, rates, etc. Wages and salaries due but unpaid at the last day of the accounting year also would have to be accrued.

Example 2

A business obtains all its petrol and oil from Monton Garages Ltd. Invoices are received detailing the supplies and are paid at the end of the following month. In these circumstances the bookkeeping entries would be—

Dr   Motor expenses   } with the sums stated in the invoices
Cr   Monton Garages Ltd } received

and later when the actual payment is made—

Dr   Monton Garages Ltd } with the sum of the monthly
Cr   Bank account   } settlement

If a less complete recording system is in use, as is the case with many smaller businesses which keep their accounts on a cash basis only, the accrual procedure is used to record amounts unpaid at the end of the year. Thus, it can be seen that this procedure has two uses. First, to correctly accrue expenses to an accounting period in the case of complete recording systems. Second, to correct less complete recording systems to take account of unpaid expenses at the end of the accounting period.

Expenses paid in advance

The complete reverse of an accrual occurs in those situations where expenses have to be paid in advance. The most common of these are rents and lease payments, rates and insurance premiums.

Example 3

Assume that a business leases shop premises at an annual rental of £2,400 payable in one sum in advance on 1 January each year. It is clear that one quarter of the rent would be 'unused' at 30 September 19X0, the date of the profit and loss account, and would be shown as an asset. The rent account in the business books for the financial year to 30 September 19X0 would be as follows:

Rent account

19X0	£	19X0	£
Jan 1 Cash[1]	2,400	Sept 30 Profit and loss a/c[4]	1,800
		Sept 30 Prepayment c/d[2]	600
	2,400		2,400
Oct 1 Prepayment b/d[3]	600		

The following points should be noted:

(1) The rent paid on 1 January was paid by cheque.
(2) The repayment is carried down and debited to the next accounting period.
(3) The prepayment is shown on the balance sheet as an asset and is usually included with the balance of debtors.
(4) The rent appropriate to the period under review is transferred to the profit and loss account of that period.

Assuming that the rent due on the following 1 January remains unchanged, the rent account for the subsequent year will be as follows:

Rent account

19X0	£	19X1	£
Oct 1 Prepayment b/d	600	Sept 30 Profit and loss a/c	2,400
		Sept 30 Prepayment c/d	600
19X1			
Jan 1 Cash	2,400		
	3,000		3,000
Oct 1 Prepayment b/d	600		

The effect of these adjustments is to bring into coincidence the rental year which runs from 1 January with the accounting year which runs from 1 October. Thus, the rent transferred to the profit and loss account for the year ended 30 September 19X1 is in the form of a prepayment of £600 made in the previous year and sum of £1,800 representing a portion of the payment of £2,400 made in the current year.

Two further points should be noted:

(1) The accounting equation is maintained by the increase of £600 in the assets caused by the creation of a debt to the business represented by the prepayment and by a decrease of £600 in the expenses charged against profit.
(2) If profit were calculated simply by measuring the changes in the capital between two dates, then the inclusion of this sum as an

asset would obviously increase the capital standing to the credit of the owner on the last date of the accounting period.

Accrued expenses summary

The adjustments required to deal with the accrual of expenses and the exclusion of prepayment in the process of determining the profit of a particular accounting period are in the nature of internal transactions. These adjustments are summarised below:

	£
Accrued expenses	
Total expenses paid during the accounting period	xxxxxx
Add:	
Accrual of expenses incurred but not yet paid	xxxxxx
	xxxxxx
Less:	
Expenses paid during the accounting period but accrued to the previous accounting period	xxxxxx
Total expenses of the current accounting period	xxxxxx
Prepaid expenses	
Total expenses paid during the accounting period	xxxxxx
Add:	
Expenses prepaid in the previous accounting period and accrued to the current accounting period	xxxxxx
	xxxxxx
Less:	
Expenses prepaid in the current accounting period and accrued to the next accounting period	xxxxxx
Total expenses of the current accounting period	xxxxxx

The accrual of revenues

When a sale is made for cash over the counter in a store, the exchange of money and goods is immediately recognised as an event to be recorded in the bookkeeping system. If, however, a customer enters the store and says 'Will you keep that hifi set for me until next month?', it is less clear when the sale may be recognised as having been made.

The adjustments which the accountant makes to deal with the accrual or the prepayment of expenses are internal transactions which anticipate, in part, the eventual external recognition of a completed transaction. Normally, the external recognition is provided by an invoice or a formal demand for payment such as an electricity bill.

Similarly, the accountant may have to come to a decision as to how far a sales transaction may be regarded as completed for the purpose of recording it in the bookkeeping system and making the required adjustments for the accrual of revenue. Hence, the accrual of revenue is also concerned with the correct determination of periodic profit.

The need for some consistency of treatment in the recognition of transactions is a critical requirement for the process of profit measurement.

Consider the following situations:

(1) The business receives a written order from a regular and valued customer for goods which are not on hand at the moment. The order is acknowledged, and in turn the business orders the goods from the supplier. Eventually they arrive, are dispatched to the customer and an invoice is issued to him. The goods reach him two weeks after dispatch from the business. When should the business enter the transaction as a sale?

(2) A customer enters a store, pays a deposit on a washing machine and agrees to buy it under a hire-purchase agreement over the next twelve months, paying interest. The washing machine is delivered to the customer one week later. How much should be recorded as a sale and when?

These examples illustrate the problems that may be encountered. In the first illustration it is usual to consider the legal transfer of ownership as marking the realisation of the transaction, and this is usually on issue of an invoice to the customer.

Various treatments are suggested for the second type of transaction and, although the legal title may not pass until the final instalment has been paid, it is usual to recognise the sale as arising on the acceptance by both parties of the contract. The interest element is regarded as additional and is not recognised until paid, but it is assumed to be paid regularly, i.e., each instalment is assumed to include a partial payment of the pure sale price of the goods and a part of the interest payable.

The treatment of bad and doubtful debts

When goods are sold by a business to customers on credit terms there is always the potential hazard of not collecting the cash due. In accounting, this hazard is considered as involving two types of debts: those which may be classified as bad debts and those which may be classified as doubtful debts.

Bad debts

When a customer does not pay his account and circumstances indicate that no recovery is possible, the business patently has an asset in its books which is valueless. When this occurs and all recovery methods have been tried without success, or are too costly in relation to the value of the debt, there is no alternative but to write off the debt.

This is done by the simple process of transferring the balance on all such debtors accounts to a bad debts account and then transferring the total to the profit and loss account where it will be treated as an expense. As far as the accounting equation is concerned, this is maintained by the effect of a reduction in the assets of the business and an equal reduction (eventually) in the capital.

The accounting entries are as follows:

Customer 'A' account				Customer 'B' account			
	£		£		£		£
Balance b/d	30	Bad debts	30	Balance b/d	110	Bad debts	110

Customer 'C' account				Customer 'D' account			
	£		£		£		£
Balance b/d	50	Bad debts	50	Balance b/d	60	Bad debts	60

Bad debts account			
	£		£
Customer A transfer	30	Profit and Loss A/c	250
Customer B transfer	110		
Customer C transfer	50		
Customer D transfer	60		
	250		250

Fig. 4.1

Notes

(1) The balance on the customers' accounts are debts to the business in respect of credit sales to these customers. Hence, prior to being written off as bad debts, these debtor balances would have been classified as asset balances.

(2) The bad debts account is a summary account to which all bad debts are transferred and aggregated in one total before being transferred to the profit and loss account.

Doubtful debts

In addition to the problem of dealing with debtor balances which will clearly not be recovered, there is the separate question of debtor balances which are doubtful of payment. Underlying the approach to doubtful debts is the conservatism which surrounds all accounting activities, and the need to keep a balance between optimism and pessimism. Doubtful debts are debts which, at the close of the accounting period, are not considered as being bad debts, although there is sufficient evidence to suggest that they may eventually prove to be such. When the evidence available is inconclusive that debts are good or bad, treating them as doubtful enables a decision to be deferred till the position becomes clear. Further, the doubtful debts account is also a safeguard against the excessive optimism of treating such debts as good, since it creates a provision against the likelihood that they may turn out to be irrecoverable.

There are two methods of estimating doubtful debts:

(a) To inspect each and every debtor account and to estimate the extent to which each debt may be doubtful.

(b) To rely on statistical evidence of past experience to reveal some consistent percentage of total debtors which ultimately proves to be irrecoverable.

The former method takes the form of a specific provision for doubtful debts, and the latter takes the form of a general provision for doubtful debts. In the United Kingdom, there are taxation objections to the use of a general provision inasmuch as they are not usually allowed in calculating taxable profits, whereas specific provisions are allowed within reason. It is, of course, much easier to rely on the second method and to create a general provision, but large numbers of accounts are needed before any statistical method of determining doubtful debts can be argued to have any degree of reliability.

The necessary bookkeeping entries are as follows:

Dr   Profit and loss account   } with the total amount of all deb-
Cr   Provision for doubtful debts } tors considered doubtful

These entries effectively take some of the profit out of the profit and loss account and place it as a credit balance in the provision for doubtful debts account. For balance sheet purposes, this provision is deducted from the total of debtors. It is essential to note that when doubtful debts are being examined in this way, no entries or adjustments are made to individual debtors' accounts until the point at which they are declared to be completely bad and irrecoverable. The provision for doubtful debts appears on the balance sheet as follows:

	£	£
Debtors (accounts receivable)	14,624	
less: Provision for doubtful debts	348	14,276

Example 4

A business which commenced on 1 January 19X1 had accumulated the following total of debtors in respect of each accounting period ended on the following dates—

	£
31 December 19X1	60,000
31 December 19X2	80,000
31 December 19X3	90,000
31 December 19X4	75,000

Relying on experience gained in the particular area of trading activity, it is believed appropriate to create and maintain a general provision for doubtful debts at the rate of 6%. Accordingly, the provision for doubtful debtors is as under:

Provision for doubtful debts account

		£			£
Dec 31 19X2	Balance c/d	4,800	Dec 31 19X1	Profit and loss a/c	3,600
			Dec 31 19X2	Profit and loss a/c	1,200
		4,800			4,800
Dec 31 19X3	Balance c/d	5,400	Jan 1 19X3	Balance b/d	4,800
			Dec 31 19X3	Profit and loss a/c	600
		5,400			5,400
Dec 31 19X4	Profit and loss a/c	900	Jan 1 19X4	Balance b/d	5,400
	19X4 Balance c/d	4,500			
		5,400			5,400
			Jan 1 19X5	Balance b/d	4,500

Bad and doubtful debts: additional considerations

Before leaving the question of bad debts, a further matter should be considered. The methods described for the treatment both imply that bad debts and the provision for doubtful debts should be treated as expenses charged against the profit of the year in which the decision was taken to treat such debts as bad and doubtful respectively.

It may be argued that no event has really taken place in the current period that effects the profit measurement process of this period.

If we attempt to analyse the situation in this way the following conclusions may be drawn.

Bad debts

(a) By the very nature of the processes involved in the recovery of bad debts, the date when the debt is regarded as irrecoverable may be in a completely different accounting period from that which includes the date on which the sale took place.

(b) It would be more appropriate to adjust the profit and loss accounts of prior periods rather than to charge and hence 'distort' the net profit for the current period under review. This, it will be found, is mentioned in a 'Standard' about which more will be said in a later chapter. (A 'Standard' in this context is, briefly, an agreed method of dealing with certain transactions where more than one such method exists.)

(c) The above treatment may not be necessary if the amounts are so small as not to be material.

Doubtful debts

The following suggested treatment of doubtful debts would be considered appropriate also for bad debts when the sale and the decision to regard the consequent debt as bad take place in the same period.

(a) Since a provision for doubtful debts implies that some part of the transfer of goods to debtors was not, in fact, true sales, it could be considered more correct to regard the adjustment as a deduction from sales rather than as an expense.

(b) The disclosure of the provision would still be achieved by the suggested following presentation:

Profit and loss account for year ended.....	
	£
Gross sales	xxxxx
Less: Deduction for doubtful debts	xxxx
Net sales	xxxxx

Depreciation

Fixed assets may be viewed as service potentials which are exhausted over a period of time through use, the passage of time or obsolescence. Accounting seeks to allocate their cost, as an expense, to the accounting periods which benefit from their use. Depreciation is an estimate of the service potential exhausted during an accounting period.

As in the case of the provision for doubtful debts, the provision for depreciation of fixed assets is an estimate since the exact amount of usage cannot be determined. When fixed assets are purchased, it is known that ultimately they will be sold or scrapped. When that event occurs, the value of the asset is likely to be much less than the original historical cost. It is that difference which is the true cost to the business of the service potential exhausted during its use in the business. As part of the process of making a reasonably accurate forecast of the depreciation to be provided for, it is neccessary to estimate the probable life of the asset, and its ultimate scrap value in order to determine the depreciation which should be charged to the several periods of its use.

Example 5

A firm purchased for £5,500 a machine, which it expects to use for five years. At the end of this period, it is expected that the trade-in allowance will be £500. It follows that, based on these estimates, the firm has purchased £5,000 of service potential. The service potential is exhausted evenly over the five years at the rate of £1,000 per annum. The procedure for recording depreciation is as follows:

> Dr Profit and loss account
> Cr Provision for depreciation account

with £1,000 per annum being the annual depreciation which has been calculated.

It will be noted that the debit to the profit and loss account has the effect of reducing the net profit. The credit to the provision for depreciation account accumulates each year, until at the end of five years, it will equal the original historical cost of the asset.

Adjustments and the extended trial balance

In Chapter 3 use was made of the technique of extending the figures from the trial balance into additional columns in order to produce a rough draft form of the profit and loss account and balance sheet. This enables a check to be kept on all the figures on one work sheet, and the formal presentation of the profit and loss account and balance sheet is reduced to a simple task of copying out. This method of using the trial balance may be extended to deal with all the required adjustments.

The extended trial balance

In the previous use of this technique no adjustments were made to the figures actually recorded as a result of external transactions. Now, in order to incorporate these adjustments, an additional column is interposed between the trial balance and the profit and loss account. As there may well be a need to distinguish between the profit and loss account to the point of the gross margin and the profit and loss account to net income, there are two columns devoted to the profit and loss account, one for each aspect.

The basic procedure still remains the same. Every item in the trial balance must be transferred to either the profit and loss account or the balance sheet columns, but now incorporating any necessary modifications in the adjustment column.

Example 6

The following trial balance was extracted from the books of J. Halsall trading as a retail haberdasher:

Trial balance as at 31 December 19X1

	Dr £	Cr £
Stock	3,670	
Sales		28,620
Purchases	13,745	
Rent	1,000	
Rates	240	
Electricity	127	
Wages	4,600	
Motor expenses	824	
Motor cars	5,200	
Fixtures and fittings	1,400	
Debtors	6,210	
Creditors		2,450
Drawings	2,500	
Capital at 1 January 19X1		8,446
	39,516	39,516

In addition, the following information is available:

(1) The closing stock at 31 December 19X1 at cost is £4,340.
(2) No provision has been made for due and unpaid rent amounting to £250.
(3) Rates prepaid totalled £60.
(4) No provision has been made for the usage of electricity estimated to cost £46.
(5) Bad debts amount to £185.
(6) Provision is to be made for depreciation of motor cars of £1,300.

It is required to prepare a profit and loss account for the year ended 31 December 19X1 and a balance sheet as at that date.

The first step is to enter all the adjustments in both the debit and the credit side of the adjustment column so as to maintain the accounting equation. Thus, the closing stock is shown once as a debit which will go into the balance sheet as an asset and once as a credit which will go into the profit and loss account. Note 2 regarding £250 rent due will need an adjustment which (Dr) increases rent and (Cr) increases creditors. Once all the adjustments are entered and the columns added to see if the debit and credit sides agree, the next column is added, and the difference between the totals is the gross margin of £15,545. This figure is entered on the debit side of the gross margin column of the profit and loss account and the credit side of the profit and loss account and the process is repeated to find the net profit. This net profit figure is transferred to the balance sheet where it should cause the two sides to be equal. (See Fig. 4.2.)

	Trial balance			Adjustments		Profit and Loss Account				Balance sheet	
	Dr (£)	Cr (£)		Dr (£)	Cr (£)	Dr (£)	Cr (£)	Dr (£)	Cr (£)	Dr (£)	Cr (£)
Opening stock	3,670		Note 1	4,340	4,340	3,670	4,340			4,340	
Sales		28,620					28,620				
Purchases	13,745					13,745					
			Gross margin			15,545			15,545		
Rent	1,000		Note 2	250				1,250			
Rates	240		Note 3		60			180			
Electricity	127		Note 4	46				173			
Wages	4,600							4,600			
Motor expenses	824							824			
Motor cars	5,200				1,300					3,900	
Fixtures and fittings	1,400									1,400	
Debtors	6,210		Note 5		185					6,025	
Creditors		2,450	Note 2 Note 4		250 46						2,746
Drawings J. Halsall	2,500									2,500	
Capital J. Halsall		8,446									8,446
Prepayments			Note 3	60						60	
Bad debts			Note 5	185				185			
Depreciation			Note 6	1,300				1,300			
			Net profit					7,033			7,033
	39,516	39,516		6,181	6,181	32,960	32,960	15,545	15,545	18,225	18,225

Fig. 4.2

Questions

1. Complete the accounts shown below by calculating the missing numbers.

Accounts	Electricity Dr (£)	Electricity Cr (£)	Telephone Dr (£)	Telephone Cr (£)	Wages Dr (£)	Wages Cr (£)	Rates Dr (£)	Rates Cr (£)	Motor expenses Dr (£)	Motor expenses Cr (£)	Insurance Dr (£)	Insurance Cr (£)
Accrual/prepayment b/d		120		.....		1,242	900			195	350	
Cash	800		654		.....		2,700		799		.....	
Profit and loss account		.....		670		8,963		.....		1,015		890
Accrual/prepayment c/d	70		47		1,380			600	.....			420
	.....	.....	.....	.....	.....	.....	.....	.....	.....	.....	.....	.....

2. C. Aspin, a jobbing carpenter, undertakes work for small builders. He commenced business on 1 July 19X2 with a van which he had just bought for £2,800, tools worth £235 and cash at the bank of £2,100.

A summary of his transactions for the year is as follows:

	£
Purchased timber for various jobs	3,670
Received from Reed & Co. (Builders) Ltd for work done on new houses	1,650
Received from Studio Holiday Homes Ltd for work on the conversion of old houses	4,650
Cash received for casual small jobs undertaken	1,246
Motor expenses paid during the year	930
Replacement of tools	65
Paid for casual labour	750
Withdrew per week from the bank for personal expenses	30
Received from Melvin Estates for various repairs to property	2,400
Entered into a contract with Studio Holiday Homes Ltd for futher conversion work. Payment is to be made on the completion of the work, which was half completed on 30 June 19X2. Payment due on completion	3,500

Required:

(1) Prepare a trial balance as at 30 June 19X3.

(2) After making the necessary adjustments in respect of the items detailed below, prepare a profit and loss account for the year ended 30 June 19X3 and a balance sheet as at that date.

	£
(a) Motor expenses due but not yet paid	46
(b) Closing stock of timber at cost	1,643
(c) Reed and Co., are dissatisfied with work done and are demanding a refund of	1,500

Note

The adjustment for drawings should be by way of a credit to the bank account (£30 × 52 = £1,560) and a corresponding debit to the capital account. The usual practice is to debit drawings to a drawings account which is transferred at the end of the accounting period to the debit of the capital account. Hence, the procedure suggested above is a short cut for the purpose of this question only.

(3) Assume that C. Aspin, to apply to his bank for a loan, has to use the accounts you have prepared.

Examine the various items appearing on the profit and loss account and discuss any alternative treatment which could apply to the manner in which they could be represented to the bank.

3. You are required to enter the following transactions in the records of M. Plant, who started trading as a shoe retailer on 1 July 19X4 with a capital of £8,000 in cash.

19X4

July 1 Purchased shop fittings for £1,500 by cheque

2 Bought goods to the value of £2,400 on credit terms from D. K. Ltd

3 Paid £75 being three months' advance rent for the shop
4 Cash sales £85
5 Sold boots on credit to the Hamilton Construction Co., Ltd for £350
6 Cash sales £84
7 Paid wages of £22 to shop assistant
8 Purchased goods for £270 by cheque
9 Paid postage £3 cash
10 Paid £500 to D. K. Ltd
11 Received cheque for £200 from the Hamilton Construction Co., Ltd
13 Weekly cash sales £242
13 Paid wages £22
20 Weekly cash sales £384
20 Paid wages £22
23 Sold sports shoes on credit to the Midborough Education Committee for £330
23 Paid £23 for fuel supplies
24 Paid £12 to Shop Cleaners Ltd for cleaning
27 Weekly cash sales £170
27 Paid wages £22
29 Received an invoice for £28 for wrapping paper from B. W. Paper Ltd
30 Paid £8 for deliveries to customers
31 Weekly cash sales £142

After recording these transactions, prepare a trial balance as at 31 July 19X4 and, using the extended trial balance method, prepare a profit and loss account for July 19X4 and a balance sheet as at 31 July 19X4. The additional information which you require for this purpose is that the closing stock at 31 July 19X4 was valued at £1,210 at cost. Unrecorded use of electricity was estimated at £25.

4. Norman Coates commenced business as a furniture dealer on 1 October 19X2 with £11,000 in the bank. Transactions for October 19X2 were as follows:

			£
Oct	1	Bought goods by cheque	510
	2	Bought goods on credit from Dobson	945
		Bridges	1,422
		Gates	365
		Ryan	850
	3	Bought packaging from Boxed Ltd on credit	510
	6	Sold goods on credit to Murgatroyd	212
		Archer	400
		Hornby	700
		Atkins	605
	7	Paid rent for October and November	200
	8	Bought fittings on credit from Sampson	1,400
	9	Paid salaries	310
	14	Purchased goods returned to Dobson	210
	15	Bought van by cheque	2,300
	16	Received loan from S. Small	1,800

16	Goods returned by Archer	40
16	Atkins	110
19	Cash sales	270
20	Sold goods on credit to Archer	300
20	Atkins	940
20	Smart	420
21	Paid by cheque outstanding accounts of Dobson and Bridges	
22	Received cheques from Smart and Archer in settlement of their accounts	
26	Paid electricity account by cheque	80
27	Received further loan from S. Small	200
28	Received cheque from Atkins	1,000

Required:
(1) Enter these transactions in the books of the business.
(2) Prepare a trial balance as at the 31 October 19X2.
(3) Using the extended trial balance method, prepare a profit and loss account for the month of October 19X2 and a balance sheet as at 31 October 19X2. For this purpose the following additional information is provided:
  (a) The closing stock at 31 October 19X2 was valued at cost at £1,500.
  (b) The unrecorded usage of electricity was estimated at £70.
  (c) Wages due but not paid at 31 October 19X2 amounted to £200.

5. The following trial balance was extracted from the books of P. Earnshaw.

Trial balance as at 31 May 19X5

	£	£
Purchases	67,800	
Sales		112,960
Stock	16,540	
Postages and telephone	912	
Motor expenses	1,596	
Salaries	17,456	
Sundry expenses	332	
Rent	1,560	
Rates	620	
Debtors	28,792	
Creditors		16,696
Premises at cost	30,000	
Motor vehicles at cost	9,400	
Fixtures and fittings at cost	4,480	
Bank overdraft		1,832
Drawings	15,400	
Capital at 1 June 19X4		63,400
	194,888	194,888

The following additional information is available:
(1) Closing stock at 31 May 19X5 was valued at cost at £13,436.

(2) Expenses owing were: Sundry expenses £95,
Motor expenses £121.
(3) Expenses prepaid: Rates   £90,
Telephone £35.
(4) Bad debts totalled £624.
(5) Provision is to be made for depreciation of motor vehicles of £1,500 and fixtures and fittings of £480.

Required:
(a) Prepare a profit and loss account for the year ended 31 May 19X5.
(b) A balance sheet on that date.

6. The following trial balance was extracted from the book of C. Hopley.

Trial balance as at 31 December 19X1

	£	£
Capital at 1 January 19X1		20,932
Furniture and fittings	1,450	
Motor vans	4,160	
Purchases	122,400	
Sales		153,000
Stock	14,000	
Trade debtors and creditors	16,300	13,228
General expenses	4,400	
Bank balance	1,930	
Lighting and heating	642	
Drawings	4,200	
Wages and salaries	13,498	
Bad debts	1,132	
Provision for bad debts at 1 January 19X1		300
Motor expenses	1,350	
Rent and rates	1,650	
Printing and stationery	180	
Insurances	168	
	187,460	187,460

The following additional information is given:
(1) Closing stock at the 31 December 19X1 was valued at cost at £13,200.
(2) Wages and salaries unpaid at 31 December 19X1 amounted to £116.
(3) Insurance paid in advance at 31 December 19X1 amounted to £40.
(4) The provision for bad debts is to be increased to £500.
(5) The provision for depreciation on the motor vans is £500.

Required
(a) Prepare a profit and loss account for the year 19X1.
(b) A balance sheet as at 31 December 19X1.

7. H. Latham started business on 1 January 19X4 by paying £6,000 into a business bank account. He rented premises and purchased fittings and furniture for £3,000 and paid by cheque.

At 31 December 19X4 the following figures were available from his records for the year.

	£
Sales on credit	44,800
Purchases on credit	39,300
Cost of goods sold	33,600
Receipts from trade debtors	39,936
Payment to trade creditors	32,408
Business expenses paid	5,500
Business expenses due but not paid	212
Business expenses prepaid	144
Drawings	4,400

There were no cash sales and all amounts received were paid into the bank. All payments were made by cheque.

Required:
(a) Calculate the cost value of the stock at 31 December 19X4.
(b) Calculate the balance of trade debtors at 31 December 19X4.
(c) Calculate the balance of trade creditors at 31 December 19X4.
(d) Calculate the balance at the bank at 31 December 19X4.
(e) Show the business expense account as it would appear at the close of business on 31 December 19X4.
(f) Prepare a profit and loss account for the year 19X4.
(g) Prepare a balance sheet as at 31 December 19X4.

5 Data Processing Systems

A data processing system comprises three basic elements for converting raw data into information: input, process and output. Input consists of raw data introduced into the system. It is derived from the originating documents generated by transactions, such as invoices, cheques, etc. Processing involves the treatment of raw data through several stages which include the initial storage of raw data into appropriate files, designing instructions for the operations to be performed on the raw data, and performing the necessary calculations. Output is the processed information presented in the desired format for the intended use.

> This chapter deals with a manual data processing system for converting accounting data into information in which the steps in processing are separate and distinct. Computerised systems accomplish the same result, although the sequence of operations is different. Irrespective of the type of equipment used, however, the basic elements themselves are common to all systems.

The most significant influence on manual data processing systems has been the growth of businesses in size and complexity. To deal with the corresponding growth in the number of transactions, accountants have devised special methods for speeding up and simplifying the accumulation and processing of data. Two most important developments have been

(1) the division of the journal into several books of original entry,
(2) the division of the ledger into several ledgers.

The division of the journal: books of original entry

It is a traditional rule in bookkeeping not to make entries direct into the ledger, but to record all transactions initially in the journal or day book prior to posting to the ledger. The journal existed, therefore, as a book of original entry. It enabled transactions to be checked prior to being formally recorded in the ledger. With the expansion of business, the journal was split up into several books of original entry in which transactions of the same type could be recorded. Accordingly, the purchases day book, the sales day book and the cash book were segregated from the journal. The journal now has a restricted use, which includes the following transactions:

(1) recording credit transactions relating to the acquisition of assets,
(2) writing off bad debts,
(3) end of year accounting transactions, defined as transactions resulting from accounting operations and not supported by base documents such as invoices. They include the creation of provisions, writing off depreciation, and the transfer of balances to the profit and loss account.
(4) recording the purchase of a business,
(5) recording the opening entries at the commencement of a trading period.

Journal entries are in the form illustrated below. It should be noted that each entry has an explanatory note of the circumstances attaching to the event being recorded.

Date	Detail		Folio	Dr	Cr
19X4				£	£
Jan 18	S. Green	Dr	DL145	114	
	To Bank account				114
	Being cheque dishonoured received from S. Green		CB67		
				114	114
19X4				£	£
Jan 30	Bad Debts account	Dr	GL36	65	
	To L. Brown				65
	Being amount owing by L. Brown now written off as irrecoverable		DL92		
				65	65

* DL = Debtor's Ledger
CB = Cash Book
GL = General Ledger

The day book

Credit transactions relating to the purchase and sale of goods are recorded separately in the four day books illustrated in Fig. 5.1.

Fig. 5.1 Recording transactions

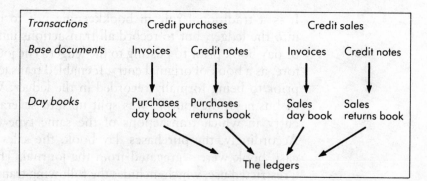

Transactions	Credit purchases		Credit sales	
Base documents	Invoices	Credit notes	Invoices	Credit notes
	↓	↓	↓	↓
Day books	Purchases day book	Purchases returns book	Sales day book	Sales returns book

The ledgers

In form, the day books are similar to each other, the format for the purchases day book shown below being typical:

Date	Invoice Number	Supplier	Folio	Amount

The day books may be designed to permit analysis by the provision of separate columns showing the purchase or sale of different stock items.

The day books are posted to the ledgers. In the case of the purchases day book, the personal account of the supplier in the creditors ledger is credited: in the case of the sales day book, the personal account of the client in the debtors ledger is debited. The general ledger is used to record total purchases and sales, and it is posted periodically, usually on a monthly basis. The purchases account is debited with total monthly purchases and the sales account is credited with total monthly sales. The purchases and sales returns day books are also posted in the same way, there being credit entries recorded in the personal account of the supplier in respect of purchases returns, and debit entries in the personal account of the client in respect of sales returns. The total purchases returns and sales returns are posted monthly to the purchases returns and sales returns accounts in the general ledger.

The cash book

Unlike the day books, the cash book is both a book of original entry and a ledger account. The existence of the book obviates the need to have a cash account in the general ledger. Most businesses effect transactions by cheques. In the case of large stores and shops, there will also be considerable cash receipts. The cash book may be adapted to record both cash and cheque transactions—cash being recorded in a cash column and cheques recorded in a bank column. Whenever cash is paid into the bank or drawn from the bank, there is a double entry transaction to be recorded in the cash book. Thus, when cash is received as a result of a cash sale, it is recorded as a debit in the cash column, and when cash is paid into the bank, the amount paid in is credited to the cash column and debited in the bank column. The cash and the bank column are balanced independently. The balance on the cash column is checked against the cash lying on the premises in the various tills, and the balance on the bank column is reconciled with the bank statement.

The format of a double column cash book is as shown below:

Cash book

Receipts									Payments
Date	Details	Folio	Cash	Bank	Date	Details	Folio	Cash	Bank

It should be noted that transfers between the cash and the bank columns are complete double entry transactions in themselves. No other account is involved. Accordingly, when cash is paid into the bank, there will be what is known as a 'contra entry' recorded in the cash column. This means that the reference in the folio column 'C' indicates that the credit shown on the cash column corresponds to the debit shown in the bank column—both being in the cash book.

Contra entries are restricted to those involving transfers between the cash and the bank columns. Normal commercial transactions would involve entries in different accounts. For example, the receipt of a loan from the bank where the business has an account, would be recorded by a debit in the bank column of the cash book, indicating that the amount of the loan has been transferred to the business's bank account, and in the general ledger a credit entry would be shown in the loan account. Similarly, bank interest received or charged would be recorded as a debit or credit in the bank column of the cash book, as the case may be, and the corresponding credit or debit entry would be shown in the interest received or interest paid account in the general ledger. For example, overdraft interest charged by the bank would appear as a credit in the bank column of the cash book and as a debit in the interest payable account in the general ledger.

Occasionally, problems arise when a cheque paid into the bank is dishonoured. The so-called 'bounced cheque' means that the bank has been unable to obtain payment on clearing it with the drawer's bank, and it is returned to the person who accepted it in payment in the first place. When the cheque had been accepted from the client, it had been paid into the bank, the entries being a debit in the bank column of the cash book and a credit to the sales account. Should the cheque be dishonoured subsequently, the procedure is to reverse the original debit in the cash book—crediting the bank column with the amount of the cheque dishonoured and debiting a dishonoured cheque account with the amount involved. Clearly, the person who presented the bounced cheque will be contacted and an attempt will be made to obtain settlement.

Cash discounts

Cash discounts are inducements to customers to settle their accounts promptly. They should be distinguished from trade discounts, which are reductions granted to dealers as distinct from customers. Trade discounts are always deducted from the invoice, and only the net amount is posted to the personal account.

Example 1

J. Berg, a customer of Midtown Supplies Company Ltd, has bought goods on credit for £100. To encourage prompt payment, Midtown Supplies Company Ltd allows a cash discount of 5%. Accordingly, Berg pays £95 in settlement of his account. The entry in the company's books would be:

J. Berg account

	£		£
Goods	100	Cash	95

To close the account, an entry must be effected in respect of the discount allowed as follows:

Dr   Discount allowed account
Cr   J. Berg account } with £5

Accordingly, J. Berg's account would be closed as follows:

J. Berg account

	£		£
Goods	100	Cash	95
		Discount allowed	5
	100		100

The procedure used to streamline the recording of discounts allowed is simply to add an additional column on the debit side of the cash book and to record only the discounts allowed in that column. At the end of each month, the total of the discount column is transferred to the discount allowed account in the general ledger. It is important to remember that the discount column is a memorandum column only: the transfer to the discount allowed account completes the double entry and corresponds to the credit entry shown on the personal account. Discount received from suppliers are treated in a similar manner.

The division of the ledger: control accounts

In the same way as the volume of transactions eventually gave rise to the need to divide the journal into several day books, the cash book and the journal itself, so too was the ledger itself divided into several ledgers. Associated with the purchases day book is the creditors ledger which records the personal accounts of suppliers. The debtors ledger is associated with the sales day book, and records the personal accounts of debtors arising from sales. The existence of the cash book as both a book of original entry and a ledger is an exception to this development.

The division of the ledger in this way allows for the sectionalisation of the accounting records, and for an appropriate specialisation of work to be made possible in the accounting department.

The personal accounts of debtors and creditors found in the debtors and creditors ledgers respectively are posted periodically from the sales and purchases day books. It was noted earlier that the total of the sales and purchases day books was also posted to the sales account and the purchases account in the general ledger, thereby completing the double entry relating to these transactions.

The problem which arises, however, is that the double entry of these transactions is spread over several ledgers. Control accounts are, in effect, summary accounts of the debtors and creditors ledgers found in the general ledger. The presence of a debtors control account and of a creditors control account in the general ledger means that the double entry is completed in the general ledger. In this situation, the debtors and creditors ledgers exist as subsidiary ledgers.

Control accounts provide an effective check on the arithmetical accuracy of postings from the day books, and can speed up the discovery of errors. The existence of a discrepancy between the control account in the general ledger and the summary of entries in a subsidiary ledger locates the sector where an error is likely to be found. Control accounts will not, however, reveal certain types of posting errors; for example, postings to incorrect personal accounts, or errors in the data recorded in the day books or compensating errors.

The debtors control account

The debtors control account is a summary or total of all the transactions effected in the debtors ledger. These procedures are based on the use of individual sales invoices which indicate both the amount of the sale and the customer's indebtedness for this amount. It is evident that the process of entering each transaction invoice by invoice would become an onerous burden on the accountant's department.

To streamline the recording process, all invoices are entered in the sales day book. The accounts of individual debtors in the debtors ledger are debited directly from the sales day book to provide an accurate record of their individual indebtedness at any time. The books of original entry may be adapted with columns to suit the control system in force. For example, the cash book may contain an additional column to record cash received from debtors, thereby distinguishing them from other receipts.

The exclusion of individual debtor accounts from the general ledger enables the control account to be used to represent the total balance of debtors outstanding. Figure 5.2 below illustrates the use of the

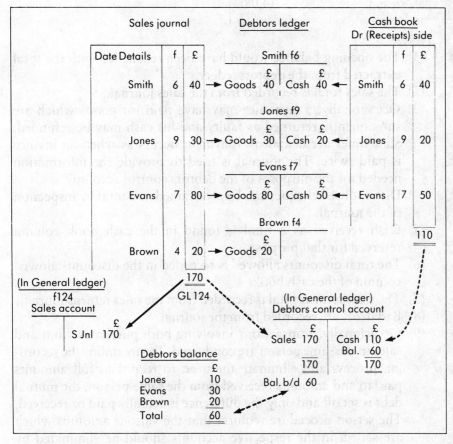

Fig. 5.2 Schematic outline of a debtors control system

debtors control account in the general ledger as representing the total transactions recorded in the individual debtor accounts found in the debtors ledger. The debtors control account shows at a glance the total balance of debtors outstanding as well as the level of cash receipts from debtors in relation to the total debtors outstanding.

The different types of entries to be found in the debtors control account are illustrated below together with explanatory notes.

Debtors control account

	£		£
(1) Balance b/d	14,732	(5) Cash received	80,320
(2) Goods—Sales	83,214	(6) Discount allowed	843
(3) Cash refund	62	(7) Returns	1,714
(4) Dishonoured cheques	117	(8) Bad debts	620
		(9) Contra items—Creditors	540
		(10) Balance c/d	14,088
	98,125		98,125
Balance b/d	14,088		

Notes:

(1) The opening balance would have been reconciled with the total extracted from the debtors ledger.

(2) The sales total is recorded from the sales journal.

(3) Occasionally, a customer may have paid for goods which are subsequently returned as faulty and his cash may be refunded. Sometimes accidental overpayment occurs as when an invoice is paid twice. The journal is used to provide the information needed for the purposes of the debtors control account.

(4) Dishonoured cheques can be ascertained as a total by inspection of the journal.

(5) Cash received as a total is found in the cash book column reserved for that purpose.

(6) The total discounts allowed is recorded in the discount-allowed column of the cash book.

(7) The sales returns total is recorded from the sales returns journal.

(8) Bad debts are recorded from the journal.

(9) Occasionally, transactions involving both purchases from and sales to the same person are conducted. To streamline the recording process and eliminate the need to record in full amounts paid to and amounts received from the same person, the mutual debt is set off and only the difference is actually paid or received. The set-off procedure requires that the various amounts which are set off in the respective accounts should be eliminated by the use of 'contra' entries. The journal will normally supply the details of the totals of contra entries to be made in the ledgers.

(10) The closing balances of debtors outstanding in the debtors control account must agree with the sum of the individual balances extracted from the individual debtor accounts in the debtors ledger.

Example 2

The following information is available from the books and records of Friedel and Company Limited as at 31 December 19X8:

	£
Total debtors outstanding at 1 January 19X8	64,369
Sales for the year to 31 December 19X8	237,426
Returns for the year to 31 December 19X8	2,690
Cash received from debtors during year	214,894
Discount allowed to debtors during year	8,316
Bad debts written off in the year	975
Settlements by contra–Suppliers' accounts	2,810

The total debtors outstanding at the 31 December 19X8 may be obtained from the debtors control account as follows:

Debtors control account

19X8		£	19X8		£
Jan 1	Balance b/d	64,369	Dec 31	Returns	2,690
Dec 31	Sales	237,426	Dec 31	Cash	214,894
			Dec 31	Discounts allowed	8,316
			Dec 31	Bad debts	975
			Dec 31	Contras	2,810
			Dec 31	Balance c/d	72,110
		301,795			301,795
19X9					
Jan 1	Balance b/d	72,110			

The balance of outstanding debtors of £72,110 should agree with the total of the balances of the individual debtor accounts in the debtors ledger.

The creditors control account

The procedure for facilitating the process of recording credit purchases and for the process of controlling total creditor balances is similar in nature to that applied to debtors. An additional problem is involved in the need to distinguish creditors in respect of goods supplied and creditors in respect of services provided. This distinction is required since total credit purchases are included in the total purchases shown in the trading section of the profit and loss account for the purpose of calculating the gross profit, whereas the various expenses charged in the calculation of net profit include services rendered but unpaid at the end of the accounting period. This additional problem is resolved by using an extended column analysis in the purchases journal to classify the nature of the goods or services supplied. The totals of the various columns are debited to the different expense accounts, and the total of goods purchased is debited periodically to the purchases account. Postings to the individual creditors accounts in the creditors ledger and the posting of the total credit balance to the creditors control account in the general ledger are also made periodically.

Discounts for prompt payment may also be received as well as allowed. A separate column is required in the cash book to record discounts received, the total of which is credited to the discount received account and shown as a debit in the creditors control account. The discount received from individual creditors is debited to their account in the creditors ledger.

Example 3
A typical creditors control account is set out below with notes on the origins of the entries.

Creditors control account

	£		£
(3) Returns	4,620	(1) Balance b/d	74,691
(4) Cash	218,110	(2) Purchases and supplies	210,360
(5) Discounts received	6,180		
(6) Contras (debtors)	1,470		
(7) Balance c/d	54,671		
	285,051		285,051
		Balance b/d	54,671

Notes:
(1) The balance brought down will have been agreed with a list of balances extracted from the creditors ledger.
(2) Purchases, etc., will be obtained from the total in the purchase journal which itself uses the suppliers' invoices as a basis for entries.
(3) The total purchases returned is obtained from the purchases returns journal which is based on suppliers' credit notes.
(4) Cash will be the figure shown as a total in the cash paid to creditors column in the cash book.
(5) The total discounts received are recorded in the cash book, as explained earlier.
(6) The 'contra' entries arise from the cancellation of mutual indebtedness.

(7) The balance of total creditors outstanding must agree with the total extracted from the creditors ledger.

A schematic outline of a creditors control system is shown in Fig. 5.3 below.

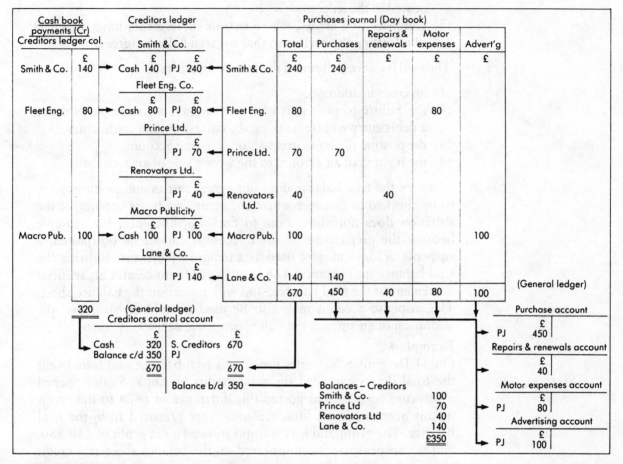

Fig. 5.3 Schematic outline of a creditors control system

Suspense accounts and the correction of errors

Numerous forms of errors may occur in a data processing system. Some of these errors may not manifest themselves at the trial balance stage, in particular the following types of errors:

(1) errors of principle, for example where the purchase of an asset is treated as a debit to the purchases account,

(2) errors of omission, where an entire transaction is unrecorded,

(3) errors of commission, for example where the double entry is correct with regard to the amount involved, but the amount is posted to the wrong account,

(4) errors of original entry, for example where a transaction has been incorrectly recorded in a book of original entry, and thereafter posted in the ledger,

(5) compensating errors, where two or more errors have the effect of offsetting themselves so that the trial balance agrees.

The trial balance will reveal the following errors:

(1) an error in addition,

(2) the failure to post part of a transaction, for example effecting a debit entry without making the corresponding credit entry,

(3) the posting of an incorrect amount to one account,

(4) the posting of an amount to the wrong side of an account.

Where the trial balance does not agree, entries and postings have to be checked to discover where the error lies. If the urgency of the situation does not allow time to find the difference, for example because the preparation of final accounts cannot be postponed, a suspense account may be used as a temporary measure to bring the trial balance into balance. The suspense account creates an artificial agreement of the trial balance, and will appear on the balance sheet. The suspense account may also be used to hold 'in suspense' the allocation of an amount until an appropriate decision is taken.

Example 4

On 31 December, S. Smiles drew up a trial balance and found that the total debits exceeded the total credits by £608. Smiles opened a suspense account and posted this difference of £608 to the credit of this account. Draft final accounts were prepared from the trial balance. The profit and loss account showed a net profit of £10,580, and the suspense account appeared on the balance sheet as a credit balance. Subsequently, the following errors came to light:

(1) the sales journal had been undercast by £150,

(2) the discounts received and discounts allowed for the year amounting to £110 and £35 respectively had been posted from the cash book to the wrong side of these accounts, £110 being posted as a debit to the discounts received account, and £35 being posted as a credit to the discounts allowed account,

(3) an invoice for £112 from R. Ryan had been entered correctly in the purchases day book, but had been posted as £211 to Ryan's account,

(4) a cash register costing £400 had been debited to the purchases account instead of to the office equipment account,

(5) a cheque for £284 received as rent had been entered in the cash book, but had not been posted to the rent receivable account.

It is required to:

(1) prepare journal entries to correct these errors,
(2) write up the suspense account to dispose of these errors,
(3) prepare a statement showing the amended net profit for the year.

Journal

		Dr £	Cr £
(1)	Suspense account	150	
	Sales account		150
	Being undercasting error in the sales day book		
(2)	Suspense account	110	
	Discounts received account		110
	Being correction of posting error from the cash book to discounts received		
	Discounts allowed account	35	
	Suspense account		35
	Being correction of posting error from the cash book to discounts allowed		
(3)	Suspense account	99	
	R. Ryan account		99
	Being correction of over-credit		
(4)	Office equipment account	400	
	Purchases account		400
	Being cash paid wrongly debited to purchases account		
(5)	Suspense account	284	
	Rent receivable account		284
	Being rent receivable not posted from the cash book		

Suspense account

	£			£
(1) Sales	150		Balance b/d	608
(2) Discounts received	110	(2)	Discounts allowed	35
(3) R. Ryan	99			
(4) Rent receivable	284			
	643			643

Note that only those errors creating a difference in the trial balance need be cleared in the suspense account. For example, the sum of £400 incorrectly posted to purchases account instead of office equipment account did not create a difference in the trial balance. The correction of this error does not require an entry in the suspense account.

Statement of amended profit for the year

	£
Net profit for the year as per draft accounts	10,580
Add: Adjustment to sales	150
Adjustment to discounts received	110
Adjustment to purchases account	400
Rent receivable omitted	284
	11,524
Less: Adjustment to discounts allowed	35
Amended net profit for the year	11,489

Questions

1. The following balances, details and totals were taken from the various books of Baker Bargains Ltd as at 30 September 19X4.

	£
Debtor balances at 1 October 19X3	6,120
Cash paid to creditors	29,600
Bad debts written off	380
Sales returns	810
Purchases	36,114
Discount allowed	1,440
Debtor balances at 30 September 19X4	7,830
Creditor balances at 1 October 19X3	4,390
Discounts received	967
Cash received from debtors	42,150
Contra items—purchases and sales	870
Sales	47,360
Purchases returns	1,960
Creditor balances at 30 September 19X4	7,107

Required:
Prepare the debtors control and the creditors control accounts for the year to 30 September 19X4.

2. The following balances appear in the general ledger of a company as at 1 July 19X3.

	£
Debtors control account	60,000
Creditors control account	32,000
Provision for doubtful debts	2,000

The following transactions occurred during the year ended 30 June 19X4:

	£
Credit sales	380,000
Return of goods previously sold on credit	14,000
Cash received from sundry debtors	285,400
Discounts allowed	5,600
Bad debts written off	5,000
Debtors and creditors accounts settled by contra	50,000
Credit purchases	186,000
Return of goods previously bought on credit	3,800
Discount received	2,200
Cash paid to sundry creditors	122,000

The balance on the provision for doubtful debts account at 30 June 19X4 is to be made equal to 5% of the balance on the total sundry debtors at that date.

Required:
Using the information given, prepared the following accounts for the year ended 30 June 19X4:
(1) Debtors control account.
(2) Creditors control account.
(3) Provision for doubtful debts account.

3. The following entries appear in the debtors ledger of a company for the year ended 31 December 19X4:

	£
Sales as per posting summaries	149,506
Receipts from debtors	138,942
Discounts allowed	3,634
Balance on control account as at 1 January 19X4	17,904

The clerk in charge of the debtors ledger listed the balances outstanding on 31 December 19X4 as amounting to £19,326, but this did not agree with the balance on the debtors control account. There were no credit balances on the ledger cards.

Investigation of the differences revealed the following:
(1) The bank statement showed cheques received from debtors amounting to £396 which had been completely overlooked.
(2) The following journal entries had been correctly posted to the debtors ledger but had not been posted to the debtors control account in the general ledger:

	£
Debtor balances set off against creditor balances	5,792
Bed debts written off	1,280

(3) When listing the debtors balances in the debtors ledger, the clerk had overlooked three debtors accounts with debit balances totalling £382.
(4) An opening debit balance of £427 on a debtor account in the debtors ledger had been discovered by the clerk in charge as having been included as £27 only.
(5) A receipt of £2,346 from J. Spruce had been recorded in the debtors'

column of the cash book, but had not been posted, since no account under that name could be traced. On investigation, it was discovered that it was in payment for a car used by the sales department and which had been sold to Spruce.

Required:

(a) Prepare the debtors control account for the year ended 31 December 19X4, taking into account the above adjustments.

(b) Reconcile the clerk's balance of £19,326 with the corrected balance on the debtors control account in the general ledger.

(c) Explain the benefits that accrue from using control accounts.

4. A business maintains a manual record of debtors' accounts, posting entries to the sales ledger from copies of invoices and credit notes. Cheques and discounts allowed are posted to the sales ledger from copies of daily cash sheets. Copy invoices and credit notes and daily cash sheets are totalled to provide for entries in the control account. All transfers into and out of the sales ledger are recorded through a transfer journal, which is totalled to provide for further entries in the control account.

At the end of March 1975, the balances appearing in the sales ledger totalled to Dr £9,275, and the balance in the sales ledger control account was Dr £9,905.

An investigation of the difference revealed the following errors:

(1) A copy invoice for £80 has been posted to a customer's account as £8.

(2) A copy credit note for £22 has been debited to a customer's account.

(3) Discounts allowed of £14 shown on the daily cash sheets have not been posted to the customer's accounts.

(4) An invoice for £135 for J. Brown has been posted to the debit of R. Brown's account.

(5) Two debit balances of £45 and £27 have been omitted from the list extracted from the Sales Ledger.

(6) An account for £110 in the Sales Ledger has been settled by contra entry to the Purchase Ledger, but not record has been made of this in the Transfer Journal.

(7) A balance of £59 in a Sales Ledger account has been written off as irrecoverable, but has not been entered through the Transfer Journal.

(8) The copy invoices were over-added by £325.

(9) Cash of £25 paid in settlement of a customer's credit balance has been entered on the wrong side of the customer's account.

Required:

Prepare a statement reconciling the sales ledger total with the sales ledger control account.

(Association of Certified Accountants)

5. The balances extracted from the records of Perrod and Company at 31 December 19X8 were as follows:

	£
Premises (cost)	7,000
Capital	8,440
Drawings	1,935
Provision for depreciation of office equipment at 1 January 19X8	480

	£
Debtor's control account	1,891
Creditors' control account	2,130
Stock at 1 January 19X8	1,200
Purchases	9,480
Sales	14,003
Returns inwards	310
Office equipment (cost) (balance at 1 January 19X8)	1,600
Wages	1,540
Commission	160
Discount allowed	210
Discount received	121
Bank (credit balance)	980
Cash in hand	56
Heating and lighting	375
Postage and stationery	224
Bad debts	68

A preliminary trial balance was prepared, but, although no arithmetical errors were made, the trial balance did not balance. In seeking the reasons for the difference, the following facts emerged.

(1) *Debtors' control account*

(a) No entry had been made in the control account in respect of the debts written off as bad;

(b) A cheque paid by a debtor for £110 had been returned on 31 December 19X8 by the bank marked 'return to drawer'. An entry had been made in both the bank account and the debtors' account for this, but no entry had been made in the control account.

(c) Sales on credit of £97 to A. Jones had been correctly entered in his account but nothing had been entered in the control account.

(d) M. Smith had been allowed a cash discount of £43, but no corresponding entry had appeared in the control account.

(2) *Creditors' control account*

This exceeded the balance of the individual creditors' accounts by £12. The difference was caused by:

(a) Goods returned to R. Hardy costing £69 had been entered correctly in the control account, but no entry had been made in Mr Hardy's account.

(b) An invoice for £56 had been incorrectly entered in the control account as £65.

(c) Two credit balances of £45 and £27 had been omitted from the list extracted from the creditors ledger.

(3) Some office equipment which had cost £240 had been debited to the purchase account.

(4) The wages (£1,540) included £320 of personal drawings by the owner of the business.

(5) The provision for depreciation of office equipment had been credited in 19X7 with straight line depreciation of 10%, i.e. £160 but the depreciation should have been charged at $12\frac{1}{2}\%$ per annum.

(6) The account for stationery (£224) included £45 of personal notepaper for the owner.

(7) The returns inwards account had been credited with £90 for some goods returned to a creditor.

Required:

(*a*) Prepare the debtors' and creditors' control accounts taking into account where appropriate the facts ascertained in (1) and (2) above.

(*b*) Prepare journal entries to correct the errors and omissions enumerated in (3) to (7) above.

(*c*) Given that Perrod and Company's stock at 31 December 19X8 was valued at £1,400 and the depreciation on office equipment for the year was £230, prepare a Balance Sheet as at 31 December 19X8, showing clearly the net profit for the year.

(*Note:* A trading profit and loss account is NOT required.)

(*Association of Certified Accountants*)

6. After the preparation of a trial balance, an unexplained difference of Dr £218 remains, and a suspense account is opened for that amount. Subsequent investigations reveal:

(1) £35 received from A. Jones and credited to his account has not been entered in the bank account.

(2) The owner of the business has taken goods which cost £69 for his own use. No entries have been made for this at all.

(3) A payment of £47 to M. Smith has been credited to that account.

(4) Discounts allowed (£198) and discounts received (£213) have been posted to the discount accounts as credits and debits respectively.

(5) Bank interest received of £111 has not been entered in the bank account.

(6) £211 owing by A. Able has been debited incorrectly to B. Able.

(7) The carriage outwards (£98) has been treated as a revenue.

Required:

Prepare the suspense account making the entries necessary to eliminate the debit balance there is. Indicate clearly how you would deal with *all* of the errors discovered. (*Association of Certified Accountants*)

7. (*a*) An inexperienced bookkeeper has drawn up a trial balance for the year ended 30 June 19X7:

	Dr £	Cr £
Provision for doubtful debts	200	
Bank overdraft	1,654	
Capital		4,591
Creditors		1,637
Debtors	2,983	
Discount received	252	
Discount allowed		733
Drawings	1,200	
Office furniture	2,155	
General expenses		829
Purchases	10,923	
Returns inwards		330
Rent and rates	314	
Salaries	2,520	
Sales		16,882
Stock	2,418	
Provision for depreciation of furniture	364	
	£24,983	£25,002

Required:

Draw up a 'corrected' trial balance, debiting or crediting any residual error to a suspense account.

(*b*) Further investigation of the suspense account, ascertained in (a) above, reveals the following errors.

(1) Goods bought from J. Jones amounting to £13 had been posted to his account as £33.

(2) Furniture which had cost £173 had been debited to the general expense account.

(3) An invoice from Suppliers Ltd, for £370 had been omitted from the purchase account, but credited to Suppliers Ltd account.

(4) Sales on credit to A. Hope Ltd, for £450 had been posted to the sales account, but not to the debtors ledger.

(5) The balance on the capital account had been incorrectly brought forward in the ledger, and should have been £4,291.

(6) An amount of £86 received from A. Blunt, a debtor, in settlement of his account had been treated as a cash sale.

(7) Discount allowed has been undertotalled by £35.

Required:

Prepare journal entries correcting each of the above errors and write up the suspense account.

(*c*) There are several types of error which will not effect the balancing of a trial balance; these include errors of omission, commission and principle. Explain what is meant by these terms and give an example of each.

(Association of Certified Accountants)

6 Accounting Concepts and the Need for Standards ——

Previous chapters have been concerned with the examination of the practices of financial accounting, and in particular those relating to record keeping and the use of recorded data for profit determination, representations of asset values and the control of working capital.

Underpinning these practices are a set of concepts which not only have a deterministic influence on the manner in which accounting procedures are carried out but also have a profound influence on the meaning and usefulness of the information resulting from these procedures.

Some of the most important concepts have already been mentioned, for example, the entity concept, the concept of periodicity, the accruals and the matching concepts. It has been noted that they lend a particular characteristic to the manner in which accountants conceptualise accounting events.

In the search for rationality which is a feature of the scientific method increasingly applied in the study of accounting, many authors have been concerned at the evident lack of *general* theory of accounting which would provide a coherent framework of reference for the continued development of accounting knowledge. In particular, such a theory would assist in the analysis of the objectives of accounting and would provide criteria for evaluating the validity of accounting practices. As a result, it is argued, accounting would become more 'scientific' in its approach to the analysis of its problems and in the formulation of appropriate solutions and methods.

Recent criticisms of financial accounting information have drawn public attention to what accountants were content to regard as matters of purely professional interest and concern. Criticism has centred particularly on the treatment of inflation, the representation of asset values, and the wide variations in the measurement of the profits of the *same* company resulting simply from the application of different valuation concepts.

In essence, the debate has now focused on the need to re-examine the substance of some important accounting concepts and to provide *standards* for regulating the manner in which they are applied in the practice of accounting. The significance of such standards, therefore, lies in the fact that they act as a substitute for rules which would otherwise emanate from a *Theory* of Accounting in which rationality rather than consensus would act as the deterministic influence.

This chapter is divided into five sections as follows:

Accounting concepts
Accounting standards
International accounting standards
Statements of standard accounting practice
Standards and Companies Acts.

Accounting concepts

Accounting is a man-made discipline. Its methods cannot be validated by reference to 'natural laws' as in the physical sciences or to the internal logic of numbers as in mathematics. Yet, accountants cannot avoid the need for reference to rules which not only provide a unity of understanding but also a uniformity of approach in the practice of accounting. This significance of such rules is evident when one considers that accountants attach meaning to events by representing them as numbers. Such meaning would be lost entirely if the compilation and the communication of accounting numbers did not conform to a generally accepted set of rules. Accounting rules are sometimes referred to as 'concepts'.

The entity concept

The entity concept defines the limits of the financial process by its identification with an organisation deemed to have a separate existence from its owner(s). The accounting process is concerned with the activities of the entity and not the activities of its owner or other persons.

There are two interpretations of the entity concept:

(1) The proprietary concept which views the entity as a vehicle through which the owner engages in economic activity with a view to profit. Assets are regarded as belonging to the owner, and the balance sheet reflects the owner's interest in the entity as being the net worth stated as the owner's equity.

(2) The entity concept, as distinct from the proprietary concept, views the entity as having a separate identity with its own objectives. This interpretation may be termed the pure entity concept. Hence, the owner is treated as being merely another interested party having claims against the entity. In line with this view, the assets are regarded as belonging properly to the entity, and the claims against it are all classified as equities.

The sole trader is the best example of the manifestation of the proprietary concept, and the limited liability company is the foremost example of the pure entity concept.

The money measurement concept

This important concept limits the recognition of accounting events to those which may be described in money terms. As a result, many factors of considerable economic importance to the entity are not recorded, for example, management expertise, technical competence of employees, good industrial and customer relations.

The failure to recognise these factors arises principally from the fact that the accounting process is transaction-based, and money value tends to arise mainly from transactions giving rise to rights and obligations susceptible of expression in money values.

Although non-monetary measurements bring further clarity and meaning to purely monetary measurements, the major obstacles to widening the basis of the accounting process in this respect are as follows:

(1) Monetary measurements have a unity of meaning which makes them readily understood when communicated as information.
(2) Monetary measurements provide a basis for quite complex financial analysis which rely on numbers having a common denominator.
(3) Non-monetary measurements cannot be integrated meaningfully with monetary measurements to provide a generalised calculus of the value of the firm and its activities.

The dual aspect concept

The essence of double-entry bookkeeping is the concept that all transactions are classified twice. The manifestation of this concept is the fact that they are entered twice: once as debits and once as credits. This allows the accounting equation to be maintained throughout the bookkeeping system.

The detailed application of this concept has been examined in preceding chapters. Advanced data recording systems based on computers have been developed to process accounting information in great detail and integrate the activities of complex organisations, but these systems still rely on the dual aspect concept.

Although the dual aspect concept relies on faultless mathematical principles, which we noted ensured that the total debit and credit entries balance when extracted in the form of a trial balance, errors may still occur even in computerised data-processing systems. These errors may not only be attributed to input errors but also to erroneous interpretations of the economic events which accounts purport to show.

The cost concept

In seeking for objectivity in attaching values to inputs of economic resources, accountants use the acquisition price as the most objective measurement since it is supported by the evidence of a transaction. Accountants have been accused of confusing verifiability with objectivity. Nevertheless, the cost concept provides uniformity in the treatment of inputs and provides a reliable valuation under conditions of stable prices. Price instability associated with specific inflation and the debasement in the value of money associated with general inflation undermine the validity of the assumptions upon which the cost concept is based. In particular, it leads to serious distortions in the measurement of profits when historic costs are allocated against current revenues. As a result, this concept has suffered increasing criticism when used for financial reporting purposes, and an alternative system based on replacement cost has been recommended for adoption in the United Kingdom.

The going concern concept

This concept is of great importance for asset valuation, for it reflects the assumption that the firm is to be valued on the basis that it is a going concern, and is not likely to terminate in the period immediately ahead. In effect, this concept underpins the asset values shown on the balance sheet and the other conventions associated with the representation of liabilities. To abandon this concept would imply that assets should be valued on a realisable value basis. Nevertheless, the following observations may be made:

(1) It is not necessarily true that firms do not cease trading. Therefore, balance sheet valuation based on the going concern assumption may give investors an incorrect view of the value of assets, particularly when firms cease trading shortly after the last published balance sheet. In this connection, decisions to cease trading may be taken quite abruptly in the face of a perception of radically changed circumstances.

(2) It is misleading to suppose that the going concern concept applies equally to continuity in the firm's operations in a particular sector or as regards a particular product. In this respect, the going concern concept finds no support in any other formal study of economic behaviour.

(3) The concept precludes the consideration of alternative courses of action and prevents the provision of relevant accounting information for this purpose.

The realisation concept

The realisation concept influences financial accounting in two ways. First, it acts to mark the recognition of an accounting event and to regulate the timing of entries in the bookkeeping system. Second, it prevents undue optimism in business affairs by restricting the recognition of gains to those which have been actually realised through a transaction giving rise to legal rights to receive monetary payments.

In essence, the realisation concept reflects the spirit of caution and conservatism which marks the accountant's approach to the analysis of business activities. It reinforces the cost concept by requiring costs to be accumulated until they may be allocated to the revenues with which they are associated.

The realisation concept is criticised because it may distort the process of profit determination in cases where gains may have accrued over a long period but are not recognised until a sale has occurred. By refusing to recognise 'holding gains', it is argued that the accounting process rejects a cardinal feature of profit measurement which is to measure increases in wealth between two points in time.

To prevent excessive distortions in certain cases, the realisation concept is modified. This is particularly the case in large building and engineering projects, where gains are accrued on the certification of work. As regards routine trading operations involving the receipt of an order, the issue of an invoice, the despatch of goods and the receipt of payment, the issue of the invoice marks the timing of an entry in the bookkeeping system.

The concept of periodicity

It may be argued that the only correct measure of enterprise profit is the surplus arising over its entire life and determined at that point of time when all business transactions have been completed and the only remaining asset is cash. This view would be inconsistent with the going concern concept and with the need to assess the financial status and performance of the firm from time to time.

Hence, an arbitrary time period, usually a year, is chosen as a basis for the measurement of *periodic* profit. The assumption underlying the concept of periodicity is that business events can be identified with particular periods.

This concept induces the necessity for supporting concepts for example, the realisation, the matching and the accruals concept which have their logic in the measurement of periodic profit.

The concept of periodicity assumes a degree of homogeneity in the pattern of business activities and a corresponding smoothness in the time profile of a periodic profit stream. Neither of these assumptions is confirmed by the evidence of business activities.

The additional problem induced by this concept relates to the depreciation of fixed asset values over successive accounting periods. As we shall note in Chapter 7, depreciation poses complex theoretical and practical problems.

The matching concept

This concept supports that of periodicity in assuming that particular items of expense can be associated with the revenues of particular periods. It also subscribes to the accounting view that cost is an appropriate measure of economic value. Moreover, it assumes that cost flows parallel the physical flow of goods, thereby inducing the various stock valuation methods to be discussed in Chapter 8.

Cost allocation procedures implicitly required by the matching concept result in a great variety in cost numbers matched against periodic revenue. Thus, the allocation of fixed asset costs and other costs incurred over protracted time make it impossible to cost numbers which are free of bias. Indeed, accounting procedures for allocating and apportioning *current* production costs are themselves the source of distortions in cost measurements. These costing procedures are directly related to the matching concept and result from the application of this concept to the measurement of product costs.

The accruals concept

Together with the realisation and the matching concept, the accruals concept has its origin in the concept of periodicity. It requires that revenues and expenses associated with a particular accounting period be brought into the calculus of the profit of that period *whether or not* cash has been received or paid.

The importance of the accruals concept has already been made explicit in earlier chapters. From a bookkeeping point of view, recorded receipts and expenditure must be carefully scrutinised in the process of determining periodic revenues and expenses. Payments in advance, both of the nature of revenue and expense, must be excluded and carried forward to the next accounting period to which they belong. Amounts receivable and payable in respect of which no entries in the books have been made must be accrued at the close of the accounting period so that they may be reflected in the revenues and expenses of the year to which they properly belong. As a result, payments received and made in respect to amounts accrued in the previous period are treated as payments from debtors and payments to creditors, and do not affect the measurement of current periodic profit. Accrual accounting represents the conventional accounting approach to profit determination.

Criticisms of the accrual concept are that it introduces complexity into accounting numbers and renders accounting results difficult to interpret by users who are non-accountants. Accordingly, proponents of cash flow accounting argue that it reduces complexity and allows a more general understanding of accounting information. Moreover, they argue that cash flow accounting is more relevant to the decisions which businessmen and investors wish to make. In this connection, it should be noted that one important attribute of the accrual concept is that it smoothes the time profile of periodic cash flows and for this reason alone provides a more accurate view of the trend of periodic profit.

The concept of consistency

This concept is directed at providing a degree of uniformity in accounting numbers to enable realistic comparisons to be made by requiring that methods of treating particular items should be followed consistently once they have been adopted.

Uniformity is required in accounting for two reasons. First, to permit comparisons to be made by reference to the results of previous years by a company in the process of evaluating its own performance and making decisions about the future. Second, to permit useful inter-firm comparisons to be made by investors in the process of selecting and evaluating investment alternatives.

The concept of consistency is at variance with the practice of accounting in several important respects. First, accounting practice permits alternative valuation methods to coexist within the same firm and as between different firms. For example, closing stock may be valued at the 'lower of cost or net realisable value'. Additionally, different firms may select entirely different valuation methods in the allocation and apportionment of costs to stock values. Second, the practice of accounting requires the exercise of judgement in considering the manner in which particular events should be represented. This has led to serious misunderstanding in the past as regards, for example, the valuation of stock items. It is possible for one firm of accountants to give a radically different treatment to a stock item from that of another firm called to give an opinion on the same matter. As a result, disputes have occurred in which the accounting profession has suffered a measure of criticism for not seeming able to keep its own house in order. These criticisms led to a demand for some degree of standardisation of accounting practice, and the establishment in the United Kingdom of the Accounting Standards Committee to deal with this problem.

The concept of prudence

This concept has a pervasive influence on accounting practice. As regards financial accounting, it is manifested in the following propositions:

(a) The accountant should under no circumstances anticipate profit but should provide for potential losses,

(b) Where alternative valuation methods are available that method should be selected which leads to the lowest value.

In a real sense, the concept of prudence reflects the social role which accountants play in providing information to businessmen and investors. Given that optimism tends to cloud the judgement of businessmen, the accountant acts as a foil by discounting risk factors in any information which he provides.

Accounting standards

The variety of different procedures and valuations permitted under generally accepted accounting practice which has given rise to the problems referred to in the previous section, has eroded to some extent their basic accounting purpose. This purpose is to provide a set of rules for ensuring that accounting information has an identity of meaning to all its users. A prerequisite to this condition is that accounting procedures should themselves be standardised in such a way as to guarantee that the information resulting from the application of these procedures to data will be identical in meaning to all users.

Underlying the debate about accounting standards are a number of very important issues for the accounting profession. These issues are as follows:

(1) *Reliability.* Accounting information should be reliable in use. This implies that users should be able to rely on some basic assumptions about the quality of accounting information produced by accountants. The ultimate criterion of reliability is one which satisfies the following conditions:

(a) That users know precisely the meaning of information, and are not deceived in their analysis of its relevance to their own needs.

(b) That users know precisely the limits to the knowledge content of the information provided.

It is evident that in considering the range of public expectations from accounting information, a degree of reliability which satisfies the minimum conditions stated above must be regarded as a fundamental requirement.

(2) *Uniformity.* Accounting information is used for making informed judgements about the affairs of a business, and also for making informed comparisons between the performance of different businesses. Where these judgements are used by the public for the purpose of making investment decisions, it follows that the degree of uniformity which is required should enable *reliable comparisons* to be made. The pressure for the standardisation of accounting practices is to ensure a uniformity of treatment of data and hence an identity of the meaning of information.

(3) *Comparability.* Reliability and uniformity are integrated in the notion of comparability. This debate about comparability is more complex than is implicit in the assumption that uniformity of accounting practice will secure perfect comparability. In a real sense, the activities and the circumstances of different firms are not comparable because they are not identical. Indeed the activities and the circumstances of the same firm may not be identical from year to year. Hence, the issue of comparability is not really concerned with discovering an *identity* of meaning about the activities and circumstances of firms, but it is concerned with revealing the *differences* between them. Some assert, therefore, that these differences may well be lost to view if accountants are not allowed to select their own procedure for revealing these differences.

(4) *Judgement.* Accountants assert that they should be allowed to exercise some judgement in interpreting data. This implies that some variety should be allowed for in the procedures available for transforming data into information. This point is made particularly as regards alternative valuation methods and ways of treating depreciation.

These several issues do not form part of a restricted discussion within the accounting profession. Both in the USA and in the UK, the criticisms levelled in the press against the accounting profession has been associated with the failure to disclose important information to investors about the true state of affairs in a number of celebrated company reports. Although accountants have been able to formulate their own rules about what is 'true and fair', their interpretation of truth and fairness has not seemed convincing to the public. In the wake of public concern and the fear that governments might intervene to impose a measure of state control in the affairs of the profession, the pressure for standardisation has become overwhelming.

The discussion of accounting standards has taken place at a national and at an international level. Given the growing interdependency of nation states, the appearance of unified capital markets and supranational bodies to formulate international laws, it is to be expected that there will ultimately be a set of international accounting standards which will be universally applicable. The processes by which these international accounting standards are currently being forged are interesting in themselves. Some countries, for example the USA and the UK, have a long tradition of professional independence. Others, for example France, have a long experience of state control.

In the USA, an early interest in accounting standards resulted from the Securities Exchange Commission (SEC) which was established under the Securities Exchange Act of 1934. It has power to intervene in the accounting practices adopted by corporations seeking listings on the stock exchanges. Although the SEC has a powerful influence in this respect, it has been concerned essentially with the protection of shareholders and investors and fair dealings on the stock exchanges rather than with accounting theory as such. At a professional level, the American Institute of Certified Public Accountants formed the Financial Accounting Standards Board (FASB) in 1973 with the objective of formulating financial accounting standards. Indications so far are that a pragmatic approach will be adopted towards pressures for standards emanating from different sources. The possibility of intervention by Congress either directly or through empowered agencies does exist.

In the UK, too, an early interest in accounting standards is evident in previous endeavours by the Institute of Chartered Accountants in England and Wales to obtain a measure of agreement on accounting principles. A series of Recommendations on Accounting Principles has been issued on matters of professional interest. This endeavour was never a comprehensive approach to the problem, nor did it produce anything comparable in scope to the Inventory of Generally Accepted Accounting Principles of Business Enterprise issued by the American Institute of Certified Public Accountants in 1965. In 1971, the Accounting Standards Committee was established and has since issued a series of Statements of Standard Accounting Practice (SSAPs).

At an international level, progress has been made and agreement has been reached in several areas and a number of International Accounting Standards have been published since the International Accounting Standards Board was established in 1973.

It is evident that the issues involved in the debate about accounting standards have deeper roots than the superficial absence of uniformity in accounting procedures. It is clear that it is really the absence of a *theory of financial accounting* which is the root cause of problems. There is already evidence of a search towards a methodology essential to the formulation of such a theory in current discussions about the objectives of financial reporting. A theory of financial accounting would provide a framework for evaluating alternative accounting practices in a systematic and coherent manner consistent with the scientific method used in other sciences for formulating theories. In this analysis, the approach to the superficial absence of uniformity by the diktat of accounting standards would not appear to be an appropriate way of solving the more fundamental problem. Nevertheless, it may be regarded as affording partial solutions to problems which cannot be presently solved, bearing in mind the current state of the art.

International accounting standards

There are several influences at work in the process of welding together an international set of agreed standards of accounting practice. These reflect a tendency towards a common view of the problems involved. In many cases, it is obvious that legislation governing the disclosure of accounting information to shareholders in the form of annual balance sheets and profit statements has a broad similarity from country to country. Tax laws also tend to develop a set of rules for the assessment of taxable corporate profit, and these laws have a degree of similarity. The existence of capital markets and the operation of stock exchanges also have an influence on the nature of published financial accounting information.

It is really at the level of professional practice, and in particular where accounting conventions allow scope for the discretionary treatment of data, that the formulation of International Accounting Standards has a particular significance. In addition to laying down a framework of basic rules, their influence for the evolution of a unified profession cannot be overlooked. This is important, for example, in the evolution of an integrated European Common Market where eventually the executive function for regulating a unified European accounting profession may rest with the European Commission.

The initial impetus for the establishment of the International Accounting Standards Board came from the accounting profession itself. Its founder members were predominantly representative of advanced industrial nations, excluding the Communist block, as follows:

Australia   France
Canada   Germany

Japan   Netherlands
Mexico   United Kingdom and Ireland
                               United States of America

Many countries have subsequently associated themselves with the International Accounting Standards Board, ranging alphabetically from Bangladesh to Zambia, and including economies as diverse as those of Fiji and Finland, Tobago and Yugoslavia.

Statements of standard accounting practice (SSAPs)

The formulation of International Accounting Standards may be seen as a process emanating from the efforts of individual countries in formulating accounting standards. Given the interest of the IASB in the future development of International Accounting Standards, it follows that no country which is associated with IASB will proceed to formulate standards which will directly conflict with possible future IAS. Obviously, the possibility of conflict and redundancy cannot be overlooked.

The approach to the formulation of SSAPs in the United Kingdom may be taken as representative of a conscious development of accounting standards in keeping with the spirit which the IASB has adopted. The accounting bodies in the United Kingdom formed an Accounting Standards Committee with technical support staff. The deliberations of topics has led to the issue of a series of Exposure Drafts (ED) setting forth the particular solutions recommended by the ASC and inviting comment. After the elapse of sufficient time for comment and discussion, the Exposure Draft is re-examined and modified as required, and formally issued as a Statement of Standard Accounting Practice (SSAP) which members of the profession are expected to observe.

The uneasy reception which has been accorded to some of the SSAPs which have been issued in the United Kingdom presages the difficulties facing the IASB. The dangers in the approach adopted are:

(a) The response by a professional body to an external need may be slow.
(b) It may be difficult for a professional body to institute disciplinary procedures against its members who do not conform to an accounting standard in respect of which there is not unanimous agreement. This problem has manifested itself already in the United Kingdom.
(c) In an extreme case, a professional body may be forced to expose an SSAP to an adoption or rejection decision by its members.

Issues of importance should be decided by force of argument and logic rather than a straight vote in which other influences may be at work.

To date, the ASC has issued the following standards:

SSAP 1 *Accounting for the Results of Associated Companies*
SSAP 2 *Disclosure of Accounting Policies*
SSAP 3 *Earnings Per Share*
SSAP 4 *The Accounting Treatment of Government Grants*
SSAP 5 *Accounting for Value Added Tax*
SSAP 6 *Extraordinary Items and Prior Year Adjustments*
SSAP 8 *The Treatment of Taxation under the Imputation System in the Accounts of Companies*
SSAP 9 *Stocks and Work in Progress*
SSAP 10 *Statements of Source and Application of Funds*
SSAP 12 *Accounting for Depreciation*
SSAP 13 *Accounting for Research and Development*
SSAP 14 *Group Accounts*
SSAP 15 *Accounting for Deferred Taxation*
SSAP 16 *Current Cost Accounting*
SSAP 17 *Accounting for Post Balance Sheet Events*
SSAP 18 *Accounting for Contingencies*
SSAP 19 *Accounting for Investment Properties*
SSAP 20 *Foreign Currency Translation*
SSAP 21 *Accounting for Leases and Hire Purchase Contracts*
SSAP 22 *Accounting for Goodwill*
SSAP 23 *Accounting for Acquisitions and Mergers*

The prime concern underlying these SSAPs is with quoted companies, and the procedures adopted to report financial information to investors. Perhaps the most useful SSAP for the purpose of this text is SSAP 2 *Disclosure of Accounting Policies*, which is reproduced in its entirety below.

SSAP 2 *Disclosure of Accounting Policies*

Contents   *Paragraphs*

2. *Disclosure of accounting policies (Issued November 1971)*

© The Institute of Chartered Accountants in England and Wales.

It is fundamental to the understanding of financial accounts that those who use them should be aware of the main assumptions on which they are based. The purpose of the Statement which follows is to assist such understanding by promoting improvement in the quality of information disclosed. It seeks to achieve this by establishing as standard accounting practice the disclosure in financial accounts of clear explanations of the accounting policies followed in so far as these are significant for the purpose of giving a true and fair view. The Statement does not seek to establish accounting standards for individual items; these will be dealt with in separate Statements of Standard Accounting Practice issued from time to time.

PART 1—EXPLANATORY NOTE

Fundamental accounting concepts, accounting bases and accounting policies

1   In accounting usage terms such as 'accounting principles', 'practices', 'rules', 'conventions', 'methods' or 'procedures' have often been treated as interchangeable.[1] For the purpose of this Statement it is convenient to distinguish between *fundamental accounting concepts, accounting bases* and *accounting policies.*

2   *Fundamental accounting concepts* are here defined as broad basic assumptions which underlie the periodic financial accounts of

---

[1] In this series 'accounting practices' has been adopted as a generic term to encompass all aspects of financial accounting methods and presentation.

business enterprises. It is expedient to single out for special mention four in particular: (a) the 'going concern' concept (b) the 'accruals' concept (c) the 'consistency' concept and (d) the 'prudence' concept.*² The use of these concepts is not necessarily self-evident from an examination of accounts, but they have such general acceptance that they call for no explanation in published accounts and their observance is presumed unless stated otherwise. They are practical rules rather than theoretical ideals and are capable of variation and evolution as accounting thought and practice develop, but their present generally accepted meanings are restated in paragraph 14 below.

3   *Accounting bases* are the methods which have been developed for expressing or applying fundamental accounting concepts to financial transactions and items. By their nature accounting bases are more diverse and numerous than fundamental concepts, since they have evolved in response to the variety and complexity of types of business and business transactions, and for this reason there may justifiably exist more than one recognised accounting basis for dealing with particular items.

4   *Accounting policies* are the specific accounting bases judged by business enterprises to be most appropriate to their circumstances and adopted by them for the purpose of preparing their financial accounts.

Particular problems in application of the fundamental concepts

5   The main difficulty in applying the fundamental accounting concepts arises from the fact that many business transactions have financial effects spreading over a number of years. Decisions have to be made on the extent to which expenditure incurred in one year can reasonably be expected to produce benefits in the form of revenue in other years and should therefore be carried forward, in whole or in part; that is, should be dealt with in the closing balance sheet, as distinct from being dealt with as an expense of the current year in the profit and loss account because the benefit has been exhausted in that year.

---

*² It is emphasised that it is not the purpose of this Statement to develop a basic theory of accounting. An exhaustive theoretical approach would take an entirely different form and would include, for instance, many more propositions than the four fundamental concepts referred to here. It is, however, expedient to recognise them as working assumptions having general acceptance at the present time.

6   In some cases revenue is received for goods or services the production or supply of which will involve some later expenditure. In this case a decision must be made regarding how much of the revenue should be carried forward, to be dealt with in subsequent profit and loss accounts when the relevant costs are incurred.

7   All such decisions require consideration of future events of uncertain financial effect, and to this extent an element of commercial judgements is unavoidable in the assessment.

8   Examples of matters which give rise to particular difficulty are: the future benefits to be derived from stocks and all types of work in progress at the end of the year; the future benefits to be derived from fixed assets, and the period of years over which these will be fruitful; the extent to which expenditure on research and development can be expected to produce future benefits.

Purpose and limitations of accounting bases

9   In the course of practice there have developed a variety of accounting bases designed to provide consistent, fair and as nearly as possible objective solutions to these problems in particular circumstances; for instance bases for calculating such items as depreciation, the amounts at which stocks and work in progress are to be stated, and deferred taxation.

10   Accounting bases provide an orderly and consistent framework for periodic reporting of a concern's results and financial position, but they do not, and are not intended to, substitute for the exercise of commercial judgement in the preparation of financial reports. Where a choice of acceptable accounting bases is available judgement must be exercised in choosing those which are appropriate to the circumstances and are best suited to present fairly the concern's results and financial position; the bases thus adopted then become the concern's accounting policies. The significance of accounting bases is that they provide limits to the area subject to the exercise of judgement, and a check against arbitrary, excessive or unjustifiable adjustments where no other objective yardstick is available. By definition it is not possible to develop generalised rules for the exercise of judgement, though practical working rules may be evolved on a pragmatic basis for limited use in particular circumstances. Broadly, the longer a concern's normal business cycle—the period

between initiation of business transactions and their completion—the greater the area subject to judgement and its effect on periodic financial accounts, and the less its susceptibility to close regulation by accounting bases. These limitations to the regulating powers of accounting bases must be recognised.

Significance of disclosure of accounting policies

11   In circumstances where more than one accounting basis is acceptable in principle, the accounting policy followed can significantly affect a concern's reported results and financial position and the view presented can be properly appreciated only if the policies followed in dealing with material items are also explained. For this reason adequate disclosure of the accounting policies is essential to the fair presentation of financial accounts. As accounting standards become established through publication of Statements of Standard Accounting Practice, the choice of accounting bases regarded as generally available will diminish, but it has to be recognised that the complexity and diversity of business renders total and rigid uniformity of bases impracticable.

12   The items with which this Statement is mainly concerned are those which are subject to the exercise of judgement as to how far they should be dealt with in the profit and loss account for the period under review or how far all or part should be carried forward in the balance sheet as attributable to the operations of future periods. The determination of the annual profit or loss of nearly every business substantially depends on a systematic approach to a few material items of this type. For the better appreciation of the view they give, annual accounts should include a clear explanation of the accounting policies followed for dealing with these few key items (some examples of which are given in paragraph 13 below). The intention and spirit of this Statement are that management should identify those items of the type described which are judged material or critical for the purpose of determining and fully appreciating the company's profit or loss and its financial position, and should make clear the accounting policies followed for dealing with them.

Examples of matters for which different accounting bases are recognised

13   Significant matters for which different accounting bases are recognised and which may have a material effect on reported

results and financial position include:

—depreciation of fixed assets
—treatment and amortisation of intangibles such as research and development expenditure, patents and trademarks
—stocks and work in progress
—long-term contracts
—deferred taxation
—hire-purchase or instalment transactions
—leasing and rental transactions
—conversion of foreign currencies
—repairs and renewals
—consolidation policies
—property development transactions
—warranties for products or services.

This list is not exhaustive, and may vary according to the nature of the operations conducted.

PART 2—DEFINITION OF TERMS

14 *Fundamental accounting concepts* are the broad basic assumptions which underlie the periodic financial accounts of business enterprises. At the present time the four following fundamental concepts (the relative importance of which will vary according to the circumstances of the particular case) are regarded as having general acceptability:

(*a*) The 'going concern' concept: the enterprise will continue in operational existence for the foreseeable future. This means in particular that the profit and loss account and balance sheet assume no intention or necessity to liquidate or curtail significantly the scale of operation;

(*b*) the 'accruals' concept: revenue and costs are accrued (that is, recognised as they are earned or incurred, not as money is received or paid), matched with one another so far as their relationship can be established or justifiably assumed, and dealt with in the profit and loss account of the period to which they relate; provided that where the accruals concept is inconsistent with the 'prudence' concept (paragraph (*d*) below), the latter prevails. The accruals concept implies that the profit and loss account reflects changes in the amount of new assets that arise out of the transactions of the relevant period (other than distributions or subscriptions of capital and unrealised surpluses arising on revaluation of fixed assets). Revenue and profits dealt with in the profit and loss account are matched with associated costs and expenses by including in the same account the costs incurred in earning them (so far as these are material and identifiable);

(c) the 'consistency' concept: there is consistency of accounting treatment of like items within each accounting period and from one period to the next;

(d) the concept of 'prudence': revenue and profits are not anticipated, but are recognised by inclusion in the profit and loss account only when realised in the form either of cash or of other assets the ultimate cash realisation of which can be assessed with reasonable certainty; provision is made for all known liabilities (expenses and losses) whether the amount of these is known with certainty or is a best estimate in the light of the information available.

15 *Accounting bases* are the methods developed for applying fundamental accounting concepts to financial transactions and items, for the purpose of financial accounts, and in particular (a) for determining the accounting periods in which revenue and costs should be recognised in the profit and loss account and (b) for determining the amounts at which material items should be stated in the balance sheet.

16 *Accounting policies* are the specific accounting bases selected and consistently followed by a business enterprise as being, in the opinion of the management, appropriate to its circumstances and best suited to present fairly its results and financial position.

PART 3—STANDARD ACCOUNTING PRACTICE

Disclosure of adoption of concepts which differ from those generally accepted

17 If accounts are prepared on the basis of assumptions which differ in material respects from any of the generally accepted fundamental concepts defined in paragraph 14 above, the facts should be explained. In the absence of a clear statement to the contrary, there is a presumption that the four fundamental concepts have been observed.

Disclosure of accounting policies

18   The accounting policies (as defined in paragraph 16 above) followed for dealing with items which are judged material or critical in determining profit or loss for the year and in stating the financial position should be disclosed by way of note to the accounts. The explanations should be clear, fair, and as brief as possible.

Date from which effective

19   The accounting practices set out in this statement should be adopted as soon as possible regarded as standard in respect of reports relating to accounting periods starting on or after 1st January, 1972.

Standards and Companies Acts

In Chapter 13 we examine the legal requirements which apply to the financial reporting procedures of companies and the manner in which financial accounting information must be disclosed in the profit and loss accounts and balance sheets. Two aspects of these requirements are directly related to the accounting concepts and standards considered in this chapter.

First, the four fundamental accounting concepts of SSAP 2 have become enshrined in law by the Companies Act 1985. Final accounts prepared within the terms of this Act must follow these concepts.

Secondly, since 1948 all final accounts prepared for the purpose of compliance with the Companies Acts have been required to give a 'true and fair view'. The 1985 Companies Act declares that the obligation to give a true and fair view is 'overriding'. This means that if the final accounts are to contain the information which is sufficient in quantity and quality to satisfy the reasonable expectations of users they should be prepared in accordance with the concepts and standards that have been formulated by the accountancy profession.

Questions

1. Discuss the influence of accounting concepts on the nature of accounting information. Illustrate your analysis by reference to any three concepts.

2. 'Accounting concepts reflect the result of long experience of the complexity of business life acquired by accountants. They offer guidelines for dealing with situations in which these are not simple answers. They permit the exercise of judgement and they allow the necessary variety in current accounting practice. Accordingly, the standardisation of accounting practices is a negation of accumulated wisdom.' Discuss this comment.

3. 'Accounting standards are concerned with establishing an underlying identity of meaning in the information produced by accountants. They should not be concerned with establishing a rigid uniformity in accounting practices which would rob accountants of the ability to interpret accounting events.' Evaluate this comment.

4. David Lawrence owns 5 houses which he leases to students on an annual basis. The rentals fixed for the year ending 30 June are as follows:

	£
Properties 1 and 2	2,000 per annum each
Properties 3 and 4	2,500 per annum each
Property 5	3,000 per annum

Lawrence prepared his income statement for every year to 30 June for the purpose of computing his tax liability. The following information is available at 30 June 19X7:

(1) Rates paid in full for 19X7/19X8,
   i.e. to 31 March 19X8 to rating year:

	£
Properties 1 and 2	820 each
Properties 3 and 4	960 each
Property 5	1020

The balance of prepaid rates at
30 June 19X6 was £1,080.

(2) Repairs and renewals paid for the year to
   30 June 19X7   267
(3) Insurance paid for the year to 30 June 19X7   68
(4) Electricity paid for the year to 30 June 19X7   692
   Estimate of electricity used and unpaid at
   30 June 19X6   118
   Estimate of electricity used and unpaid at
   30 June 19X7   78
   Estimate of monies collectible from metered
   coin boxes at 30 June 19X7   95
(5) All rents due for the year ended 30 June 19X7 had been collected with the exception of the rent for the last quarter on property 4 which had been occupied by third-year students who had graduated and left. The students in property 5 had paid a quarter in advance for the period to 30 September 19X7 to secure the tenancy for the next year.

Required:
Prepare a profit and loss account for the year to 30 June 19X7 on:

(1) An accrual basis.
(2) A cash basis.

5. On 1 January 19X1, George Frobisher commenced business as a market gardener with an initial injection of capital of £5,000 in cash, and using land which he had purchased three years ago for £6,500. The following summary relates to transactions for the six months to 30 June 19X1:

	£
Purchased seeds—lettuce, radish, etc.	150
Purchased sunflower seeds	500
Purchased manure and fertilizer	300
Purchased van	1,600
Purchased tractor and implements	2,000
Purchased herb plants	250
Withdrawn for personal use £50 per week	1,300
Sold to local health store—herbs, etc.	600
Sold to greengrocers—lettuce, etc.	1,200
Motor and tractor expenses paid	610

On 30 June 19X1, Frobisher received his bank statement which showed that he had only £50 left in hand. Realising that he would have to borrow from the bank, Frobisher drew up the following profit and loss account to 30 June 19X1:

Profit and loss account for the period ended 30 June 19X1

		£	£
Income:	Herbs ½ sold	600	
	½ to be sold	600	1,200
	Lettuces etc. ⅓ sold	1,200	
	⅔ to be sold	2,400	3,600
	Sunflower seeds—expected to be sold for:		3,500
	Increase in the value of land		
	£(9,000 − 6,500)		2,500
			10,800
Expenses:	Cost of seeds and manure	1,200	
	Motor and tractor expenses	610	
	Loss in value of:		
	(i) Van £(1,600 − 1,500)	100	
	(ii) Tractor £(2,000 − 1,750)	250	
	Wages—self	1,300	
			3,460
	Net profit		7,340

Having prepared the profit and loss account, Frobisher asks for your comments, and in particular for your opinion as to his chances of obtaining borrowing facilities from the bank on the basis of the information shown in that statement. During conversation with Frobisher, you learn that some people have become mildly ill after consuming herbs which he had sold to the health store and that the store was now asking Frobisher for a refund.

Required:
Redraft Frobisher's profit and loss account to 30 June 19X1 in accordance with recognised accounting conventions.

6. George Whiteside graduated from university with a degree in business studies, and an idea for putting his recently acquired knowledge of computers to profitable use. Using £250 which he had saved from vacation earnings and £1,000 borrowed from his mother, he commenced business under the name 'Mainchance Computer Dating'. The business offered to pair couples by scientific matching.

He leased premises on 1 September 19X9, the day on which he commenced trading, and paid £200 being six months' rent in advance. He then inserted advertisements in various student magazines and placed cards in shop windows, all of which cost £620. He paid £480 immediately and secured monthly credit terms for the balance which was to be paid at the end of October 19X9.

To his delight, within a fortnight he had received over 600 replies of which 400 contained the requested fee of £6. Quickly settling down to the job of classifying the applications, he proceeded to set up the necessary programmes and, buying computer time for £500 which he paid at once, he matched up the applicants and wrote to them all giving them a selection of suitable persons with the address and the relevant information.

In the course of the following week, he received the following information:

(a) Eight of the cheques for £6 each had been returned marked 'unpaid'.
(b) Six couples had met and come to immediate matrimonial arrangements. His fee for this additional success was to be £25, but none of the couples had yet paid.
(c) Fourteen people had turned up for appointments which had not been kept by the other party, and George Whiteside had promised to arrange alternative dates or refund the fee.
(d) One retired businessman was so delighted with his date that a marriage had been arranged and he promised to send a cheque for £1,000 to Mainchance Computer Dating out of gratitude.
(e) Thirty men had turned up to one date organised by George's programme and fighting had broken out in the pub when just one girl appeared. Two broken noses had been reported so far and property in the pub had been damaged. A preliminary estimate of claims against the service came to £75.
(f) Inexplicably, George's mother's name had been included in the computer programme, and she was demanding to know why so many men were calling at her flat. She asked him for an account of his business to 31 October 19X9.

Required:
Prepare an accounting statement in any suitable form in respect of the activities of Mainchance Computer Dating, and explain your reason for the treatment of all items shown on this statement.

7 Accounting for Fixed Assets

This chapter is addressed to one of the most important areas of financial accounting, namely the recognition and treatment of asset values. Accounting for asset values impinges on the problems of profit measurement in a number of ways. First, the recognition of expenditure involving the acquisition of assets means that such expenditure must be excluded from expenses charged against revenue in arriving at periodic profit. Second, certain assets are taken into account in the calculus of periodic profit. Thus, stocks of raw materials existing at the end of the accounting period are taken into account in the calculation of the gross margin of the following period. Third, certain fixed assets are depreciated over time. In effect, this means that the process of depreciation is a method of allocating the cost of acquiring fixed assets over the economic life of these assets, which will span a number of years. Finally, the disposal of assets may involve a gain or loss which will appear in the profit and loss account.

A number of other problems exists in relation to the treatment of assets, which this chapter introduces. These problems include the selection of the appropriate basis for depreciation, and the financial implications of provisions for depreciations.

This chapter is divided into the following sections:

The meaning and nature of assets.
The concept of depreciation.
Depreciation and profit measurement.
Methods of depreciation.
Depreciation and the valuation of assets.
The economic life of an asset.
The disposal of fixed assets.
SSAP 12: *Accounting for Depreciation.*
Asset values and cash flows.
Intangible assets.
Leases.

The meaning and nature of assets

The term 'asset' is usually associated with proprietary rights, both tangible and intangible; that is, rights to tangible property such as motor cars, plant and machinery, and rights to intangible property such as rights to the enjoyment of land, trade marks and patents. Accounting has its traditional concern with recording rights of property and the control of such rights, and in the exercise of this concern it follows the law as regards the interpretation of the term 'asset'.

The purpose of this section is to examine in detail the importance of asset definition in accounting, and in particular to analyse the distinction between different forms of assets and the manner in which these distinctions are significant to the accounting process. Lying at the root of much of the accounting debate about the meaning of asset is the process of profit measurement. In this context, the term 'asset' has a strict meaning in accounting which is associated with the 'use' of assets in an operational sense. In this analysis, the existence of 'asset values' on the balance sheet is conditional upon an expectation of future benefits to the firm arising from such values. Hence, the exact meaning of the term 'asset' is a conditional interpretation of a legal concept.

From the foregoing, the term 'asset' is used in accounting to refer to a legal right which offers the prospect of future benefits to the accounting entity in which the right is vested. Initially, therefore, the recognition of an asset in accounting depends upon a transaction which confers legal rights to the entity to the use of the asset in its business operations. Next, the continued recognition of an asset depends upon the possibility that it will continue to have a use in the profit-generating process.

It is important to note, however, that asset recognition in accounting is *generally* limited to a range of economic resources over which ownership rights *can* be acquired and *are* acquired by contract. Accounting theory, however, does not recognise as assets an important class of economic advantages of crucial importance to the profitability of a business. The technical expertise of the employees of the firm, a monopoly position in the market, good industrial relations, etc., are all economic advantages which are not formally expressed in accounting as 'assets', although in nearly every case they depend upon a legal contract; for example, employees have contracts of employment and the conditions attached to such contract may well be crucial to good industrial relations. Monopoly rights may arise from patents, but may well be associated with distribution agreements.

Finally, it is important to note that asset recognition is *generally* limited to the payments made for the acquisition of the legal rights implied in the term 'asset'. Thus, accountants have difficulty in recognising assets except by the process of acquisition by purchase. The need to revalue the historic cost of acquisition to reflect a revised realisable and revised replacement cost is the subject matter of inflation accounting.

The meaning of the term 'asset' is extended by the classification systems adopted for accounting purposes. Fixed assets are distinguished from current assets, and this distinction has particular significance in explaining the operational context in which the assets are intended to be employed. In general terms, fixed assets represent the collection of assets which provide the *profit-generating structure* of the business and have a degree of permanence in that role. By contrast, current assets represent the collection of assets which are associated with the *profit-generating operations*, and are usually defined as those assets which have a service potential to the business not exceeding one accounting period.

Fixed assets

The association of fixed assets with the profit-generating structure of the business hinges to a considerable extent upon the distinction between capital and revenue expenditure which is central to the process of profit measurement. Essentially, fixed assets represent expenditure which has been treated as capital expenditure in the process of determining the profit of the current or previous years. The concepts of accounting which are related to the recognition of expenditure as representing the acquisition of fixed assets provide a set of elementary rules of thumb to guide accountants in bookkeeping and in the preparation of annual financial statements. The simple rule is to recognise a series of assets as appertaining to a class denoted fixed assets. Among these assets are land and buildings, plant and equipment, motor vehicles, tools, furniture and fittings, etc. Their common characteristic lies in their *long-term* use in the operations of the business. It is for this reason principally that they are regarded as providing the capital structure of the business. Accordingly, the reason which underlines the simple rule associates the term 'fixed assets' with all expenditure that is incurred in the acquisition of assets which will have a use in the business extending beyond one year.

At a more sophisticated level, the term 'fixed asset' may be seen as representing an implicit forecast of future net cash flows flowing to the firm associated with expenditure which has been capitalised rather than written off against revenues.

From a practical viewpoint, it is sometimes difficult to identify particular items of expenditure. An additional factor in this problem are the rules applied by the income tax authorities towards classes of expenditure. For example, it is possible to undertake repairs either through the activity of restoring an asset by repair or simply by replacement. Often, it is cheaper to replace than to repair. Expenditure on repairs is written off against profit, but expenditure on replacement is capitalised both under accounting and taxation rules. Difficulties arise, moreover, where there is both an element of repair and improvement; for example, when in the course of repairing an entire central heating system, a new boiler is installed. Is the expenditure on the boiler a part of repairing the central heating system or should it be treated as an item separate from the system? Some typical problem areas are listed below, with a brief note on the reasoning involved in a decision to treat the item as involving capital or revenue expenditure.

Transaction	*Discussion*
1. Purchase of a secondhand machine.	So long as the acquisition implies future usefulness, it does not matter that the item purchased is new or secondhand. Hence, in this case, the machine must be treated as a fixed asset.
2. Repair a secondhand machine which has just been purchased in order to use it in the business.	The act of repairing disguises the true purpose of the expenditure which is to improve the item purchased. Hence, the repair must be capitalised and added to the value of the machine.
3. Transport and installation costs of machinery.	*All* costs normally associated with putting an asset into a condition ready for use are capitalised and added to the purchase cost of the asset.
4. Painting and partitioning new offices.	Any initial expenditure carried out on an asset, which would otherwise be treated as current expenditure, must be capitalised when it relates directly to placing an asset into use.
5. Hire purchase charges of £1,000 involved in the purchase of machinery costing £10,000, and included in the total price of £11,000.	The asset value is recorded as £10,000 and the charges of £1,000 are treated as an immediate financial expense related to the credit service rendered to the business.

6. During a slack period of trading, employing staff on the construction of a new warehouse, rather than laying them off. An outside contractor has quoted £25,000 for the construction of the warehouse.

Under normal circumstances, the wages would be treated as revenue expenditure. But since the men are employed in creating a capital asset, their wages and all other expenditure related to constructing the warehouse should be capitalised.

From the foregoing discussion, it is clear that the nature of expenditure is only *prima facie* evidence of its correct accounting definition and of the manner in which it should be recorded and treated in the process of profit measurement. A business may choose to use its labour to build its own factory or machinery, and the labour and other costs which would otherwise be included under wages, purchases and other expenses should be capitalised under the heading of the appropriate asset account. In the case of a warehouse, for example, all associated labour and material expenses would merely appear as debits to warehouse building account. In this connection, it should be noted that both capital and current expenses involve debit entries in the books. Hence, the process of using the double-entry bookkeeping system for measuring profit requires the ability to distinguish the debit entries, which should be classified as assets and excluded from expenses chargeable against revenues, from those debit entries which are properly chargeable against revenues in the process of profit measurement.

The concept of depreciation

The concept of depreciation raises a number of complex issues in accounting. The issues which are discussed in this section relate to the notion of capital maintenance in the process of profit measurement, the manner in which depreciation should be represented, the financial implication of depreciation, and the problem of allocating costs over time.

The maintenance of capital

The problem involved in the maintenance of capital are illustrated in Example 1 below.

Example 1

James Cavendish started business on 1 April 19X0 as a hot-dog vendor. His initial capital was £2,600. He purchased a van already converted for use as a hot-dog stall at a cost of £2,400 and applied the balance of £200 to the purchase of foodstuff for sale. Hence, the van represented the fixed capital and the £200 represented the working capital of the business. Each day, he would acquire £200-worth of foodstuff for sale during that day. For reasons of hygiene, Cavendish never bought more than he required, since the foodstuff purchased was of a perishable nature. Hence, no stock of unsold foodstuff remained at the close of each day's trading. Cavendish's policy was to treat as profit any surplus over £200 which was left after meeting daily expenses and to withdraw that surplus immediately for his own private use. The balance sheet on 1 April 19X0 was as follows:

Assets	=	Capital account
Van £2,400 + Cash £200	=	£2,600

In view of the policy adopted by Cavendish, it is evident that his balance sheet at the end of any day would be exactly as above. His capital account would remain at £2,600 since profit is immediately withdrawn.

At the end of the fourth year of trading, the van fails to pass a road test and is pronounced unroadworthy. Owing to its particular features, it had no scrap value. The balance sheet at 31 March 19X4 is as follows:

Assets	=	Capital account
Cash £200	=	£200

In effect, Cavendish has failed to maintain the value of the business and the value of the capital invested in that business, since over the period of four years that value has dropped from £2,600 to £200. The difference of £2,400 represents the original value of the van. Hence, the failure to maintain the value of capital is caused by the failure to provide for the depreciating value of the van out of annual profit. Thus, the sums withdrawn daily by Cavendish represented not only profit but also a withdrawal of capital. To restore the value of the capital invested in the business to the position existing at 1 April 19X0, Cavendish would have to invest a further £2,400.

It is evident that the perception of the gradual loss in value of the van over its life in use would have induced Cavendish to make an appropriate provision out of 'profit' for the replacement of the van at the end of its life. Assuming constant prices over the four-year period, the replacement cost of the van is equal to its historic cost. Had Cavendish estimated the life of the van at four years, he should have created a reserve of $\frac{£2,400}{4} = £600$ per annum and reduced his withdrawals by that sum annually. Accordingly, the accounting equation would have been maintained by a decreasing value of the van and a corresponding increase in the amount reserved out of profit. Assuming that this reserve is held in cash, the revised balance sheets for each of the four years to 31 March 19X4 would have been as follows:

		Assets						Capital account
		£			£		=	£
31 March 19X1	Van	1,800	+	Cash	800	=		2,600
31 March 19X2	Van	1,200	+	Cash	1,400	=		2,600
31 March 19X3	Van	600	+	Cash	2,000	=		2,600
31 March 19X4	Van	0	+	Cash	2,600	=		2,600

Providing for depreciation

The provision for depreciation in the accounts system deals with the replacement of fixed assets at the termination of their useful life. It should be noted that its purpose is limited to fixed assets which experience a loss in value through use. For example, plant and machinery are fixed assets which generally lose their usefulness through use, whereas land may well retain its value and indeed increase in value in relation to other assets.

The procedure involved in creating a provision for depreciation is relatively simple as regards bookkeeping:

Dr   Profit and loss account   ⎫ with the annual amount
Cr   Provision for depreciation account ⎭ of depreciation

The debit to the profit and loss account reduces the net profit of the business and hence the amount which may be withdrawn. The credit is normally shown as a deduction from the relevant asset account on the balance sheet.

The provision for depreciation account increases yearly by the amount transferred from the profit and loss account as depreciation.

Example 2

The creation of a provision for depreciation of the van used by Cavendish in Example 1 would be as follows:

Provision for depreciation—motor van

	£			£
31 March 19X1 Balance c/d	600		31 March 19X1 Profit and loss a/c	600
31 March 19X2 Balance c/d	1,200		1 April 19X1 Balance b/d	600
			31 March 19X2 Profit and loss a/c	600
	1,200			1,200
31 March 19X3 Balance c/d	1,800		1 April 19X2 Balance b/d	1,200
			31 March 19X3 Profit and loss a/c	600
	1,800			1,800
31 March 19X4 Balance c/d	2,400		1 April 19X3 Balance c/d	1,800
			31 March 19X4 Profit and loss a/c	600
	2,400			2,400
			1 April 19X4 Balance b/d	2,400

The entry on the motor van account remains as £2,400, being the acquisition cost, for the four-year period involved, as follows:

Motor van account

	£			£
1 April 19X0 Cash	2,400		31 March 19X1 Balance c/d	2,400
1 April 19X1 Balance b/d	2,400			
	....			
	....			
1 April 19X4 Balance b/d	2,400			

The balance sheet for each of the four years would reflect the following positions:

	Balance sheets as at 31 March			
	19X1	19X2	19X3	19X4
	£	£	£	£
Fixed assets				
Motor van at cost	2,400	2,400	2,400	2,400
Accumulated depreciation	600	1,200	1,800	2,400
	1,800	1,200	600	0
Current assets				
Cash	800	1,400	2,000	2,600
	2,600	2,600	2,600	2,600
Financed by				
Capital account	2,600	2,600	2,600	2,600

Financial implications of depreciation

Although the foregoing example shows a connection between the depreciation and an increase in the cash balance, this situation is unlikely ever to be found in practice. Indeed, there is no reason why depreciation should be associated with a provision out of profit in the form of cash. Depreciation is not a source of funds, and it is misleading to consider it as such.

Example 3

Assume for simplicity that at the end of an accounting period in which all transactions were conducted in cash, that the net profit is £100. Evidently, this profit is reflected in a cash balance of £100. A decision to create a provision for the depreciation of fixtures and fittings of £50 does not result in a decrease in the cash balance from £100 to £50, though it results in a decrease in the net profit from £100 to £50. The effect of the decision to introduce a provision for depreciation of £50 is to restrict the distributable profit to £50 from £100.

Depreciation and the allocation of costs over time

An important aspect of the concept of depreciation is the allocation of the cost of fixed assets over the several accounting periods during which they are used in the production of profit.

Example 4

A newly formed mining company requires substantial supplies of electricity, and is faced with two alternative means of obtaining those supplies. The first alternative is to enter into a contract with the local electricity supply board and buy electricity on a metered basis. The second alternative is to install an electricity generating plant and to produce the electricity required.

Clearly, the outcome of the first alternative method of obtaining electricity would be the receipt of periodic bills which would be debited to the electricity account. As regards the second alternative, the only visible costs associated with the periodic supply of electricity would be in the form of the costs of operating the electricity generating plant. The major costs would be involved in the installation of the plant, and the problem is how to represent those costs as part of the cost of obtaining supplies of electricity? This problem arises in every case where assets are purchased. This is because the services associated with the use of assets may be obtained either by the purchase of the assets or by leasing or buying the services themselves. Accordingly, the depreciating value of the electricity generating plant may be seen as representing an annual charge for the provision of the services implied in the acquisition of the asset.

The recognition of assets as representing the acquisition of service potential and the treatment of depreciation as a charge for the periodic services provided by assets is an indication of the manner in which accounting theory is moving from a strictly legal base to an economic interpretation of the nature of assets. The bookkeeping entries for dealing with depreciation in this way are the same as shown earlier.

Depreciation and profit measurement

Depreciation is concerned with two critical issues regarding the measurement of profit:

(1) The maintenance of capital.
(2) The allocation of costs over different accounting periods.

The useful economic life of an asset is an important consideration in both cases, and the failure to take account of the economic life of an asset when calculating depreciation may lead to underestimating the required provision for depreciation with consequential effects on the maintenance of capital and the allocation of fixed asset costs over time.

Accounting practice is to rely on technical estimates of the life of an asset as a basis for allocating the cost of the asset against the profits of different accounting periods. These are discussed below.

It should be noted, however, that depreciation is only one element of the cost of obtaining asset services. Running costs and the cost of repairs should be included perhaps in the overall consideration of the relationship between depreciation and profit measurement. For example, the effective economic life of an asset may be shortened if running costs suddenly were to increase, whereas—given that running costs remain at a normal and expected level—the economic life of an asset may well be prolonged by careful maintenance.

Methods of depreciation

The various methods for dealing with depreciation are set out below. It is important to note that whichever methods are used, the net

Table 1. Depreciation methods which depend on a prior estimate of asset life

Method	Annual depreciation	Comment
(1) Straight line	Equal amount per annum	Implies that the routine operating efficiency of the asset remains constant throughout its life and that repairs are also constant. Much used for plant and machinery
(2) Declining balance (also known as reducing balance)	Highest in the first year and declining year by year	Implies that operating efficiency is declining and that repairs are increasing. Frequently adopted for motor vehicles, fixtures and fittings
(3) Sum-of-years digits	Very high in the first few years but declining rapidly	A method of providing a rapid build-up in the provision for depreciation, and is a more extreme form of the declining balance method. Considered to be appropriate for assets with high risks of obsolescence
(4) Annuity	Lowest in first year but increasing year by year	Introduces the time value of money into the depreciation concept. This method is the reverse of the declining balance and the sum-of-years digits methods, which is unlikely to represent reality for most assets. It is considered appropriate for assets, such as property, with a long life

figures shown on the balance sheet do not necessarily indicate that the realisable or replacement values of the assets involved correspond with the actual market values. Tables 1 and 2 briefly describe methods of depreciation and Table 3 presents the formulae for calculating depreciation.

Variants of the methods described in Table 1 do exist, but the fundamental purpose of all methods of depreciation in accounting is to allocate costs over different time periods.

Table 2. Depreciation methods which depend upon technical knowledge of the usage capacity of an asset

Method	Annual depreciation	Comment
(1) Production	Varies with production	Used where an asset has an expected total output, for example stamping and pressing machines. Repairs do not enter into the choice of this method
(2) Revenue	Varies with revenue raised	May be appropriate for assets used directly in raising revenue, such as assets hired out
(3) Depletion	Varies with extraction	Relevant to dealing with natural resources, such as mines and oil wells, where the life of the asset is related to the known mineral reserves

The formula for computing depreciation under the methods described in Tables 1 and 2 are shown in Table 3 below. The following symbols are used in these fomulae:

C = Original cost of the asset
D = Annual charge for depreciation
A = Accumulated depreciation
S = Scrap value
n = Number of years of expected life of asset

Table 3. Formulae for depreciation methods

Method	Formula
(1) Straight line	$D = \dfrac{C - S}{n}$
(2) Declining balance	(a) To determine the rate r to be applied in the formula: $$r = 1 - \sqrt[n]{\dfrac{S}{C}}$$ (b) $D = r(C - A)$
(3) Sum-of-years digits	$D = \dfrac{t}{n(n + 1)/2} \times (C - S)$ where t = number of years of asset life left.
(4) Annuity	$D = \dfrac{C}{a_{\overline{n}|^i}} - i(C - A)$

Method	Formula
	where $\overline{a_n}|^i$ is the present value factor of an annuity of £1 discounted at $i\%$ for n years, and i is the appropriate interest rate for the business. The scrap value is ignored in this example as it introduces a minor difficulty which is beyond the scope of this text.
(5) Production	$D = \dfrac{\text{No. of units produced}}{\text{Total potential usage}} \times (C - S)$
(6) Revenue	$D = \dfrac{\text{No. of units sold}}{\text{Total potential sales}} \times (C - S)$
(7) Depletion	$D = \dfrac{\text{No. of units extracted}}{\text{Total potential output}} \times (C - S)$

Depreciation and the valuation of assets

A few brief examples are given below of the manner in which the charge for depreciation affects the written-down value of assets. For the sake of completeness, an example is given of the manner in which the annuity method affects the written-down value of assets, but the implications of this method are not pursued.

Table 4. Written-down asset values under various depreciation methods (the figures given assume that the original asset cost is £12,000, the expected life 5 years and the expected scrap value is £2,000)

Method	Written-down values
(1) Straight-line	(a) Depreciation $= \dfrac{C - S}{n}$
	$= \dfrac{£12,000 - 2,000}{5}$
	$= £2,000$ per annum
	(b) Written-down value:

Year	Original cost (£)	Annual depreciation (£)	Accumulated depreciation (£)	Written-down value at year end (£)
1	12,000	2,000	2,000	10,000
2	—	2,000	4,000	8,000
3	—	2,000	6,000	6,000
4	—	2,000	8,000	4,000
5	—	2,000	10,000	2,000 = Scrap value

Method	Written-down values

(2) Declining balance

(a) Rate $r = 1 - \sqrt[n]{\dfrac{S}{C}}$

$= 1 - \sqrt[5]{\dfrac{2,000}{12,000}}$

$= 0.31$ or 31%

Depreciation $= r(C - A)$

$= 0.31(12,000 - $ Accumulated depreciation at the end of each year, viz. 31% of £12,000 at end of year 1, etc.)

(b) Written-down value

Year	Original cost (£)	Annual depreciation (£)	Accumulated depreciation (£)	Written-down value at year end (£)
1	12,000	3,720	3,720	8,280
2	—	2,567	6,287	5,713
3	—	1,770	8,057	3,943
4	—	1,222	9,279	2,721
5	—	721*	10,000	2,000

* This figure is adjusted to account for approximations

(3) Sum-of-years digits

(a) Depreciation $= \dfrac{t}{(n + 1)/2} \times (C - S)$

year 1 $= \dfrac{5}{5(5 + 1)/2} \times (12,000 - 2,000)$

$= £3,333$

year 2 $= \dfrac{4}{5(5 + 1)/2} \times (12,000 - 2,000)$

$= £2,666$, etc.

(b) Written-down value:

Year	Original cost (£)	Annual depreciation (£)	Accumulated depreciation (£)	Written-down value at year end (£)
1	12,000	3,333	3,333	8,667
2	—	2,666	5,999	6,001
3	—	2,000	7,999	4,001
4	—	1,333	9,332	2,668
5	—	668*	10,000	2,000

* Adjusted for approximation

(4) Annuity

(a) Depreciation $= \dfrac{C}{a_{\overline{n}|}^i} - i(C - A)$

Method	Written-down values

(*Note:* for simplicity, it is assumed that $C = £10,000$, thereby eliminating the scrap value, and that $i = 12\%$.)

The calculation of depreciation involves two stages:

(1) Calculating the annual depreciation.
(2) Calculating the annual interest imputed against the written-down value of the asset.

The annual depreciation is calculated as follows:

$$\frac{10,000}{a_{\overline{5}|}0.12} = \frac{10,000}{3.605} \text{ (from tables)} = £2,774$$

The annual interest imputed against the written-down value of the asset is shown below in the valuation of the written-down value.

(b) Written-down value:

Year	Original cost (£)	Annual depreciation (£)	Interest Base (£)	Interest Rate (%)	Imputed interest (£)	Net depreciation (£)	Written-down value at year end (£)
1	10,000	2,774	10,000 ×	12	1,200	1,574	8,426
2	—	2,774	8,426 ×	12	1,011	1,763	6,663
3	—	2,774	6,663 ×	12	800	1,974	4,689
4	—	2,774	4,689 ×	12	563	2,211	2,478
5	—	2,774	2,478 ×	12	296	2,478	0

The method of calculating the depreciation charge under the production, revenue and depletion methods are similar. The following example illustrates the depletion method.

Example 5

The Longlump Slate Company purchased a quarry for £100,000 having estimate reserves of 500,000 tons. The output of the quarry in the first year was 25,000 tons and it rose to 50,000 tons in the second year. The following depreciation calculated on the depletion method should be charged against the profits of years 1 and 2 respectively:

$$\text{Depreciation} = \frac{\text{No. of units extracted}}{\text{Total potential output}} \times (C - S)$$

$$\text{Year 1} \quad = \frac{25,000}{500,000} \times £100,000$$

$$= \underline{£5,000}$$

$$\text{Year 2} \quad = \frac{50,000}{500,000} \times £100,000$$

$$= \underline{£10,000}$$

The economic life of an asset

Accounting practice relies on a technical estimate of the life of an asset. Thus, a lorry may be given a life of five years on the basis that it will be worn out by the end of that period. The analysis of the effective life in use of an asset must obviously take into consideration its potential physical life. It is also clear that other factors impinge upon the analysis of the economic life of an asset. Such factors as obsolescence resulting from technological improvement, falling output associated with increasing repairs are typical considerations indicating the need to view the problem of assessing the economic life of an asset as being associated with establishing a cycle of asset renewal aimed at securing the lowest overall annual asset costs.

Example 6

Consider the case of a small engineering firm faced with the problem of buying a new lathe, which has a technical life of four years. The following data is available:

	£
Cost of lathe	10,000
Estimated annual repairs:	
Year 1	900
Year 2	1,300
Year 3	1,600
Year 4	3,000
Estimated disposal value at end of:	
Year 1	5,000
Year 2	4,000
Year 3	600
Year 4	—

The total average cost per year of operating the lathe may be calculated as follows:

	At end of			
	Year 1 (£)	Year 2 (£)	Year 3 (£)	Year 4 (£)
Original cost	10,000	10,000	10,000	10,000
Repairs: Year 1	900	900	900	900
Year 2	—	1,300	1,300	1,300
Year 3	—	—	1,600	1,600
Year 4	—	—	—	3,000
Net cost	10,900	12,200	13,800	16,800
Disposal value	5,000	4,000	600	0
Annual cost	5,900	8,200	13,200	16,800
Average annual cost	5,900	4,100	4,300	4,200

It is clear that since the lowest average annual cost of operating the lathe occurs over a two-year period, the firm should adopt an economic life for the lathe of two years and replace the lathe at the end of each two-year period.

The disposal of fixed assets

Fixed assets are either sold or scrapped at the end of their useful life. The accounting implications are twofold. First, entries are required to record the sale or scrapping of the assets in the appropriate accounts. Second, any difference between the disposal value and the written-down book value is regarded either as a profit or loss, as may be, on the disposal of asset and is shown on the profit and loss account in the year of disposal. Although the amount transferred to the profit and loss account is conventionally referred to as 'gains' or 'losses' they are almost always, in effect, a final adjustment of depreciation. Infrequently, an asset may be disposed of for a sum greater than original cost and hence a 'gain' may be recognised.

Example 7

During the year ended 31 March 19X7, a business sold for £70 a typewriter which originally cost £300, and in respect of which the provision for depreciation stood at £250.

The bookkeeping entries required to record the disposal of the typewriter are concerned with the following three points:

(a) Removing the asset from the office equipment account.
(b) Eliminating the provision for depreciation in respect of the asset.
(c) Posting the difference between the written-down book value and the disposal value to the profit and loss account of the year 19X7.

The means by which these three objectives are met is through an asset disposal account, as follows:

(a) Transfer the original cost of the typewriter from the office equipment account to the asset disposal account as follows:

Dr. Asset disposal account ⎫
Cr Office equipment account ⎬ with £300

(b) Transfer the provision for depreciation in respect of the typewriter from the provision for depreciation (office equipment) account to the asset disposal account as follows:

Dr Provision for depreciation (office ⎫
    equipment) account ⎬ with £250
Cr Asset disposal account ⎭

(c) Record the sale of the typewriter in the asset disposal account and transfer the difference between the disposal value and the written down value to the profit and loss account as follows:

Dr   Cash
Cr   Asset disposal account   } with £70

Dr   Asset disposal account
Cr   Profit and loss account   } with £20 being gain on disposal

The bookkeeping entries are as follows:

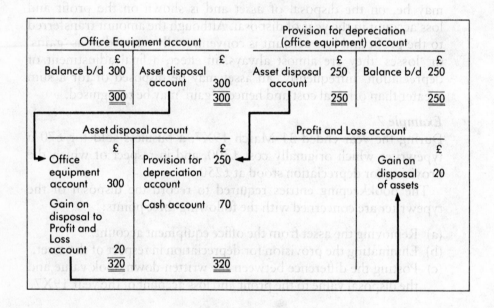

Notes:

(1) The only external transaction is the receipt of cash from the sale of the typewriter.

(2) The gain or loss on disposal represents the final adjustment for depreciation. A true gain would only arise where the asset is sold for more than it originally cost.

(3) With rare exceptions, assets are found in accounts for whole categories of assets. Equally, the provision for depreciation applies to all assets in the category denoted. Thus, all motor vehicles will be found in the motor vehicle account, and there will not be an account for each individual motor vehicle. Similarly, the provision for depreciation (motor vehicle) account will relate to all motor vehicles.

SSAP 12: *Accounting for Depreciation* (1977, revised 1981)

To a large extent, SSAP 12 summarises generally understood concepts with regard to depreciation. For example, it states that depreciation arises from several possible factors—use, time or obsolescence. These factors, either singly or together, make it necessary for provision to be made for depreciation with regard to all fixed assets, except land.

Depreciation is an allocation of costs related to the accruals concept of accounting, whereby revenues and costs are matched in the process of periodic accounting. According to SSAP 12, 'depreciation should be allocated to accounting periods so as to charge a fair proportion to each accounting period during the expected life of the asset'.

SSAP 12 does not discuss the various methods of depreciation which are in use, for example, the straight line, the depreciating percentage, etc. Instead, it states that management should 'select the method regarded as the most appropriate to the type of asset and its use in the business'.

SSAP 12 requires the following information to be disclosed in financial statements for each major class of assets:

(1) the depreciation method used,
(2) the useful life or the depreciation rate used,
(3) the total depreciation allocated to the period,
(4) the gross amount of depreciable assets and the related accumulated balance.

Prior to SSAP 12, it was common practice for depreciation not to be provided for buildings on the ground that market values tended to exceed net book values shown on the balance sheet. SSAP 12 takes the view that because buildings have a limited life, they should be depreciated using the same criteria applied to other fixed assets. This requirement provoked strong objection from property investment companies. SSAP 19: *Accounting for Investment Properties* (1981) allows companies not to provide for depreciation in respect of investment properties.

Asset values and cash flows

Transactions concerned with the acquisition and disposal of assets give rise to cash flows and non-cash flows. Thus, the sale of a typewriter which had already been substantially depreciated gives rise to a net non-cash flow of £20 shown as a gain on disposal in the profit and loss account, where the cash flow associated with the actual sale of the typewriter was £70, which was the sum of money received.

It is important, therefore, to distinguish these different accounting flows that lie behind the aggregated asset figures on the balance sheet.

Example 8

The summary of the plant and machinery account shown on the balance sheet of Transcot Co. on 31 March 19X1 is as follows:

	19X0	19X1
	£000	£000
Plant and machinery at cost	424	506
Accumulated depreciation to date	214	282
	210	224

According to the profit and loss account for the year ended 31 March 19X1, the depreciation charged for the year amounted to £105,000 and a loss of £8,000 was sustained on the disposal of machinery which originally cost £56,000.

From this information, the following information may be ascertained:

(a) The cash which was received on the disposal of the machinery.
(b) The cash which was expended on the purchase of new plant and machinery during the year ended 31 March 19X1.

The procedure relies on a reconstruction of the accounts lying behind this data.

Asset disposal account

	£		£
Plant and machinery	56,000	Provision for depreciation	37,000
		Loss on disposal	8,000
		Cash (b)	11,000
	56,000		56,000

Plant and machinery account

	£		£
Balance b/d	424,000	Asset disposal account transfer	56,000
Cash (c)	138,000	Balance c/d	506,000
	562,000		562,000
Balance b/d	506,000		

Provision for depreciation—plant and machinery account

	£		£
Asset disposal account transfer (a)	37,000	Balance b/d	214,000
Balance c/d	282,000	Profit and loss account	105,000
	319,000		319,000
		Balance b/d	282,000

Notes

(a) The amount of depreciation transferred out relates to assets sold. This figure is obtained from the opening and closing figures and the amount added to the provision by the depreciation charged in the profit and loss account for the year ended 31 March 19X1.

(b) Cash received from plant and machinery sold is derived from the other three components in the asset disposal account.

(c) Cash paid for new plant and machinery is derived from the other known figures in the plant and machinery account.

Intangible assets

Intangible assets do not have any physical features; rather they represent legal rights and relationships which are beneficial to their owner. The most common examples of intangible assets are:

(1) patents, copyrights and trade marks,
(2) goodwill,
(3) research and development expenditure.

Patents

A patent is a legal right to exploit a new invention, and is obtained after the registration of its specification with the Department of Trade. Patents are recorded at cost and are amortised (written off) over their effective life, usually on a straight-line basis. A similar treatment is applied to other such exclusive rights which are granted by government authority, for example, copyrights and trade marks.

Goodwill

Goodwill is an intangible asset value attached to an entity as a consequence of such factors as the skill of its management, product reputation, technical know-how and marketing organisation. The value of goodwill is often defined as the excess of the value of the entity as a whole over the sum of the fair value of its accountable net identifiable assets.

A firm may be creating goodwill continuously, but it is recorded in the accounts only when an existing enterprise is purchased. As a result, in accounting, goodwill is acquired at a particular time and through a market transaction. The goodwill debited to the goodwill account will be equal to the difference between the total price paid for the enterprise and the fair market value assigned to the net assets (assets less liabilities).

The treatment of goodwill has been the subject of considerable controversy over many years. SSAP 22: *Accounting for Goodwill* (1984) requires goodwill to be written off immediately against reserves or amortised over the period of its useful life.

Research and development expenditure (R & D)

A particular problem of accounting for research and development expenditure is that of associating expenditure with benefits resulting from such expenditure. SSAP 13: *Accounting for Research and Development* (1977) distinguishes clearly between research and development as follows:

(1) research is original investigation undertaken to gain new scientific or technical knowledge. A distinction is drawn between (a) pure research, which is not directed towards any specific practical aim or application and (b) applied research, which has a more practical aim;
(2) development is work directed towards the introduction or improvement of specific products or processes.

SSAP 13 requires that all research expenditure be written off as it is incurred. It takes the view that expenditure incurred on pure and applied research may be regarded as part of a continuing operation to maintain a company's business and its competitive position. In general, it is not to be expected that one period rather than another will benefit from such expenditure. Therefore, it is appropriate that such expenditure should be written off as incurred.

Development expenditure should also be written off as incurred, unless it may clearly be related to a project which is technically feasible and commercially viable. Deferred development expenditure should be disclosed separately and should not be included under current assets.

Leases

A lease is a contract which grants the right to operate or use property for a specified period of time. The lessor retains the ownership of the asset, but conveys to the lessee the right of use in consideration of a payment of a specified rent.

The traditional approach to accounting for leases has been to record the transactions in their legal form. Thus, the lessee merely debits the rent due and payable in the profit and loss account. Since the lessee has no ownership right, no asset is shown on the balance sheet. The lessor, on the other hand, remains the owner of the asset leased, which he records as an asset on his balance sheet. At the same time, the rent receivable is recorded as revenue in his profit and loss account.

Seen from a business viewpoint, the lessee acquires the use of an asset without needing to buy it. Therefore, he avoids the necessity of raising finance for its acquisition. Had the lessee acquired the asset, and borrowed money to that end, both the assets and the debt would have been recorded on the balance sheet. For this reason, leasing is frequently referred to as 'off balance sheet financing'. The leasing of assets is a practice which is increasing. The traditional treatment of leases in accounting may be misleading to users of financial statements wishing to assess a company's state of affairs.

SSAP 21: *Accounting for Leases and Hire Purchase Contracts* (1984) prescribes an alternative treatment, which seeks to reflect the economic nature of a leasing transaction by bringing leases on to balance sheets. Future commitments to finance leases are recorded as liabilities, and assets leased are shown as fixed assets. The corresponding treatment in the lessor's accounts is altered accordingly: assets subject to leases are no longer treated as fixed assets, but as debtors corresponding in value to future rental income.

Questions

1. Indicate how you believe the following transactions should be treated in the accounting records. State the reasons for your decision.

(*a*) Delivery van with a written down value of £260 traded in for an allowance of £400 against the purchase of a new van costing £2,800.

(*b*) Overhaul of machinery costing £1,500 which has extended its working life.

(*c*) The purchase of three old cars for £100 each for use as spares by a garage.

(*d*) The construction of new storage bins from metal which was regarded as scrap.

(*e*) The replacement of all the mechanical adding machines used in the offices of a business by electronic calculators at a net cost of £950.

(*f*) Repainting all the delivery vans of a business to conform with a new and distinctive style at a cost of £2,600.

(*g*) Replacement of a factory heating system, from coal-fired steam boilers to a hot-air ducted system costing £3,200 and the sale of scrap from the old system resulting in the receipt of £850 although the written down value of the old system was zero.

(*h*) Build a new fire escape to comply with office safety regulations at a cost of £985.

2. Ron Stalker, the owner of a printing firm, is contemplating the purchase of new printing machinery costing £8,000, and having a technical life of four years. The following estimates of repairs and maintenance costs over a four-year period have been prepared from experience of similar machines in the past.

	£
Year 1	200
Year 2	850
Year 3	1,200
Year 4	1,300

The disposal value of the new machinery has been estimated as follows:

	£
At the end of year 1	3,500
At the end of year 2	2,800
At the end of year 3	2,000
At the end of year 4	0

Required:
(1) Advise Stalker on the length of economic life which he should attach to the machinery which he proposes to purchase.
(2) Suggest a method of depreciation which would be appropriate to your recommendation.

(Support your recommendation with the calculations you have made.)

3. You are required to show the provision for depreciation (fixed assets) account in respect of the machine mentioned below as it would appear in the accounting records of the business during the five relevant years by each of the following methods:

(*a*) Straight-line.
(*b*) Declining balance.
(*c*) Sum-of-years digits.
(*d*) Production usage.

The machinery was bought for £12,000 on 1 January 19X2, and at that date it was estimated that the scrap value at 31 December 19X6 would be £1,500. The number of operating hours per annum were:

Year ended 31 December	Hours
19X2	2,500
19X3	5,000
19X4	3,000
19X5	3,000
19X6	1,500

It may be assumed that the useful life of the machine is represented by the total hours shown above

4. On 1 January 19X4, a manufacturer acquired two identical machine tools at a cost of £8,000 each, and a reprographic machine for the office at a cost of £4,000. The machine tools are depreciated at 25% per annum on a declining balance basis, and the reprographic machine, which has an estimated residual value of £400 and a life of six years, is depreciated on a straight line basis. On 1 January 19X5, one of the machine tools was sold for £4,500 and a new one acquired for £11,000.

Required:
(1) Prepare the relevant asset accounts, the provision for depreciation accounts and the asset disposal account, for the year ended 31 December 19X5.
(2) The manufacturer, observing the data given in the asset disposal account and noting the cost of the new machine, ruled that 'in future we must increase the depreciation rate because we underestimated the amount of cash needed to replace the asset'. Discuss this statement.

5. On 1 January 19X1, a manufacturing business bought three machines at a cost of £20,000 each. The business normally provided depreciation at 20% per year on the decreasing balance basis. On 1 January 19X3, a further machine was acquired at a cost of £22,000. On 30 June 19X3, one of the machines originally acquired on 1 January 19X1 was sold for £8,000. A full year's depreciation is charged in the year of purchase of any asset, but none is charged in the year of disposal.

Required:
(1) Prepare the following accounts for each of the years ended 31 December 19X1, 19X2 and 19X3:
　　Machinery account.
　　Provision for depreciation (machinery) account.
　　Asset disposal account.
(2) According to the owner of the business, 'if depreciation had not been charged in 19X3, then the loss for the year could have turned into a profit which would have been much better for the business. Why, therefore, do we have to charge depreciation?'
Write a brief memorandum in reply to this question.

6. J. Martin commenced business as a house builder on 1 January 19X0 with a capital of £70,000. A summary of the transactions for the year ended 31 December 19X0 is given below:
(1) Purchased: £
　　Fixed assets 36,000
　　Materials 92,046
(2) Payments made:
　　Creditors 120,722
　　Wages 37,168
　　General expenses 5,838
(3) Drawings by Martin for his own use: £8,234
(4) Details of work undertaken by Martin on contract were as follows:

	Materials used (£)	Wages incurred (£)	Sales invoiced (£)	Cash received (£)
Moss Estates	19,296	14,932	40,698	40,698
Waverly Homes	23,960	12,126	42,172	42,172
Gorse Hill	14,910	4,702	22,614	14,068

	Materials used (£)	Wages incurred (£)	Sales invoiced (£)	Cash received (£)
Rush Homes Ltd	17,584	3,528	—	—
Poole Villas	10,288	2,464	—	10,000
	86,038	37,752	105,484	106,938

The Rush Homes Ltd and Poole Villas contracts were uncompleted at 31 December 19X0.

(5) At 31 December 19X0:
  The balance of cash in hand and at the bank was £4,976.
  The work-in-progress is to be valued on the basis of the cost of materials used and wages incurred plus 25% of wages for general expenses.

(6) Depreciation is to be provided on fixed assets at the rate of 10% per annum on cost for a full year.

Required:
Prepare a profit and loss account for the year ended 31 December 19X0 and a balance sheet as at that date.

7. S. Cummins traded as a merchant. His trial balance at 31 December 19X6 revealed the following:

	£
Capital account as at 1 January 19X6	67,042
Trade debtors	19,200
Rent and rates	1,676
Fittings and equipment at cost	35,200
Provision for depreciation	5,292
Purchases	117,354
Drawings	5,000
Trade creditors	14,864
Provision for doubtful debts	754
Stock	13,868
Motoring expenses	832
Sales	136,426
Advertising	2,750
Delivery vans at cost	6,000
Provision for depreciation	1,500
Salesmen's salaries	10,524
Lighting and heating	1,982
Bad debts	152
Audit and professional charges	86
Cash at bank and in hand	10,296
Postage and office expenses	958

The following adjustments are to be made:

(1) The closing stock at 31 December 19X6 at cost was estimated at £7,832.

(2) Depreciation is to be provided at 10% of fittings and equipment and at 25% on delivery vans.

(3) Prepayments at 31 December 19X6 were:

	£
Rates	120
Motoring expenses (insurance for van)	116

(4) Accruals at 31 December 19X6 were:

	£
Rent	200
Electricity	54
Repairs to delivery vans	78
Audit fee	210
Telephone	56

(5) The provision for doubtful debts is to be made equal to 5% of trade debtors.

Required:
Prepare a profit and loss account for the year ended 31 December 19X6 and a balance sheet as at that date.

8. The following balances were extracted from the books of B. Baker, timber importer, on 30 September 19X1:

	£
Capital account at 1 October 19X0	48,478
Office furniture and equipment	2,880
Drawings	9,776
Stock	29,944
Purchases	335,520
Sales	409,600
Rent	2,700
Lighting and heating	950
Insurances	608
Salaries	12,704
Stationery and printing	1,474
Telephone and postages	1,034
General expenses	5,122
Travellers' commission and expenses	19,850
Bad debts	662
Trade debtors	38,200
Trade creditors	16,324
Cash at bank	13,208
Cash in hand	58
Provision for doubtful debts	288

The following additional information is given:

(1) Closing stock at 30 September 19X1 was estimated at cost at £12,972.
(2) Provision is to be made for the following accrued expenses at 30 September 19X1:

	£
Rent	900
Lighting and heating	272
Travellers' commission and expenses	900
Audit charge	400

(3) The provision for doubtful debts is to be raised to 3% of closing debtors.
(4) Office furniture and equipment is to be depreciated by 10% on book value.

(5) B. Baker has withdrawn goods costing £112 for his own use during the year.

Required:
Prepare a profit and loss account for the year ended 30 September 19X1 and a balance sheet as at that date.

9. You have been given the task, by one of the partners of the firm of accountants for which you work, of assisting in the preparation of a trend statement for a client.

The client's business has been in existence for four years. Figures for the three previous years are known but those for the fourth year need to be calculated. Unfortunately, the supporting workings for the previous years' figures cannot be found and the client's own ledger accounts and workings are not available.

One item in particular, plant, is causing difficulty and the following figures have been given to you.

	12 months ended 31 March			
	1979	1980	1981	1982
	(£)	(£)	(£)	(£)
(A) Plant at cost	80,000	80,000	90,000	?
(B) Accumulated depreciation	(16,000)	(28,800)	(36,720)	?
(C) Net (written down value)	64,000	51,200	53,280	?

The only other information available is that disposals have taken place at the beginning of the financial years concerned.

	Date of Disposal	Date of Original acquisition	Original cost	Sales proceeds
	12 months ended 31 March		(£)	(£)
First disposal	1981	1979	15,000	8,000
Second disposal	1982	1979	30,000	21,000

Plant sold was replaced on the same day by new plant. The cost of the plant which replaced the first disposal is not known but the replacement for the second disposal is known to have cost £50,000.

Required:
(a) Identify the method of providing for depreciation on plant employed by the client, stating how you have arrived at your conclusion.
(b) Reconstruct a working schedule to support the figures shown at line (B) for each of the years ended 31 March 1979, 1980 and 1981. Extend your workings to cover year ended 31 March 1982.
(c) Produce the figures that should be included in the blank spaces on the trend statement at lines (A), (B) and (C) for the year ended 31 March 1982.
(d) Calculate the profit or loss arising on each of the two disposals.

(Association of Certified Accountants)

10. Greenacres Limited, a well-established company, specialising in the distribution of agricultural buildings, equipment and fertilisers, commenced a machinery repair service on 1 January 19X7.

From the beginning of the new venture, the repair service used a prefabricated building which the company bought originally with the intention of selling it.

In fact, the building was included in trading stock at cost at 31 December 19X6, at £10,000 and was then displayed for retail sale at £13,000.

In preparing the building for use as a workshop on 1 January 19X7, the following expenditure was incurred:

	£
Foundations and erection costs	1,000
Interior and exterior painting	600
Heating and lighting systems	3,000

On 1 January 19X8, further work was undertaken on the repair service building's heating system at a total cost of £1,400, half of which related to repairs and the rest concerned the installation of additional thermostatic controls.

On 30 June 19X8, the following work was completed on the workshop building:

	£
Installation of partition walls	1,600
Renewal of wooden window frames	1,000

Early in 19X9, following the closure of the machinery repair service, the workshop building, including the heating and lighting systems, was sold for £8,000. It is company policy to provide depreciation annually on prefabricated buildings at the rate of 10% of cost at the end of each financial year (31 December).

Required:
(a) The following ledger accounts as they would appear in the books of Greenacres Limited for each of the financial years ended 31 December 19X7, 19X8 and 19X9:
    (1) Repair service workshop building;
    (2) Repair service workshop building provision for depreciation.
    Note: The balances on accounts should be brought down at the end of each financial year.
(b) The repair service workshop building disposal account.

(Association of Certified Accountants)

8 Accounting for Current Assets

Traditionally, current assets are defined as assets having a service potential to the business not exceeding one accounting period. They include stocks, debtors, short-term investments and cash. Their relative liquidity is considered to be of importance to the problem of financial management, and for this reason, they are ranked on the balance sheet in that order. Stocks are seen as less liquid than debtors, and debtors less liquid than short-term investments.

Stocks

The objective of a stock control system is to provide means of exercising a close control over the flow of materials or goods into stock and the flow of stock into production or sales, thereby not only preventing losses but also ensuring that adequate stock levels are maintained. The purpose of this section is to focus on the procedures applied to the control of stock on a daily basis. Policy decisions affecting minimum stock levels will not be discussed.

A feature of stock control systems is the need to maintain records of both quantities and values. In this respect, it will be recalled that stock valuations depend upon a physical stocktake combined with a valuation base, such as unit cost or unit market value. Stock control systems increase in complexity with the number of different items held. Indeed, in the case of large firms, stock control systems are completely computerised. In this section, it will be assumed for simplicity that only one item is held in stock.

Controlling the flow of stock

The flow of stock through an accounting system is as follows:

Purchases

Purchases of goods for resale are recorded in the *purchases account*, as follows:

Dr Purchases account ⎫ with the cost of the
Cr Creditor account or cash book ⎭ goods bought

It should be noted particularly that the purchases account is only used for the purpose of recording the purchase of trading stock, and is not used to record acquisitions of such items as plant, equipment and supplies. The purchases account provides a record of all purchases during the accounting period, supporting evidence for which is found in the invoices received from suppliers which will have been entered in the purchases day book.

Inventory methods

There are two methods of recording stock flows:
(i) The periodic inventory method.
(ii) The perpetual inventory method.

Periodic inventory

Under this method of accounting for the flow of stock, no record of stock is maintained during the accounting period. At the end of the accounting period, the purchases account is closed. Those purchases remaining unsold are transferred to the *stock account*: the balance representing the goods which have been sold is transferred to the *cost of goods sold account*.

The periodic inventory method requires a count of all the items unsold on the last day of the accounting period to determine the closing stock. Little is known about the exact content of the stock during the course of the year. Thus, items in the opening stock or purchased during the year which are not found present in the closing stock are presumed to have been sold.

In effect, the periodic inventory method provides virtually no control over the flow of stock. The closing stock on the last day of the accounting period becomes the opening stock on the first day of the *next* accounting period, and remains in the stock account throughout that period. Acquisitions and disposals of stock are not recorded. The only check which is made is the physical stocktake on the last day of the accounting period.

The cost of goods sold under this method is determined as follows:

$$\frac{\text{cost of}}{\text{goods sold}} = \frac{\text{opening}}{\text{stock}} + \frac{\text{cost of}}{\text{purchases}} - \frac{\text{closing}}{\text{stock}}$$

Perpetual inventory

The object of this method of stock control is to maintain a continuous record of acquisitions, disposal and balances of stock throughout the accounting period. It is to be noted particularly that under this method of stock control no separate account is kept for purchases.

Instead, each purchase is recorded as an increase in the stock account, and the following entries are made:

Dr Stock account $\left.\right\}$ with cost of goods purchased
Cr Cash or creditor

When goods are sold, the following entries are now made:

Dr Cost of goods sold account $\left.\right\}$ with the cost of the goods sold
Cr Stock account

It is evident, therefore, that the result of this method of recording both purchases and the cost of sales through the stock account means that the stock account shows the cost of stock on hand at any particular time. A further advantage of the perpetual inventory method is that the cost of goods sold account can provide a direct means of calculating the gross profit on sales, without the necessity of formally preparing a profit and loss account. Thus, a partial profit and loss account based on details available in the sales account and the cost of goods sold account can take the following simple form:

	£
Sales	800,000
Cost of goods sold	600,000
Gross profit	200,000

It should also be noted that since the perpetual inventory provides up-to-date information on the quantities and value of stock on hand, the importance of the physical count of stock is reduced to one of checking the accuracy of the information contained in the stock account. The detailed records of inflow and outflow of stock are maintained as subsidiary records to the ledger. As may be seen from Fig. 8.1 below, the perpetual inventory shows quantities, unit costs and total costs of each transaction relating to the acquisition and

Date	Received			Sold			Stock		
19X4	Quantity	Unit cost	Total cost	Quantity	Unit cost	Total cost	Quantity	Unit cost	Total cost
		£	£		£	£		£	£
Jan 1							200	4	800
Feb 21				120	4	480	80	4	320
Mar 24	300	4	1,200				380	4	1,520
Apr 11				250	4	1,000	130	4	520
Aug 28	150	4	600				280	4	1,120
Sep 14				100	4	400	180	4	720
Oct 19	200	4	800				380	4	1,520
Nov 23	350	4	1,400				730	4	2,920
Dec 10				200	4	800	530	4	2,120

Fig. 8.1 Example of a perpetual inventory account

disposal of stock. In the simplified illustration shown below, it is assumed that the firm only carries one item in stock. Where many items are involved, a record would be maintained for each item.

Figure 8.1 shows how the perpetual inventory facilitates the control of stock by showing (a) the quantity of stock which should be on hand, and (b) the cost of that stock.

The valuation of stock

Stock valuation is of considerable significance for profit determination and the valuation of the business. The closing stock is often large in proportion to other items appearing on the balance sheet. Any understatement or overstatement in the valuation of closing stock will affect the measurement of the cost of goods sold, the gross profit on sales, the net profit for the period, as well as affecting the valuation of current assets and the value of the equity in the firm.

Errors in stock valuation not only affect accounting measurements relating to the period concerned, but also they spread over into the next accounting period. Thus, if the closing stock of the current period is overstated, the gross margin will also be overstated, and, since the closing stock is the opening stock of the next period, it follows that the gross margin of that period will be understated by reason of the overvaluation of the opening stock. Accordingly, the consequential effect will reach as far as the measurement of the net profit of the following period.

In the examples given above, stock has been shown at cost, and it has been assumed that the acquisition cost of stock remained constant. Clearly, the assumption is unreal and it is likely that costs will fluctuate as well as rise through time. As a result, the transfer of stock to the cost of goods sold account poses a difficulty as to the value which should be attached to individual items transferred. This difficulty also affects the valuation of closing stock.

A ruling convention among accountants is that closing stock should be valued at the 'lower of cost or market value'. Unfortunately, there are many pitfalls in the application of this rule. Firstly, there are difficulties in defining the cost of closing stock. Moreover, the market value may mean the replacement cost or the net realisable value. Secondly, the rule reflects the conservatism of accountants concerned that closing stock should not be overvalued and that, therefore, the net profit should not be overstated. Thirdly, the rule may be applied consistently and yet permit a great variety of procedures for valuation. As regards the determination of market value, the majority of firms use the net realisable value as the lower level valuation test. Thus, if the net realisable value of stock is £5,000 and the historic cost is £6,000, the closing stock is shown as £5,000, being the net sum after deduction of realisation expenses.

There are three generally accepted methods for valuing the cost of stock, which reflect different treatments of the changing cost of acquisition of stock. These methods are commonly referred to as FIFO (First In First Out), LIFO (Last In First Out) and AVCO (Average Cost).

FIFO

This method assumes that the oldest goods on hand are those which are first to be sold. The cost of goods sold, therefore, is determined by reference to the price at which the earliest items in the stock were purchased. Consequently, the closing stock is valued at the most recent purchase price, as the most recent purchases are deemed to be still on hand. It should be noted, therefore, that FIFO reflects a traditional view of the flow of stock.

The following example illustrates the application of the FIFO method.

Example 1
The following data relates to the Marford Supply Co. Ltd for April 19X0.

Opening stock 1 April 19X0: 100 units at a cost of £4 each

Purchases:			£
April 2	200 units @	4.15	830
April 7	200 units @	4.20	840
April 15	300 units @	4.30	1,290
April 22	100 units @	4.40	440
April 28	200 units @	4.65	930
			4,330

During April the company sold 800 units. The cost of goods sold and the value of the closing stock are as follows:

	Units	Cost		
		£	£	
Cost of sales	100	4.00	400	(Opening stock)
	200	4.15	830	(Bought April 2)
	200	4.20	840	(Bought April 7)
	300	4.30	1,290	(Bought April 15)
	800		3,360	
Closing stock	100	4.40	440	(Bought April 22)
	200	4.65	930	(Bought April 28)
	300		1,370	

LIFO

This method assumes that the most recently acquired goods are the first to be sold. It assumes, therefore, an opposite viewpoint of the flow of stock to that assumed by FIFO. Under the LIFO method, the cost of goods sold is determined by reference to the price of the latest acquisitions.

The following example illustrates the application of the LIFO method.

Example 2

By taking the same data given in the previous example and using the LIFO as distinct from the FIFO method, the cost of goods sold and the value of the closing stock are as follows:

	Units	Cost £	£	
Cost of sales	200	4.65	930	(Bought April 28)
	100	4.40	440	(Bought April 22)
	300	4.30	1,290	(Bought April 15)
	200	4.20	840	(Bought April 7)
	800		3,500	
Closing stock	200	4.15	830	(Bought April 2)
	100	4.00	400	(On hand April 1)
	300		1,230	

AVCO

This method avoids the extreme assumption of the FIFO and LIFO methods and attempts to avoid the excessive distortions in either the cost of goods sold or the value of closing stock implied by these methods. This method is at best an expedient which does not really solve the problems of valuing stock.

Example 3

The first step is to calculate the weighted average cost of goods available for sale in the period under review. Using the data for the Marford Supply Co. Ltd, the weighted average cost is as follows:

		Units	Price £	£
April 1	Opening stock	100	4.00	400
2	Purchases	200	4.15	830
7	Purchases	200	4.20	840
15	Purchases	300	4.30	1,290
22	Purchases	100	4.40	440
28	Purchases	200	4.65	930
		1,100		4,730

The weighted average cost is $£\dfrac{4,730}{1,100} = £4.30$ per unit

Cost of sales is therefore: $\qquad 800 \times 4.30 = 3,440$
and closing stock: $\qquad\qquad 300 \times 4.30 = 1,290$

$$\underline{1,100} \qquad \underline{4,730}$$

The balance of the stock going into the next period will be used as part of the data used in arriving at the weighted average cost for that period.

Retail price less Gross margin

Many businesses and, in particular large retail stores, find it convenient to value stock at selling price and to reduce this valuation by the amount of the gross profit to obtain the cost value. The advantage of this method is that it avoids a considerable amount of record keeping although weakening the stock control system. Since the gross profit is fairly stable for individual classes of goods, it can be applied to the selling prices to obtain a reliable valuation of stock. For this purpose, the gross profit ratio is calculated as follows:

$$\frac{\text{Gross trading profit}}{\text{Sales}} \times 100$$

Example 4

The gross profit ratio expresses the relationship between the selling price and the cost of the goods sold. Consider the following data:

	£
Selling price of goods	100
Cost of goods	80
Gross profit	20

The gross profit ratio is: $\quad \dfrac{20}{100} \times 100 = 20\%$

It is evident on the data given above that a gross profit of 20% on sale is equivalent to 25% on cost. Expressing these relationships as fractions, if the gross profit on sales is 1/5, then it is 1/4 on cost. Accordingly, the following generalisation may be made:

If the gross profit on sales is $1/x$, then it is $1/(x-1)$ on cost. Similarly, if the gross profit is expressed as $1/y$ on cost, then it is $1/(y+1)$ on sales.

Selecting the method of valuation

Since the value of the closing stock has an immediate impact on the measurement of the net profit, it is important to understand the reasons for adopting one method of valuation rather than another.

FIFO

As indicated earlier, FIFO seeks to emulate the physical flow of goods in and out of the business. This method is used by the majority of companies in the United Kingdom. During periods of inflation, however, the value of the closing stock under this method is likely to approximate current replacement cost. Whilst this characteristic is relevant to the correct valuation of closing stock on the balance sheet, it leads to an overstatement of reported profits.

LIFO

Under LIFO valuation procedures, the closing stock will be at the value of the earliest purchases constituting stock. Accordingly stock values tend to be progressively understated. Advocates of this method claim that the most current costs are being matched against revenue, leading to more accurate representation of profit. Changes in stock levels, however, can lead to fluctuations in the cost of sales. This system is rarely used in the United Kingdom. The Inland Revenue does not regard it as an acceptable basis for tax purposes.

AVCO and retail price

These methods usually have the merit of requiring fewer clerical processes and are easy to operate. AVCO may be appropriate where purchase prices fluctuate, but seems to have little merit for dealing with conditions of constantly rising prices.

The retail price method is widely used. Its use produces valuations which are closer to FIFO than other methods, particularly when selling prices and costs are moving in the same direction.

Stock control and stock valuation

So far valuations have been placed on stocks at the end of a financial period leaving the cost of sales as a residual. This application of the method is known as *periodic inventory*. Thus, when a valuation procedure is stated as being FIFO, LIFO or AVCO, then it must be further qualified to indicate whether the periodic inventory method is being used. This is necessary because the flow assumption underlying FIFO, etc., can be applied in an alternative way which is called *perpetual inventory*. This method requires an accounting system which not only fully records each acquisition of stock in the way explained above, but also identifies, and places a value on each withdrawal of goods from stores on the date of withdrawal. If this is done, the closing stock is the residual, unlike the results of periodic inventory.

The valuation of the goods withdrawn for sale, processing, etc., is based on the same ideas of FIFO, LIFO and AVCO, whichever-method has been adopted. The distinction is that the rule is applied in the light of knowledge at the date of the withdrawal. It will be apparent that in order to use this method a control system must be in force which identifies goods withdrawn from stores. This normally takes the form of an authorised requisition note which is then used as the basis for an accounting entry, which will be:

Dr   Cost of sales account
Cr   Stock } with cost value of goods withdrawn

and similarly in the case of items withdrawn for further processing in the manufacture of a final product. Under perpetual inventory, the following consequences emerge when the method is compared with periodic inventory.

(a) *FIFO*. Under the assumption of this method of valuation, there will be no difference between the value of goods transferred out of stock and the value of goods remaining in stock, irrespective of which stock control system is used.

(b) *LIFO*. The application of LIFO to the perpetual inventory method requires the strict observance of the rule that transfers out of stock must be valued at the most recent purchase price. During periods of rising prices, the cost of goods transferred out of stock will have a total value which will be smaller in the case of the perpetual inventory method than in that of the periodic inventory method. This is because the closing stock under the latter method will be valued at the latest purchase price, whereas under the former method, it will reflect a series of progressively increasing purchase prices rather than the latest purchase price.

(c) *AVCO*. Under this method, the transfers of goods out of stock to sales must be based on the most recent weighted average cost. This means that the average cost must be calculated at the time of purchase and not at the time of sale. The application of this method under conditions of rising prices will lead to smaller valuations of the closing stock when using the perpetual inventory as distinct from the periodic inventory method.

Example 5
The following data was given in Example 1:

Opening stock 1 April 19X0		100 units at a cost of £4 each

Purchases:			£	£
April 2	200 units @	4.15		830
7	200 units @	4.20		840
15	300 units @	4.30		1,290
22	100 units @	4.40		440
28	200 units @	4.65		930
				4,330

Sales for April totalled 800 units, and goods transferred out of stock were as follows:

April 3	250 units
10	200 units
16	250 units
23	100 units

The stock records based on the perpetual inventory method under the different valuation procedures are as follows:

(a) *FIFO.* As stated earlier, no difference exists in the valuation of cost of sales and closing stock as between the two methods of stock control.

(b) *LIFO.* The effect of using the perpetual inventory method is to produce the following valuations:

	£
(1) Total cost of goods sold	3,385
(2) Closing stock	1,345

Figure 8.2 below shows how these valuations are produced. The corresponding valuation using the periodic inventory method is as follows:

	£
(1) Total cost of goods sold	3,500
(2) Closing stock	1,230

(c) *AVCO.* The corresponding record using the AVCO is shown in Fig. 8.3.

Date	Received			Sold			Stock		
19X0	Quantity	Unit cost	Total cost	Quantity	Unit cost	Total cost	Quantity	Unit cost	Total cost
		£	£		£	£		£	£
Apr 1							100	4.00	400
2	200	4.15	830				200	4.15	830
3				200	4.15	830	100	4.00	400
				50	4.00	200	50	4.00	200
7	200	4.20	840				200	4.20	840
10				200	4.20	840	50	4.00	200
15	300	4.30	1,290				300	4.30	1,290
16				250	4.30	1,075	50	4.00	200
							50	4.30	215
22	100	4.40	440				100	4.40	440
23				100	4.40	440	50	4.00	200
							50	4.30	215
28	200	4.65	930				200	4.65	930
				Total cost of sales		3,385	300	Closing stock	1,345

Fig. 8.2   Perpetual inventory—using LIFO

The effect of the AVCO method (Fig. 8.3) is to produce the following valuations:

$\qquad$ £

(1) Total cost of goods sold $\qquad$ 3,366
(2) Closing stock $\qquad$ 1,364

The corresponding valuations under the periodic inventory method are as follows:

$\qquad$ £

(1) Total cost of goods sold $\qquad$ 3,440
(2) Closing stock $\qquad$ 1,290

(d) *Comparison of valuations.* Figure 8.4 below summarises the differing valuations of the cost of goods sold and of the closing stock using the three alternative valuation methods, under the perpetual inventory method.

SSAP 9: *Stocks and Work in Progress* (1975)

The basic rule contained in SSAP 9 for the valuation of stock and work in progress is that the value adopted should be the lower of

Date	Received			Sold			Stock		
19X0	Quantity	Unit cost	Total cost	Quantity	Unit cost	Total cost	Quantity	Unit cost	Total cost
		£	£		£	£		£	£
Apr 1							100	4.00	400
2	200	4.15	830				200	4.15	830
							300	4.10	1,230
3				250	4.10	1,025	50	4.10	205
7	200	4.20	840				200	4.20	840
							250	4.18	1,045
10				200	4.18	836	50	4.18	209
15	300	4.30	1,290				300	4.30	1,290
							350	4.28	1,499
16				250	4.28	1,071	100	4.28	428
22	100	4.40	440				100	4.40	440
							200	4.34	868
23				100	4.34	434	100	4.34	434
28	200	4.65	930				200	4.65	930
				Total cost of sales		3,366			
				Closing stock			300	4.55	1,364

Fig. 8.3 Perpetual inventory—using AVCO

	FIFO £	LIFO £	AVCO £
Perpetual inventory			
Cost of goods sold	3,360	3,385	3,366
Closing stock	1,370	1,345	1,364
Periodic inventory			
Cost of goods sold	(Example 1) 3,360	(Example 2) 3,500	(Example 3) 3,440
Closing stock	(Example 1) 1,370	(Example 2) 1,230	(Example 3) 1,290

Fig. 8.4 Comparison of valuations

cost and net realisable value, taking each item or group of items separately.

Cost is further defined to mean 'expenditure incurred in the normal course of business in bringing the product or service to its present location and condition'. Related production overheads (those costs not associated directly with the product) should be included in cost, as should other overheads attributable to bringing the product or service to its present location and condition. The allocation of overheads should reflect current and expected future levels of activity.

Net realisable value is defined as the actual or estimated selling price of the stock net of any trade discount, from which is deducted any cost incurred to put the stock into a saleable condition, and to which is added all costs to be incurred in the marketing, selling and distribution of such stock.

SSAP 9 allows the use of several methods of approximating to actual cost. Permissible methods are unit cost, AVCO and FIFO. If standard (predetermined) costs are used as production costs and for the valuation of stocks, they should be reviewed frequently to ensure that they bear a reasonable relationship to actual cost. The use of selling price less the profit mark-up is allowed only if it can be shown to give a reasonably close approximation to actual cost. LIFO is not a permissible method of stock valuation because it does not normally provide a sufficiently close approximation to actual cost. In this connection, it will be remembered that under LIFO the earliest purchases remain in stock since the latest purchases are sold. As prices increase, the relative value of stock tends to fall.

SSAP 9 also requires the disclosure of the main categories of stock. The accounting policies used for stock valuation must be disclosed. As will be seen in Chapter 13, the Companies Act 1985 requires the disclosure of separate figures for (a) raw material stock, (b) work in progress and (c) finished goods stock.

Long-term contracts

Construction contracts, such as those for dams, roads, ships and industrial plants may take years to complete. At the end of a given accounting period, a contracting company has to determine the extent to which a profit or loss should be recognised with respect to the work in progress and not completed. When profit is recognised as arising only on the completion of the contract, profit realisation rests on a factual basis. On completion date, all revenues and costs are known, and the profit earned on the contract may be determined readily. If the contract covers several accounting periods, this method of accounting for profit will result in wide profit fluctuations over these periods.

SSAP 9: *Stock and Work in Progress* (1975) recognises that it is reasonable to account for a proportion of accrued profit when valuing the work in progress of a long-term contract, defined as a contract extending over a period exceeding one year. Prudence must be exercised when estimating or calculating the profit to be taken. The method recommended in SSAP 9 is as follows:

$$\text{Accrued profit} = \text{Total contract revenue} - (\text{Costs to date} + \text{estimated costs of completion}) \times \frac{\text{Work done to date}}{\text{Total work to be done}}$$

It is the normal practice in long-term contracts to have stages certified as completed for the purpose of determining progress payments. The issue of a work completed certificate justifies the calculation of the profit or loss to be taken at that point. No profit should be recognised until it may be predicted with reasonable certainty. As soon as it becomes evident that a loss on completion is likely, the entire loss, and not merely the accrued proportion, must be recognised immediately.

Debtors

For most businesses, debtors represent major current assets. They arise primarily from credit transactions associated with the sale of goods and services. The control of debtors involves policy considerations such as the creditworthiness of potential customers, the credit limit to be granted and time limit imposed for payment in individual cases. Accounting procedures for the control of debtors are designed to keep a record of individual debts to ensure that policy decisions are being applied, and to keep a running total of outstanding debts due to the firm to ensure that the firm is not investing in debtors beyond the limit of its ability.

Most of the problems in recording transactions with customers have already been discussed. Those relating to bad and doubtful debts were examined in Chapter 4: the treatment of discounts allowed and received, and the use of control accounts and subsidiary ledgers were examined in Chapter 5.

Investments

Investments made by a firm may be treated either as short-term or as long-term investments. Short-term investments may be made as a temporary but profitable refuge for surplus funds. Short-term investments include local authority deposits and the acquisition of shares for resale within a year. Long-term investments in shares and debentures may be associated with a substantial interest in another company, which amounts to the ability to examine a significant influence on the activities of that company.

Investments are usually shown on the balance sheet at cost. Stock market fluctuations are usually ignored unless there is a substantial permanent fall in value, in which case a provision should be made for that loss. The requirements of the Companies Act 1985 in that regard are dealt with in Chapter 13.

Cash

The transactions realised by the firm must eventually involve either an inflow or an outflow of cash. If the firm is to survive and prosper, the inflows of cash from its operations must exceed the outflows. Cash management is of vital importance for sound financial management. Among the most useful techniques which have been developed for this purpose are:

(a) internal control procedures for cash receipts and payments,
(b) imprest system for the control of petty cash,
(c) periodic bank reconciliations,
(d) cash forecasts.

Internal control procedures

Because cash is the asset most susceptible to misappropriation, procedures are necessary to safeguard cash receipts and prevent unauthorised cash disbursements. An adequate system of internal control over cash should possess at least three features.

First, there should be a separation of responsibilities so that staff who handle cash are not the same as those who keep the cash records. Such a division of responsibilities would make it necessary for collusion to exist before cash could be embezzled, and the embezzlement concealed in the accounting records.

Second, all cash receipts should be deposited in the bank in their totality at the end of each day.

Third, all payments should be effected by cheque, thereby providing by means of the bank's own records an independent and external control over the firm's own cash records.

Imprest system for petty cash

An exception to the rule that all cash payments should be made by cheque is that which exists in most firms for the payment in cash of items of small value, where it would be inconvenient to use the cheque system. The purchase of urgent small supplies such as postage stamps, flowers, taxi fares, etc. is normally provided for by the existence of a petty cash fund. The authorised signatories on company cheques are usually senior executives and directors. The petty cashier is normally responsible for the maintenance of the petty cash fund, from which he may make reimbursements on the presentation of vouchers which authorise the reimbursement.

The size of the petty cash depends on the estimated total petty cash disbursements likely to be effected during a short period, usually a month. The petty cashier begins the month with a petty cash float. The accounting entries are:

    Dr   Petty cash book
    Cr   Cash book (bank column)

During the following month, credit entries are made in the petty cash book to record petty cash disbursements, the latter being debited to the appropriate expenses accounts. At the end of each month, the petty cash expended by the petty cashier is refunded to him, on the presentation of properly authorised vouchers, thereby resorting the petty cash float back to its original level.

Control over the petty cash balance is maintained since at any time during the month, the petty cash balance on hand plus supporting vouchers for the petty cash disbursed should equal the petty cash float or imprest amount.

Bank reconciliation

The bank reconciliation is effected monthly, or for whatever appropriate period, upon the receipt from the bank of the statement showing the transactions which have gone through the bank account, and the balance remaining at the end of the month. The bank reconciliation statement has the purpose of effecting a reconciliation between the balance shown on the bank statement and the balance recorded in the bank column of the cash book. It is, in effect, a periodic audit of the balance recorded in the cash book by means of the bank statement which is an external and independent record.

It is usual for there to be a discrepancy between the balance shown on the bank statement and the balance shown in the bank column of the cash book. There are several possible reasons which account for the discrepancy:

(a) cheques issued by the firm, and not yet presented for payment to the bank, and cheques received by the firm but not yet credited by the bank to the firm's bank account, will account for a substantial proportion of the discrepancy,

(b) payments made by the bank on the firm's behalf under standing orders may not have been entered in the firm's cash book, although they will appear on the bank statement,

(c) sums received directly by the bank, for example, standing orders, dividends and interest receipts will appear on the bank statement but may not have been recorded in the cash book,

(d) bank charges which have been debited to the firm's account will appear on the bank statement, but may not have been entered in the cash book prior to receipt of the bank statement,

(e) amounts paid into the firm's bank account but not yet shown as credited to that account by the bank,

(f) an error made by the bank on the bank statement. This event is infrequent, but does occur.

The process of reconciling the bank statement with the cash book begins by checking each entry in the bank column of the cash book with the corresponding item in the bank statement, and marking agreement with a tick. Next, the bank statement is examined for any entries not ticked, that is, those entries which have not been recorded in the cash book. These entries will correspond to (b), (c) and (d) above. The cash book must be adjusted accordingly, and the appropriate entries made, once they are approved. Finally, there will remain a number of entries shown in the cash book which do not appear on the bank statement. These items will be shown in the bank reconciliation statement.

Example 6

On 31 January 19X5, Harry Hay's cash book showed a debit balance of £510, representing cash at bank. He received a bank statement as at that date, and on checking it with the cash book, all entries agreed except the following:

(a) during the month, the bank had debited Hay's account with £30 in respect of bank charges. No entries had been made in the cash book,

(b) the bank paid an annual subscription of £25 to a motoring organisation. This amount had not been entered in the cash book,

(c) a remittance from R. Green for £165 on 31 January had been entered in the cash book, but had not yet been credited by the bank,

(d) the following cheques drawn and credited in the cash book had not yet been presented to the bank for payment:
B. Smart   £140
T. White   £115

(e) the bank had credited H. Hays' account with £70 being dividends received, but this amount had not yet entered in the cash book.

You are required to draw up a bank reconciliation statement as at 31 January 19X5. The credit balance appearing on the bank statement at that date was £615.

The work involved in preparing the bank reconciliation has two stages:

(a) entering in the cash book amounts unrecorded but appearing in the bank statement,
(b) reconciling the adjusted cash book balance with the balance appearing in the bank statement.

Cash book (bank column)

	£		£
Balance b/d	510	Payment to motoring organisation	25
Dividends collected	70	Bank charges	30
		Balance c/d	525
	580		580
Balance b/d	525		

Bank reconciliation statement
as at 31 January 19X5

	£	£
Balance as per bank statement		615
Less: Unpresented cheques		
B. Smart	140	
T. White	115	255
		360
Add: Cheque deposited and not yet recorded		
by bank		
R. Green		165
Balance as per cash book		525

Cash forecasts

Sound financial management requires that adequate cash funds are available to meet expenditure commitments in the form of payments to suppliers, wages and other operating expenses. An adequate cash balance is also needed to maintain a good credit rating with suppliers. Excessive cash balances, however, particularly during periods of inflation, imply an inefficient management of cash.

An essential feature of a sound cash management policy lies in the forecasts made of future cash requirements with a view to ensuring that adequate funds will be available as and when expenditure is due. This is the main objective of the cash forecast.

A cash forecast is an estimate of future cash flows based on a careful analysis of prior periods and subjected to appropriate adjustments for anticipated expenditure. The steps involved in the preparation of a cash forecast are:

(a) estimating cash receipts for the forecast period,
(b) estimating cash expenditure to be effected during the forecast period,
(c) estimating the cash balance required at the end of the forecast period.

Example 7

The cash forecast for Knowles Toys for the first quarter of 19X6 is prepared from the following estimates:

(a) *Sales*

	Credit £	Cash £
January	150,000	10,000
February	100,000	5,000
March	120,000	5,000

No cash discounts are accorded to customers. From past experience, 20% of credit sales are collected at the end of the month in which the sales were effected, the balance of 80% is collected in the following month. During December 19X5, credit sales amounted to £120,000 and £96,000 remained to be collected in January 19X6.

(b) *Purchases*
All merchandise purchases are on credit terms, and the following estimates apply:

	£
January	80,000
February	60,000
March	70,000

Payment of approximately 40% of purchases is effected by the end of the month to which they relate, and the balance of 60% is paid in the following month. Purchases effected during the month of December 19X5 amounted to £90,000 and £54,000 remains to be paid during January 19X6.

(c) *Other estimated monthly cash expenditure*

	£
Wages	30,000
Advertising	5,000
Rent	10,000
Miscellaneous	2,000

(d) *Capital expenditure*

It is planned to incur expenditure on the purchase of equipment amounting to £40,000 in February and to £10,000 in March.

(e) The cash balance at 1 January 19X6 was £15,000. The firm desires to maintain this amount as the minimum cash balance.

Knowles Toys

Cash forecast for the three months ending 31 March 19X6

	January £	February £	March £
Cash balance, beginning of month	15,000	18,000	15,000
Cash receipts:			
Cash sales	10,000	5,000	5,000
Credit sales, December	96,000		
January	30,000	120,000	
February		20,000	80,000
March			24,000
Total cash available	151,000	163,000	124,000
Cash payments:			
Purchases, December	54,000		
January	32,000	48,000	
February		24,000	36,000
March			28,000
Wages	30,000	30,000	30,000
Advertising	5,000	5,000	5,000
Rent	10,000	10,000	10,000
Miscellaneous	2,000	2,000	2,000
Capital expenditure		40,000	10,000
	133,000	159,000	121,000
Cash balance, end of month	18,000	4,000	3,000
Borrowing requirement		11,000	12,000
Cash balance forecast		15,000	15,000

The cash forecast shows that the cash balance will fall below the desired minimum in February and March. Therefore, management must plan in advance for a loan to meet this shortage.

Questions

1. The following information relates to one of the items carried by the Houlgate Co. Ltd.

Purchases record of Item No. A.312 for October 19X5

			£	£
Balance on hand at start		250 units @ 1.60 =	400
October	8	Purchases	800 units @ 1.70 =	1,360
	13	Purchases	400 units @ 1.75 =	700
	20	Purchases	350 units @ 1.80 =	630
	29	Purchases	200 units @ 1.85 =	370

During October 1,700 units were sold.

Required:

Calculate the cost of sales for October and the value of closing stock based on each of the following methods:

(a) FIFO.
(b) LIFO.
(c) AVCO.

2. In addition to the data given in Question 1 above, you are given the following information concerning the dates and quantities of Item No. A.312 transferred to the cost of goods sold account:

October 5	Sales	200 units
10	Sales	700 units
15	Sales	450 units
23	Sales	300 units
30	Sales	50 units

Required:

(i) Calculate the cost of sales and the value of closing stock using perpetual inventory applied to (a) FIFO, (b) LIFO, (c) AVCO.
(ii) Prepare a perpetual inventory for each method of valuation.

3. On 9 August 19X7, a fire completely destroyed the shop and warehouse of the Portal Home Decorating Co. Ltd. The stock of goods was destroyed, but the basic ledgers of the company, which were kept in a fireproof safe, were recovered. From the ledgers, the following information was extracted:

	£
Opening stock on 1 January 19X7	35,612
Purchases at cost to 9 August 19X7	134,364
Sales to 9 August 19X7	187,200

The company's policy was to fix selling price as a mark-up of one-third on cost.

Required:

Calculate the cost of the stock destroyed for the purpose of an insurance claim against the Fire Insurance Co. Ltd.

4. The miscellaneous section of the inventory of the Speedwell Engineering Company Ltd as at 30 June 19X4 consisted of the following items:

Parts	Quantity	Unit price Cost £	Unit price Market value £
Sprockets	2,000	2.00	2.15
Flanges	1,500	3.10	3.00
Gear wheels	3,000	1.60	1.75
Drive chains	1,000	4.30	4.00
Clamps	4,000	1.20	1.25

Required:

Calculate the total value of the stock for this section at 30 June 19X4 applying the following bases of valuation:

(a) Cost base only.
(b) Lower of cost or market value by total.
(c) Lower of cost or market value by item.

5. Solo Ltd, who only deal in one product, have produced the following schedule of their transactions for purchases and sales of goods during 19X6.

			Purchases			Sales			Balance		
			Qty	Unit cost (£)	Total (£)	Qty	Unit cost (£)	Total (£)	Qty	Unit cost (£)	Total (£)
Jan	1	Stock							600	2.10	1,260
	8	Sales				400					
	23	Purchases	300	2.15	645						
Feb	2	Sales				240					
	18	Purchases	700	2.20	1,540						
	23	Sales				500					
Mar	14	Purchases	250	2.30	575						
	23	Purchases	300	2.35	705						
	27	Sales				200					
Apr	3	Sales				260					
	10	Purchases	400	2.40	960						
	15	Sales				500					
May	28	Purchases	200	2.30	460						
Jun	18	Purchases	200	2.35	470						
	24	Sales				400					
Jul	17	Purchases	300	2.40	720						
Aug	2	Sales				500					
	30	Purchases	600	2.45	1,470						
Sep	18	Sales				200					
	30	Purchases	400	2.50	1,000						
Oct	10	Sales				600					
Nov	9	Purchases	400	2.55	1,020						
	28	Sales				300					
Dec	1	Purchases	200	2.70	540						
	23	Sales				100					

The selling price up to 30 June was £5 per unit but was raised to £5.50 for the rest of the year.

Required:
Prepare the trading account up to the gross profit under the following cost flow assumptions:

(a) Periodic inventory: (i) FIFO, (ii) LIFO, (iii) AVCO.
(b) Perpetual inventory: (i) FIFO, (ii) LIFO, (iii) AVCO.
(c) Using the form shown above as your example, complete the column for sales and balance in accordance with perpetual inventory assumptions, using: (i) FIFO, (ii) LIFO, (iii) AVCO.

6. The cash book of a business shows a favourable bank balance of £3,856 at 30 June 19X7. After comparing the entries in the cash book with the entries on the related bank statement you find that:

(1) Cheques amounting to £218 entered in the cash book have not yet been presented for payment to the bank.
(2) An amount of £50 entered on the debit side of the cash book has not been banked.

(3) An amount of £95 has been credited by the bank to the account in error.

(4) The bank has credited and then debited the bank statement with an amount of £48, being A. Jones' cheque which it forwarded on 1 July 19X7 marked 'insufficient funds—return to drawer'.

(5) Interest of £10 has been charged by the bank, but not yet entered in the cash book.

(6) A cheque from a customer entered in the cash book as £88 had been correctly entered by the bank as £188.

Required:

(1) Show the additional entries to be made in the cash book and bring down the corrected balance.

(2) Prepare a bank reconciliation statement.

(Association of Certified Accountants)

7. You are given the following information extracted from the records of B. Webb.

Bank account

		Dr £			Cheq. No.	Cr £
1 Dec	Balance b/f	16,491	1 Dec	Alexander	782	857
2 Dec	Able Ltd	962	6 Dec	Burgess	783	221
2 Dec	Baker Ltd	1,103	14 Dec	Barry	784	511
10 Dec	Charlie Ltd	2,312	17 Dec	Cook	785	97
14 Dec	Delta & Co.	419	24 Dec	Hay	786	343
21 Dec	Echo Ltd	327	29 Dec	Rent	787	260
23 Dec	Cash Sales to bank	529	31 Dec	Balance c/d		19,973
30 Dec	George	119				
		£22,262				£22,262

Marrods Bank Ltd
Bank Statement
B. Webb

Detail	Payments £	Receipts £	Date	Balance £
Balance forward			1 Dec	17,478
836780	426		2 Dec	17,052
Remittance		176	2 Dec	17,228
836782	857		5 Dec	16,371
Charges	47		5 Dec	16,324
836781	737		6 Dec	15,587
Counter credit		2,065	6 Dec	17,652
Standing Order	137		10 Dec	17,515
836783	212		11 Dec	17,303
Remittance		2,312	13 Dec	19,615
836784	511		17 Dec	19,104
Counter Credit		419	17 Dec	19,523
Remittance		327	23 Dec	19,850
Counter Credit		528	24 Dec	20,378
836786	343		28 Dec	20,035
310923	297		30 Dec	19,738

Required:

(*a*) From the above data prepare a bank reconciliation as at 31 December.

(*b*) List the reasons for preparing such a statement.

(*c*) Comment briefly upon any aspects of your reconciliation which might require further investigation.

(*Association of Certified Accountants*)

8. The bank account for the month of September 19X3 for the firm of Rivers and Co. was as follows:

Bank account

	Receipts	£			Payments	Cheque No.	£
Sept			Sept				
1	Balance b/d	271.94	3	Derwent Ltd		052316	25.08
1	T. Hames	53.40	4	Severn Bros.		052317	31.72
1	Dove Enterprises	62.85	8	Clyde and Co.		052318	121.86
13	Isis PLC	1,793.48	9	Ribble Merchants		052319	1,374.29
20	Colne Electronics	2,404.37	13	Swale Associates		052320	10.35
			20	Don Engineering		052321	642.13
			24	Humber Water Authority		Direct Debit	32.00
			26	Arun Decorators		052322	90.44
			26	Tyne Borough Council		Standing Order	123.57
			27	Salaries transfers		—	940.60
			28	Wye and Sons Ltd		052323	4.30
			30	Balance c/d			1,189.70
		£4,586.04					£4,586.04
Oct							
1	Balance b/d	1,189.70					

In early October the firm's bank sent a statement for the month of September 19X3, as shown below.

Statement of account with Mersey Bank plc

Name: Rivers and Co. Current Account   *Date Issued:* 1 October 19X3

Sept	Description	Debit £	Credit £	Balance £
1	BCE			592.45
2	052315	85.16		507.29
5	052314	100.34		406.95
8	052316	25.08		381.87
12	DD (Medway Insurance)	26.26		355.61
13	CR		1,793.48	2,149.09
13	052318	121.86		2,027.23
15	052319	1,374.29		652.94
16	052317	31.72		621.22
20	CR		2,404.37	3,025.59
22	DD (Humber Water Authority)	32.00		2,993.59

(*contd*)

Sept	Description	Debit £	Credit £	Balance £
23	052320	10.35		2,983.24
26	SO	123.57		2,859.67
28	TRFR	940.60		1,919.07
29	INT (Loan Account)	11.19		1,907.88
30	Bank charges	7.37		1,900.51
30	052321	642.13		1,258.38
30	BCE			1,258.38

Abbreviations: BCE = Balance, SO = Standing Order, CR = Credit
TRFR = Transfer, INT = Interest
DD = Direct debit (to Current Account)

Required:
Prepare the firm's bank reconciliation statement as at 30 September 19X3.

(Association of Certified Accountants)

9 Incomplete Records

The term 'incomplete records' is used to describe situations where a complete double-entry bookkeeping system has not been maintained. In the absence of proper records, the accountant's task is to attempt to use the information available for the purpose of producing year end financial statements. At the same time, he will establish a basis for complete records to be kept in the future.

Typically, incomplete records are associated with the following circumstances:

(a) a small firm, which does not keep records on a systematic basis. Such a firm may have a cash book, and simply put invoices and bank statements in a cardboard box until the year end,

(b) records have been partly damaged due to fire, flood or other disaster,

(c) the wilful destruction of part of the records in an attempt to conceal fraud.

The accountant's task when faced with incomplete records is:

(a) to assess what information is missing,

(b) to reconstruct, as far as possible, the missing information,

(c) to establish, as best possible, a profit and loss account for the period affected by the incompleteness of records, and a balance sheet as at the close of the period,

(d) install a proper recordkeeping system, thereby ensuring that in future a complete recordkeeping system will be maintained in accordance with the requirement of law.

There are two general approaches to dealing with incomplete records:

(a) in the virtual absence of any records, use is made of comparative statements of wealth at two dates marking the opening and the closing dates of the accounting period affected by missing records. This is known as the *statement of affairs approach*,

(b) where records are available, but are partial and incomplete, the available information is expanded as much as is possible and used to prepare a full profit and loss account and a balance sheet for the period. This is known as the *incomplete double entry approach*.

Under both approaches, once the period affected by incomplete records has been dealt with and final accounts produced, the balance sheet is used to provide the opening balances which will enable a proper set of accounts to be maintained.

The statement of affairs

The reasoning underlying the statement of affairs is found in the accounting equation:

$$\text{Assets} = \text{Liabilities} + \text{Owners' equity}$$

Accordingly, the statement of affairs approach requires that the accounting equation at the beginning of the period be reconstructed by such means as are available. Normally, there will be fragmentary information with which the accountant will be able to discover clients who owe money, creditors to whom money is owed. More often than not, the accountant will have to rely on the memory of the owner of the business for a list of creditors and debtors, to whom he may subsequently write to obtain verification of the amounts involved. If use has been made of a separate business bank account, the analysis of that account will produce a list of receipts and expenses relating to the business. It may be used to establish the acquisition of assets, loans, etc. It frequently happens, however, that the proprietor of the business will merely use his own personal account, and a detailed analysis will be required to identify the business items.

The statement of affairs at the opening date of the period is merely a listing of assets and liabilities in the form of an opening balance sheet. It is NOT a balance sheet, however, since it is not a listing of assets and liabilities found in the balances established in a double-entry bookkeeping system.

The list of assets and liabilities established as at the date of the opening statement of affairs will determine the owners' equity at that date, again on the basis of the accounting equation:

$$\text{Owners' equity} = \text{Assets} - \text{Liabilities}$$

By a similar process, the next stage is to prepare a statement of affairs as at the closing date of the period. The owners' equity as at that date will provide an estimate of the profit or loss for the period as follows:

	£
Owners' equity as at opening date	xxxxxxxx
Less: Owners' equity as at closing date	xxxxxxxx
Profit/Loss for the period	xxxxxxxx

Example 1

Phil Lindop graduated from University in June 19X3 with a BA(Hons) degree in history, a motorbike costing £850 given to him by an uncle as a graduation present and no immediate job prospects. He became aware of a local need which existed in his home town for a fast delivery service for documents, photographs and small parcels. Borrowing £50 from his mother, and working from his parents' home, he advertised the Lindop Fast Delivery Service. Soon, he obtained a number of regular customers and business became brisk. He was paid cash for the services he provided, and likewise paid all his expenses in cash. He repaid the loan his mother had made him, and bought a new motorbike costing £1,500. He was in the habit of keeping £100 per week to cover his personal expenses, and what was left over, he accumulated in a cash box, which he kept in his bedroom.

In due course, he received a letter from the Inspector of Taxes requiring him to submit an income tax return. This letter induced him to seek the assistance of an accountant, who asked him for the following information:

(a) a list of any assets which he owned for his business, and a valuation of such assets both at the start and at the close of the first year of business,

(b) a list of any liabilities as at those two dates.

From the information which Lindop provided, the accountant prepared the following statements of affairs:

Statement of affairs as at	Start £	Close £
Assets: Motorbike	850	1,250
Cash	50	462
	900	1,712
Liabilities: Loan	50	—
Capital	850	1,712

Using the foregoing statement of affairs and the additional information given by Lindop as regards his drawings, the accountant was able to prepare the following estimates of the net profit of the Lindop Fast Delivery Service for the period:

	£
Capital as at the close of the period	1,712
Capital as at the start of the period	850
Increase in capital during the period	862
Add: Cash withdrawn by proprietor	
£100 × 52 weeks	5,200
Gain for the period	6,062

At this stage, an appropriate adjustment can be made for depreciation on the motorbike, and the gain calculated above translated into an estimate of the accounting profit for the period.

The incomplete double entry

The more usual situation facing an accountant is where some records have been kept. Many small businesses, for example, use preprinted cash books which are designed to allow cash to be balanced daily or weekly with a minimum knowledge of bookkeeping. Such cash books are set out to allow the entry of an opening cash balance, daily totals of cash takings, identified routine expenditure headings, such as purchases, wages, light and heat, etc., as well as cash deposited in the bank.

The preprinted cash book, easily obtainable in stationery stores, would normally provide an adequate basis of information for a full double-entry bookkeeping system to be kept, particularly as small businesses operate bank accounts as well as maintaining cash records.

Problems arise when, under pressure, the cash book is not properly kept. Items are forgotten, and reconciling actual cash in hand with cash balances as per the cash book becomes largely a matter of recon-struction. Accordingly, the production of year-end financial state-ments is a question of dealing with the incompleteness of proper records.

A knowledge of the techniques and use of debtors and creditors control accounts is useful in deriving 'missing' figures. For example, if there is no proper record of sales, whether made for cash or on credit, provided that the opening and closing debtors figure is ascer-tainable, the sales figure may be derived by the following procedure:

	£
All cash received from customers—both from cash sales and in settlement of accounts	xxxxxx
Less: Amounts due from customers at start of period	xxxx
	xxxxxx
Add: Amounts due from customers at close of period	xxxxx
= Total sales for period	£xxxxxx

Example 2

An analysis of the available records of P. Randle, a self-employed builder, reveals that business receipts amounted to £185,624 for the year 19X4. In addition, it has been established that he was owed £4,319 on 1 January 19X4 and £6,213 by customers for work done and invoiced to them. The amount of sales for 19X4 is:

	£
Cash received	185,624
Less: Owing at 1 January 19X4	4,319
	181,305
Add: Amount owing at 31 December 19X4	6,213
Therefore, sales for the year 19X4	£187,518

A similar procedure enables the figure for purchases of the period to be derived:

	£
Cash paid to suppliers	xxxxxx
Less: Amounts due at start of period	xxxxx
	xxxxxx
Add: Amounts due at close of period	xxxxx
Purchases for period	xxxxxx

This process will need to be repeated for all expense payments wherever transactions on credit are involved.

Example 3

J. Repton started a greengrocers business, and at the end of the first year of trading required financial statements to be prepared for tax purposes. He started business with a bank balance of £10,000, which represented his entire savings. Most major items of expenditure were paid by cheque, including all daily market purchases of produce and 'cash and carry' purchases of additional supplies. Certain other expenses were paid out of cash takings, and the balance of cash receipts were banked once a week. A cash float of £25 was kept. No accurate record of daily cash takings was kept, but receipts were kept for all cash payments and for personal cash withdrawals.

The accountant concerned with the preparation of a profit and loss account for the year ended 31 December 19X4 and a balance sheet as at that date made two initial summaries as follows:

Summary of cash payments	£
Assistant's wages	3,600
Delivery van expenses	1,240
Cleaning and sundries	420
Purchases of milk, butter and eggs for resale	4,248
Advertising	320
Postage and stationery	186
Personal drawings	4,800

There was a cash float of £80 at 31 December 19X4.

A careful analysis of Repton's bank statements for the year, together with cheque-book stubs or cancelled cheques, provided the means of preparing a summary of cheque transactions.

Summary of bank account

		£	£
1 January 19X4	Balance introduced by Repton		10,000
31 December 19X4	Cash lodgements for year from shop		96,432
	Delivery van purchased	6,400	
	Purchase of goods	61,268	
	Motor expenses	1,894	
	Insurance	130	
	Light and heat	1,260	
	Rent and rates	4,240	
	Personal drawings	6,890	
	Telephone	820	
	Advertising	2,165	
	Postage and stationery	863	
	Shop fittings	3,600	
	Balance at 31 December 19X4	16,902	
		106,432	106,432

The accountant required further details before proceeding with the preparation of the profit and loss account and balance sheet. In particular, he needed to know:

(a) the value of the year end stock,

(b) the amount owing to suppliers at the year end,

(c) the amount, if any, owing by customers at the year end.

Repton gave the accountant the following information:

(a) the value of the year end stock was £2,370,

(b) suppliers' invoices showing £862 as unpaid at the year end for trade purchases, and a further £89 unpaid for motor expenses,

(c) the amount owing by customers was £164.

From the foregoing information, the cash account was reconstructed, as a prelude to establishing the sales figure for the year.

Cash account for the year ended 31 December 19X4

	£		£
Cash takings*	111,326	Assistant's wages	3,600
		Delivery van expenses	1,240
		Cleaning and sundries	420
		Purchases of milk etc.	4,248
		Advertising	320
		Postage and stationery	186
		Drawings	4,800
		Cash deposited in bank	96,432
		Balance c/d	80
	111,326		111,326
Balance b/d	80		

* Cash takings are calculated by adding cash payments (£14,814) plus cash deposited in bank (£96,432) plus the cash float at the end of the year (£80).

The total sales for the year may now be calculated as follows:

Total sales = Cash takings + Debtors outstanding
     = £111,326   + £164
     = £111,490

It is now possible to prepare the profit and loss account for the year as follows:

Profit and loss account for the year ended

31 December 19X4

	£	£
Sales		111,490
Less: Cost of sales		
Purchases (£4,248 + 61,268 + 862)	66,378	
Less: Closing stock	2,370	64,008
Gross profit		47,482
Less: Wages	3,600	
Motor expenses (£1,240 + 1,894 + 89)	3,223	
Cleaning and sundries	420	
Advertising (£320 + 2,165)	2,485	
Postage and stationery (£186 + 863)	1,049	
Insurance	130	
Telephone	820	
Light and heat	1,260	
Rent and rates	4,240	
*Depreciation—Delivery van 1,600		
Shop fittings 360		
	1,960	19,187
Net profit transferred to capital account		28,295

* In calculating the provision for depreciation, it was regarded as necessary to estimate at 4 years the life of the delivery van, and at 10 years the life of the shop fittings. The straight-line method of depreciation was used.

The closing balance sheet was established as follows:

Balance sheet as at 31 December 19X4

	£	£
Capital account—J. Repton, Esq.,		
Capital introduced	10,000	
Net profit for the year	28,295	
	38,295	
Less: Drawings (£4,800 + 6,890)	11,690	
	26,605	

Represented by

Fixed assets	Cost	Deprecia- tion	
	£	£	£
Shop fittings	3,600	360	3,240
Delivery van	6,400	1,600	4,800
	10,000	1,960	8,040

Current assets		£	
Stock at cost		2,370	
Debtors		164	
Cash at bank		16,902	
Cash in hand		80	
		19,516	
Less: Creditors (£862 + 89)		951	18,565
			26,605

In practice, the accountant may adopt the more formal approach using a spread sheet and an extended trial balance. The following example illustrates this approach applied to the information used in preparing accounts for J. Repton. Note that stationery is available with an appropriate setting allowing the extension of the analysis through to the profit and loss account and balance sheet. The latter need only be redrafted into their final format, at the termination of the analysis.

The statement of affairs and incomplete double entry compared

The statement of affairs and the incomplete double entry approaches serve as two different models to deal with incomplete records. The statements of affairs is used when the information available is less substantial than in the example used for explaining the incomplete double entry approach.

To illustrate the relationship between these two models, consider

Example 4: Spread sheet and extended trial balance approach

J. Repton	Balance B/Fwd. Debit	Balance B/Fwd. Credit	Cash Account Debit	Cash Account Credit	Bank Account Debit	Bank Account Credit	Adjustments Debit	Adjustments Credit	Creditors Accruals	Debtors Prepayments	Profit & Loss Account Debit	Profit & Loss Account Credit	Balance Sheet Debit	Balance Sheet Credit
Amount Introduced					10,000									10,000
Wages				3,600							3,600			
Delivery Van Expenses				1,240		1,894	89 Creditor		89		3,223			
Cleaning				420							420			
Purchases				4,248		61,268	862 Creditor		862		66,378			
Advertising				320		2,165					2,485			
Postage & Stationery				186		863					1,049			
Drawings				4,800		6,890							11,690	
Bank Lodgements				96,432	96,432									
Delivery Van						6,400		1,600 Depreciation					4,800	
Insurance						130					130			
Light and Heat						1,260					1,260			
Rent and Rates						4,240					4,240			
Telephone						820					820			
Shop Fittings						3,600		360 Depreciation					3,240	
Sales			111,326					164 Debtors				111,490		
Depreciation Motors							1,600				1,600			
Depreciation Fittings							360				360			
Stock							2,370 Stock	2,370 Stock				2,370	2,370	
Balances				80		16,902							16,982	
Debtors							164			164			164	
Creditors														951
Net profit											28,295			28,295
			111,326	111,326	106,432	106,432			951	164	113,860	113,860	39,246	39,246

the case of J. Repton in the circumstances where much less information is available. The accountant would have had to use the statement
of affairs approach as follows:

Statement of affairs as at 31 December 19X4	£	£
Shop fittings		3,240
Delivery van		4,800
Stock		2,370
Debtors		164
Bank balance (as per Bank statement)		16,902
Cash in hand		80
		27,556
Less: Creditors—for goods	862	
—for motor expenses	89	951
Capital as at 31 December 19X4		26,605
Capital as at 1 January 19X4		10,000
Increase in capital during the year		16,605
Add: Drawings by Repton		11,690
Net profit for the year		28,295

It may be seen, therefore, that either the statement of affairs or the
incomplete double entry approach leads to the same estimation of
the net profit for the period.

Insurance claims

The techniques for dealing with incomplete records are also useful
for the preparation of insurance claims or other documents, relating
to losses through fire, flood or theft.

Example 5
On the night of 8 June 19X5, a fire completely destroyed a warehouse
containing the entire stock of the Cinders Co. Ltd. The value of the
stock at that date was not known. The Cinders Co. Ltd had an insurance policy under which the stock was insured against fire, flood
and theft. For the purpose of claiming against the insurance company,
the value of the stock as at 8 June 19X5 had to be established.

Accounting records kept at Head Office provided the following
information:

		£
(a)	Sales—Period 1 January to 8 June 19X5	586,740
(b)	Purchases—Period 1 January to 8 June 19X5	484,210
(c)	Stock at 31 December 19X4	52,575

The company's average gross profit ratio was 20%, and this could be substantiated from the results of previous years.

Accordingly, the following estimate of the value of the stock destroyed was prepared:

Estimated value of stock as at 8 June 19X5

	£	£
Opening stock at 1 January 19X5		52,575
Purchases 1 January to 8 June		484,210
Goods available for sale during period		536,785
Less: Cost of sales during period		
Sales 1 January to 8 June	586,740	
Gross profit thereon at 20%	117,348	
		469,392
Estimated value of stock at 8 June 19X5		67,393

Questions

1. The summarised balance sheet at 30 September 19X8, of John Bowers, retailer, is as follows:

	£		£	£
Capital account—		Fixtures and fittings:		
J. Bowers	15,600	At cost	11,000	
		Less: Aggregate		
		depreciation	6,600	4,400
		Stock in trade		9,000
Trade creditors	2,130	Trade debtors		2,100
Accrued charges		Prepayments (rates)		260
(electricity)	230	Balance at bank		2,200
	£17,960			£17,960

Although John Bowers does not keep a full set of accounting records, his business transactions during the financial year ended 30 September 19X9, are summarised as follows:

(1) Sales totalled £95,830 and sales returns £880; trade debtors at 30 September 19X9, amounted to £4,400.
(2) Gross profit amounted to 2/9ths of net sales revenue.
(3) Stock in trade, at cost, at 30 September 19X9, shows an increase of £6,000 over that of a year earlier.
(4) Trade creditors at 30 September 19X9, amounted to £3,970; discounts received from suppliers totalled £450 for the year under review.
(5) Payments for rent, rates, light and heat totalled £6,830 and wages payments £8,250 for the year ended 30 September 19X9.
(6) At 30 September 19X9, rent prepaid amounted to £320 and electricity charges accrued due were £270.
(7) On 30 September 19X9, a loan of £2,000 was received from L. Pond.
(8) Additions to fixtures and fittings during the year cost £1,500 cash.

(9) Cash drawings amounted to £4,000 and, in addition, John Bowers withdrew from the business goods for his own use which had cost £310. Whilst these goods were paid for in the payments made to suppliers, the goods withdrawn by John Bowers for his own use were not included in the cost of the goods sold or sales.

(10) It has been decided to make a provision for doubtful debts at 30 September 19X9, of 2½% of trade debtors.

(11) Depreciation is provided annually on fixtures and fittings at the rate of 10% on the cost of assets held at the relevant accounting year end.

Required:

(a) From the figures and information above compile John Bowers' trading and profit and loss account for the year ended 30 September 19X9, and a balance sheet as at that date.

(b) Give reasons which could be advanced to John Bowers in favour of keeping a full set of accounting records.

(Association of Certified Accountants)

2. Landgrab commenced business on 1 January 19X6, hiring out earth moving machines to building contractors. He failed to keep proper records for the year ended 31 December 19X6, but a summary of his business bank account for the year shows the following:

	£		£
Transfer from private bank account	150,000	Purchase of Machine A (on 1 January 19X6)	35,000
Bankings during year	87,980	Purchase of transporter lorry (on 1 January 19X6)	30,000
		Purchase of Machine B (on 28 February 19X6)	40,000
		Purchase of Machine C (on 1 March 19X6)	43,200
		Cash withdrawals	40,300
		Insurance	1,020
		Office rent and rates	1,840
		Machine repairs	2,100
		Balance on 31 December 19X6	44,520
	£237,980		£237,980

You also receive the following information:

(1) All monies received from the hire of machines are immediately paid into the bank. On 31 December 19X6, £14,560 was due from various building contractors for hire of machines.

(2) The cash withdrawn from the bank has been utilised to pay the following:

	£
Running expenses of transporter lorry	1,560
Wages and national insurance	24,960
General expenses	1,240

The balance consisted of Landgrab's drawings from the business.

(3) Depreciation is to be charged on the straight-line basis as follows:

on the transporter lorry at 20% per annum with no residual value, and

on the machines at a rate based on the assumption that they will have a residual value of 10% of cost after five years.

(4) On 31 December 19X6, £420 was outstanding for office rent. Rates were prepaid to the extent of £260.

Required:
(a) to write up the following ledger accounts for the year:

Plant and machinery,
Plant and machinery depreciation,
Transporter lorry,
Transporter lorry depreciation,

(b) To prepare a detailed profit and loss account for the year ended 31 December 19X6 and balance sheet as on that date.

(Institute of Chartered Accountants)

3. Angus, a tenant farmer, has failed to keep books of account for the year ended 31 March 19X6. A summary of his bank account for the past year shows the following:

	£		£	£
Balance on 31 March 19X5	4,920	New tractor	7,000	
Receipts from Milk Marketing Board	30,840	*Less:* Allowance on old		
Ploughing grant	1,450	tractor in part exchange	3,600	
Cereal deficiency payments	2,170			3,400
Cattle auctions	5,700	Seeds and fertilisers		7,280
Cash bankings	17,240	Feeding stuffs		12,960
		Tractor and machinery		
		expenses		5,370
		Veterinary fees		550
		Additional machinery		1,250
		Rent and rates		4,830
		Transfer to private bank		
		account		20,000
		Balance on 31 March 19X6		6,680
	£62,320			£62,320

You also obtain the following information:

(1) The amount received from cattle auctions is the net figure after taking into account purchases of £4,260.

(2) A neighbouring farmer did threshing and baling work for Angus in exchange for hay valued at £2,730 and the feeding stuffs merchant had accepted produce to the value of £7,300 in part payment of his account.

(3) Angus has sold crops and produce for cash, and has banked the balance of the proceeds after paying:

	£
Electricity	790
Wages	11,090
Own drawings	6,240
Sundry expenses	290

(4) Outstanding amounts on 31 March were:

	19X5	19X6
	£	£
Milk Marketing Board	2,670	2,940
Electricity	230	210

(5) The part exchange allowance on the old tractor was equivalent to its written down value in the balance sheet as on 31 March 19X5. The new tractor is to be written down to £6,000 and other machinery which was valued at £15,000 on 31 March 19X5, together with the additional machinery purchased during the year, is to be written down to £13,000.

(6) Stocks on hand on 31 March have been valued as follows:

	19X5	19X6
	£	£
Livestock	18,250	17,000
Crops, produce and fertilisers	2,000	2,400
	£20,250	£19,400

You are required to prepare a profit and loss account for the year ended 31 March 19X6, and a balance sheet as on that date.

(Institute of Chartered Accountants)

4. The Carnaby Wholesale Clothing Company was burgled on the night of 14 December 19X2.

The raiders stole all that day's cash takings together with the petty cash and a selection of the most expensive clothing.

On 30 November 19X2, the owner had taken a physical stock count for which the cost was evaluated at £32,540. The stock of clothing left after the burglary amounted to £11,300 at cost.

Deliveries from suppliers, of further stock items, between 1 and 14 December 19X2, were invoiced at £5,784 after deduction of trade discounts of £732.

Sales to retail customers (at selling prices) had been:

	Cash	Credit
	£	£
1 to 6 December	1,429.71	6,250.29
7 to 13 December	1,644.50	8,079.50
14 December	259.32	1,200.68

The cash and bank accounts showed that during the period 1 to 14 December 19X2:

(1) the cash takings for 1 to 13 December, inclusive, had been banked intact;

(2) cheques for £168.92 and £192.67 had been drawn to pay staff wages;

(3) credit customers had paid cheques amounting to £15,867.11 (all of which had been banked) in full settlement of accounts totalling £16,102.83;

(4) the company had paid credit suppliers a total of £17,118.36 by cheque after deducting cash discounts of £940.45;

(5) the petty cash imprest account had been restored to its established level of £25.00 on 1 December by a withdrawal from the bank of £9.74. Subsequent disbursements to 14 December had amounted to £13.69.

Account balances in the firm's books on 30 November 19X2 had been:

	£
Bank	6,625.08 (debit)
Cash	129.60
Petty cash	15.26

Gross profit on sales had been at the rate of 30% throughout 19X2 but on 7 December, as part of a sales campaign, this was reduced to 25% for the remainder of the month.

Required:
Calculate, using such of the above information as is relevant,

(a) the amount of cash and the value of stock at cost, which had been stolen;

(b) the balance on the bank account at close of business on 14 December 19X2.

(*Association of Certified Accountants*)

5. Carton, in connection with his business, keeps a cash book, carbon copies of the customers' statements, which are marked off when settled, and a file of creditors' statements.

(1) Analysis of the cash records for the year ended 30 June 19X4 shows:

	£
Debts due by customers collected	232,430
Creditors' accounts for goods paid	194,070
Cash purchases	18,230
Wages	24,190
Rent and rates paid	10,200
Trade expenses	15,360
Purchase of trade van	4,800
Cash drawn by Carton	5,600

(2) Further investigation discloses:

	30 June 19X3 £	30 June 19X4 £
Balance at bank	7,520	18,200
Till float	300	300
Debtors	12,620	14,790
Stock	17,400	19,250
Creditors for:		
Goods	11,460	16,320
Rent	1,500	1,750
Trade expenses	740	960

(3) Depreciation of $33\frac{1}{3}$% is to be written off the trade van.

Required:
(*a*) the profit and loss account for the year ended 30 June 19X4, and
(*b*) the balance sheet as on that date.
Ignore taxation.

(Institute of Chartered Accountants)

6. Ash is a wholesaler of fancy goods. On 30 September 19X9 a fire occurred at his warehouse and the greater portion of his stock was destroyed. The value of the stock salvaged was agreed at £5,500.

His books were saved and the following is an extract from his last accounts for the year ended 31 March 19X9:

Trading account

	£	£		£
Opening stock	342,400		Sales	980,000
Purchases	784,700			
	1,127,100			
Less: Closing stock	294,100			
		833,000		
Gross profit		147,000		
		980,000		980,000

The stock was fully insured against fire risks.

Trade creditors on 31 March 19X9 amounted to £123,040. Sales for the period to 30 September 19X9 were £546,000 and amounts paid for purchases £440,080. On 30 September 19X9 trade creditors amounted to £110,560.

You are required to prepare a statement showing the amount Ash should claim from the insurance company for loss of stock.

(Institute of Chartered Accountants)

10 The Accounts of Non-profit Organisations

The text, so far, has dealt with accounting procedures in the context of commercial activities. There are many organisations whose activities are not undertaken with the object of commercial gain. These may range from small clubs formed to pursue some sport or common pastime to institutions having large sums at their disposal. Examples of the former could be badminton clubs and photographic societies whilst examples of the latter are the National Trust and the large charities.

The largest accounts produced, in terms of the sums involved, are the national income accounts. These accounts are of vital interest in the formulation of national economic policy but their construction and the specialist considerations relating thereto are beyond the scope of this introductory text.

Many treasurers of clubs and similar organisations are enthusiastic volunteers who are not necessarily familiar with bookkeeping and accounting practices, as can be seen in the simplicity of the accounts kept by many clubs. These usually satisfy the informational needs of club members, for there are few complex decisions calling for sophisticated accounting information.

Receipts and payments account

The simplest form adopted is merely a summary of cash transactions. Where organisations do not own assets or deal on credit terms with suppliers, this type of presentation is adequate. The summary is generally referred to as a 'receipts and payments' account.

Example 1

A typical receipts and payments account is set out below.

Goose Feather Badminton Club

Receipts and payments account for the year ended 31 May 19X5

	£		£
Balance at bank		Northshire Badminton	
1 June 19X4	86	League affiliation fee	125
Subscriptions received:		Rent of St. Mary's	
Full members	620	Church Hall	350
Juniors	134	Shuttlecocks	298
Donations	18	Gratuity—	
Refreshment receipts		caretaker	50
		Refreshment supplies	70
	86	Balance at bank carried	
		forward	51
	944		944

This type of account will serve the purpose of allowing the members to appreciate the level of expenditure and to relate it to their own subscriptions. The balance at the bank is easily verifiable and few complications arise.

Larger organisations may seek to support their primary activity by supplementary fund raising in the form of lotteries, more sophisticated refreshment and bar facilities, one-armed bandits, etc. In such cases, the accounting system has to be able to produce more exacting analyses than a receipts and payment account.

Income and expenditure account

In the case of larger and more complex organisations, assets may be owned, full-time employees may be engaged, and there may be transactions involving purchases of goods on credit and the giving of credit. Such organisations will have accounting requirements similar to commercial enterprises. They are unlike commercial enterprises in two important respects.

First, since their primary purpose is non-profit-making, the account which summarises the activities of such organisations is called the 'income and expenditure account'. This must be distinguished from the receipts and payment account, which is confined to a cash (or bank) summary. The income and expenditure account is based on accrual accounting and closely parallels the profit and loss account of a commercial enterprise.

Second, in the accounting systems of commercial enterprises, the owners of the entity are clearly defined. They may be individuals, partners or shareholders depending upon the nature of the organisation.

Non-profit organisations may be established by a trust or the formation of a company limited by guarantee, to ensure continuity and responsibility and simply continue with a changing membership and a renewal of officers from year to year. The majority of balance sheets adopt the term 'accumulated fund' instead of 'capital account' to represent the net worth. The accumulated fund will have grown from surpluses of income over expenditure and in some cases, gifts. The members for the time being are deemed to be the owners and the accumulated fund represents the sum of their interest.

Accordingly, any differences in the accounting treatment of non-profit organisations lie in the nature of the income and expenditure account and of the accumulated fund.

It should be noted that the term 'income and expenditure account' is not restricted to use for non-profit-making organisations. It is still also widely employed in commercial and professional activities and used as synonymous with the profit and loss account.

Example 2

The Scottside Literary and Philosophical Society has prepared the following trial balance as at 31 December 19X5:

Trial balance as at 31 December 19X5	Dr £	Cr £
Balance at bank—current account	3,624	
Accumulated fund 1 January 19X5		28,856
Property account		
64, High Street at cost	18,500	
Debtors for subscription	310	
Furniture and fittings	9,370	
Provision for depreciation of furniture and fittings		1,420
Subscriptions		7,254
Lecturers' fees	4,600	
Lecturers' travel and accommodation expenses	1,790	
Donations		540
Camera and projector repairs	85	
Projectors, cameras and audio equipment	952	
Depreciation of equipment		272
Rates and water	1,385	
Lighting and heating	1,836	
Rental of rooms		2,475
Wages—caretaker	4,400	
Wages—restaurant	8,000	
Wages—bar staff	4,000	
Purchase of food	7,829	
Stock—bar cellar	2,368	
Bar receipts		20,160
Bar purchases	14,210	
Restaurant receipts		18,210
Loan—Denton Brewery plc		8,000
Deposit account—bank	5,000	
Interest payable and receivable		180
Creditors for bar and food		892
	88,259	88,259

The following additional information is available.

(1) The bar stock was valued at £3,214 as at 31 December 19X5.
(2) It is expected that, of the debtors for subscriptions, £218 will not be collectable.

(3) The interest account is net. The amount paid to Denton Brewery is at the concessional rate of 4% while 10% has been earned on the deposit account. No changes have taken place all year in the principal sums involved.

(4) An invoice for £215 of wine had been omitted from the December 19X5 records although the wine had been included in the bar stock valuation.

(5) Depreciation for the year is to be provided as follows:

Furniture and fittings £970
Projectors, cameras etc. £95

One point of general usage can be made with regard to the preparation of the income and expenditure account. When there are subsidiary activities such as bar and restaurant facilities it is usual to show the net result as a single figure in the income and expenditure account. If these activities are substantial it would be appropriate to present the details by way of supporting accounts.

Bar trading account for year ended 31 December 19X5		
	£	£
Receipts		20,160
Less: Cost of sales		
Stock—1 January 19X5	2,368	
* Purchases	14,425	
	16,793	
Stock 31 December 19X5	3,214	13,579
Gross margin		6,581
Less: Wages		4,000
Surplus for year		2,581

Restaurant trading account for year ended 31 December 19X5		
	£	£
Receipts		18,210
Less: Purchase of food	7,829	
Wages	8,000	15,829
Surplus for year		2,381

* Bar purchases =
£14,210 plus omitted item £215
= £14,425

Scottside Literary and Philosophical Society

Income and expenditure account for year ended 31 December 19X5

	£	£		£	£
Lecturers' fees	4,600		Subscriptions		7,254
Lecturers' expenses	1,790	6,390	Donations		540
Rates and water		1,385	Rents received		2,475
Lighting and heating		1,836	Surplus from		
Caretaker's wage		4,400	bar	2,581	
Depreciation			restaurant	2,381	4,962
Fixtures	970		Interest		
Equipment	95	1,065	received		500
Camera repairs		85			
Bad debts		218			
Interest paid		320			
Surplus carried to					
accumulated fund		32			
		15,731			15,731

Scottside Literary and Philosophical Society

Balance sheet as at 31 December 19X5

			£
Accumulated fund			
Balance as at 1 January 19X5			28,856
Add: Surplus for year to			
31 December 19X5			32
Balance as at 31 December 19X5			28,888
Denton Brewery plc			8,000
			36,888

Fixed assets	Cost	Depreciation	Net
	£	£	£
64 High Street Scottside	18,500	—	18,500
Furniture and fittings	9,370	2,390	6,980
Cameras and equipment	952	367	585
	28,822	2,757	26,065

Current assets		
Bar stock	3,214	
Subscriptions—Debtors	92	
Bank accounts—current account	3,624	
deposit account	5,000	
	11,930	
Less: Current liabilities		
Creditors	1,107	10,823
		36,888

Subscriptions accounts

Where non-profit organisations are financed by members' subscriptions, the subscriptions account presents special problems since:

(i) At the financial year end, there are subscriptions due but not paid.
(ii) Some members have paid their subscriptions in advance for the following year.

Unpaid subscriptions must be treated as bad debts if it is felt that they are unlikely to be paid. Subscriptions paid in advance must be carried forward to the year to which they relate.

Example 3

The records of the Marmont Rugby Club reveal the following details regarding subscriptions for the year ended 31 May 19X4:

	£
Cash received from members during year to 31 May 19X4	6,242
Subscriptions due at 1 June 19X3 for previous year	286
Subscriptions received in May 19X3 relating to the year to 31 May 19X4	94
Subscriptions due at 31 May 19X4 still not paid	310
Amounts received in advance for 19X4/5 during May 19X4	88

It is noted that of the £286 outstanding subscriptions at 1 June 19X3, £210 has been received and the balance is regarded as irrecoverable.

The subscriptions account will appear as follows:

(a) At 1 June 19X3:

Subscriptions account

	£		£
1 June 19X3 Balance (subscriptions from members) b/d	286	1 June 19X3 Balance prepaid subscriptions for 19X3/X4	94

(b) At 31 May 19X4:

Subscriptions account

	£		£
1 June 19X3 Balance b/d	286	1 June 19X3 Balance b/d	94
		31 May 19X4 Cash	6,242
31 May 19X3 Balance c/d:		31 May 19X4 Income and	
Prepaid subscriptions		Expenditure a/c	
for 19X4/X5	88	Uncollectable	76
Income and expenditure		31 May 19X4 Balance—	
a/c	6,348	subscriptions due at	
		31 May 19X4	310
	6,722		6,722
	£		£
1 June 19X4 Balance b/d	310	1 June 19X4 Balance b/d	88

Questions

1. The balance sheets of Adley Social Club at 31 December 19X7 and at 31 December 19X8 were as follows:

	19X7	19X8		19X7	19X8
	£	£		£	£
Accumulated			Premises (cost)		3,500
fund	3,462	6,739	General equip-		
Loan—			ment (cost)	2,100	2,700
C. Smith		3,000	Depreciation	(800)	(1,050)
Bar creditors	1,520	1,340	Bar stock	1,100	830
Subscriptions			Bar debtors	600	800
in advance	95	115	Subscriptions		
Accruals—			in arrears	35	25
Bar wages	45	55	Prepayments—		
Electricity	93	78	rates	90	110
Loan interest		150	insurance	40	50
			Bank—		
			deposit	890	1,930
			current	960	1,982
			Cash in hand	200	600
	£5,215	£11,477		£5,215	£11,477

Analysis of the bank current account and of the cash account for the year ended 31 December 19X8 was as follows:

Receipts	Cash	Bank	Payments	Cash	Bank
	£	£		£	£
Balance at			General Equip-		
1 Jan 19X8	200	960	ment		840
Subscriptions	2,740	390	Bar creditors		7,100
Loan		3,000	Bar purchases		
Bar sales for			for cash	950	
cash	8,200		Bar wages	585	1,145
Bar debtors		4,100	Rates		350
Receipts from			Transfer to		
social events	1,340		deposit		900
Raffle receipts	238		Electricity		680
Cash banked		9,703	Social expenses	270	840
Sale of general			Raffle expenses	153	
equipment		140	Insurance		230
			Loan interest		150
			Premises		3,500
			Heating		392
			Cleaning—		
			bar	115	75
			clubhouse	184	68
			Miscel-		
			laneous—		
			bar	87	23
			clubhouse	71	18
			Cash to bank	9,703	
			Balance at		
			31 Dec. 19X8	600	1,982
	£12,718	**£18,293**		**£12,718**	**£18,293**

(*Note:* depreciation on general equipment sold amounted to £115.)

Required:
(*a*) Prepare a bar account for the year ended 31 December 19X8, showing both the gross and the net profit.
(*b*) Prepare an income and expenditure account for the year ended 31 December 19X8.

(*Association of Certified Accountants*)

2. The Greenfinger Gardeners' Club is a member of the Countryside Gardeners' Federation. The annual subscription payable by members clubs to the federation is 5% of the total subscription income plus 5% of any profit (or less any loss) arising from the sale of seeds and fertilisers for the preceding year.

The receipts and payments account for the year ended 31 December 19X8 of the Greenfingers Gardeners' Club is as follows:

	£		£
Balance at 1 January 19X8	196	Purchase of seeds and	
Subscriptions received	1,647	fertilisers	1,640
Sale of tickets for visit to		Cost of visit to research	
research centre	232	centre	247
Sale of seeds and fertilisers	1,928	Purchase of garden equipment	738
Annual garden show:		Repairs to garden equipment	302
Sale of tickets	829	Annual garden show:	
Competition fees	410	Hire of marquee	364
		Prizes	650
		Balance at 31 December	
		19X8	1,301
	£5,242		£5,242

The following additional information is given:

At 31 December	19X7	19X8
	£	£
Subscriptions due and unpaid	164	83
Subscriptions prepaid	324	248
Sale of seeds and fertilisers—debtors	220	424
Purchase of seeds and fertilisers—creditors	804	547
Stocks of seeds and fertilisers—at cost	261	390

Required:

A computation of the membership subscription for 19X9 payable by the Greenfinger Gardeners' Club to the Countryside Gardeners' Federation.

(Association of Certified Accountants)

3. The treasurer of the Bamford Country Dancing and Rambling Society has prepared the following receipts and payments account for the year ended 31 December 19X8:

Receipts	£	*Payments*	£
Opening balance	1,760	Purchase of amplifier	
Subscriptions (*see note* (i)):		(bought 1 July 1978)	700
Country dancing	2,410	Country dancing:	
Rambling	1,690	Musicians' fees	900
Annual dinner—Ticket sales	340	Coaching fees	820
Sale of hut	670	Hall—Rent	330
Country dancing festival—		Rates for year to	
Admissions	940	31 December 19X8	800
Sales—Clothes	2,100	Decorating	110
Refreshments	8,300	Cleaning	160
		Annual rambling expedition	1,320
		Annual dinner—hotel and	
		catering	410
		Country dancing festival:	
		Prizes	170
		Adjudicator's fee	90
		Purchases—Clothes	1,800
		Refreshments	7,000
		Closing balance	3,600
	£18,210		£18,210

Additional information:

(1) (a) Subscriptions	Country Dancing £	Rambling £
Received in 19X7 for 19X8	130	60
Received in 19X8 for 19X7	10	140
for 19X8	2,300	1,520
for 19X9	100	30
	£2,410	£1,690

(b) It is not the policy of the Society to take into account subscriptions in arrears until they are paid.

(2) The hut which was sold during 19X8 had been valued at £800 on 31 December 19X7, and was used for the Society's activities until sold on 30 June 19X8.

(3) Immediately after the sale of the hut, the Society rented a new hall at £330 per annum.

(4) The above receipts and payments account is a summary of the Society's bank account for the year ended 31 December 19X8; the opening and closing balances shown above were the balances shown in the bank statement on 31 December 19X7 and 19X8 respectively.

(5) All cash is banked immediately and all payments are made by cheque.

(6) A cheque for £200 drawn by the Society on 28 December 19X8, for stationery was not paid by the bank until 4 January 19X9.

(7) The Society's assets and liabilities at 31 December 19X7 and 19X8, in addition to those mentioned earlier, were as follows:

	19X7 £	19X8 £
Stocks of goods for resale, at cost:		
Clothes	1,300	1,100
Refreshments	310	600
Sundry creditors—Annual dinner (catering)		70
Purchases—Clothes	600	400
Refreshments	300	500

The Society has now instructed its treasurer to prepare an income and expenditure account for the year ended 31 December 19X8, and a balance sheet at that date.

It is proposed to provide for depreciation on the amplifier at the rate of 20% per annum on cost, pro rata to time.

Required:

(a) The Society's income and expenditure account for the year ended 31 December 19X8, and balance sheet as at that date. Comparative figures are not required.

(b) Outline the advantages of income and expenditure accounts as compared with receipts and payments accounts.

(Association of Certified Accountants)

4. The following receipts and payments account for the year ended 31 October 19X0 has been prepared from the current account bank statements of the Country Cousins Sports Club:

19X9		£	19X0		£
1 Nov	Balance b/fwd	1,700	31 Oct	Clubhouse:	
19X0				Rates and	
31 Oct	Subscriptions	8,600		insurance	380
	Bar takings	13,800		Decorations and	
	Donations	1,168		repairs	910
	Annual dinner—			Annual dinner—	
	Sale of tickets	470		Catering	650
				Bar purchases	9,200
				Stationery and	
				printing	248
				New sports	
				equipment	2,463
				Hire of films	89
				Warden's salary	4,700
				Petty cash	94
				Balance c/fwd	7,004
		£25,738			£25,738

The following additional information has been given:

At 31 October	19X9 £	19X0 £
Clubhouse, at cost	15,000	15,000
Bar stocks, at cost	1,840	2,360
Petty cash float	30	10
Bank deposit account	600	730
Subscriptions received in advance	210	360
Creditors for bar supplies	2,400	1,900

It has been decided to provide for depreciation annually on the clubhouse at the rate of 10% of cost and on the new sports equipment at the rate of $33\frac{1}{3}\%$ of cost.

The petty cash float is used exclusively for postages.

The only entry in the bank deposit account during the year ended 31 October 1980 concerns interest.

One-quarter of the warden's salary and one-half of the clubhouse costs, including depreciation, are to be apportioned to the bar.

The donations received during the year ended 31 October 19X0 are for the new coaching bursary fund which will be utilised for the provision of training facilities for promising young sportsmen and sportswomen. It is expected to make the first award during 19X1.

Required:
(a) An account showing the results for the year ended 31 October 19X0 on the operation of the bar.
(b) An income and expenditure account for the year ended 31 October 19X0 and a balance sheet at that date for the Country Cousins Sports Club.

(*Association of Certified Accountants*)

11 Partnership Accounts

In previous chapters we have examined in detail the procedures associated with double-entry bookkeeping and the basic problems to which financial accounting is addressed. For this purpose, reference was made generally to the most simple form of accounting entity described as the sole trader. This form of business organisation is very prevalent, but the more significant forms of business organisations from an accounting viewpoint are those which have harnessed much greater capital, and control much greater economic resources. Such organisations pose complex financial accounting problems.

> The initial expansion of a business organisation is often by way of an extension to the sole trader form of organisation effected by the admission to the business of a co-owner, who is known as a partner. Partnerships remain the most common form of business organisations for a variety of activities, including those represented by the professions, such as doctors, architects, stockbrokers and accountants.
>
> The Partnership Act 1890, whilst not containing all the law relating to the subject, is the main source of authority for the principles relating to the conduct of partnerships. Partners may draw up their own agreements as to their partnership but wherever such agreements are silent on a point or where there is no agreement, then the Act must be observed should disputes occur.
>
> Section 1 of the Partnership Act 1890 defines partnership as follows:
>
> 'Partnership is the relation which subsists between persons carrying on a business with a view of profit'.
>
> The purpose of this chapter is to examine the financial accounting implications of partnerships, and the manner in which their formation and dissolution is treated in accounting.

Financial accounting for partnerships

The financial accounting aspects of partnerships are concerned with the following problems:

(1) The formation of a partnership and the admission of a new partner.

(2) The division of partnership profit among the partners, and the subdivision of the equity in the partnership to reflect the rights of the individual partners.

(3) The dissolution of a partnership or the retirement of a partner.

These problems really fall into two categories. The first category covers changes in ownership and includes both (1) and (3) above. These important events occur infrequently. The second category deals with profit measurement and includes (2) above. The measurement of partnership profits is an on-going process. For this reason, attention will be focused initially on the implications of the partnership form of organisation for the process of profit determination.

The measurement and treatment of partnership profits

The proprietary theory and partnerships

In the case of the sole trader form of business, the owner's equity is represented by the capital account and is the residual balance expressed in the accounting equation as follows:

$$Capital = Assets - Liabilities$$

The capital account is used to aggregate the accounting numbers which affect the value of the owner's equity. Thus, the opening and closing balances on the capital account are reconciled by taking into account the net profit and drawings made during the accounting period as follows:

Summary of account	£
J. Bloggs	
Capital as at 1 January 19X1	32,467
Net profit for the year	8,620
	41,087
Drawings	7,400
Capital as at 31 December 19X1	33,687

In the case of a partnership, the equity of the partners is analysed in order to distinguish:

(a) The original capital brought into the partnership by each partner.
(b) Any loans by a partner to the partnership over and above the agreed capital.
(c) The net profit accruing to each partner less drawings.

Three separate accounts must be maintained to reflect these requirements, as follows:

(a) A capital account for each partner showing the original capital contributed.
(b) A loan account when a partner makes a loan to the partnership.
(c) A current account for each partner to which his share of the partnership profit is credited and to which his drawings and share of losses are debited.

The appropriation of net profit or losses

In the case of the sole trader form of business, the whole of the net profit of loss is deemed to be attributable to the owner and his capital account is automatically credited or debited with the net result of the business. An important distinction introduced by the partnership is the manner in which the net profit is appropriated, requiring an additional section to the profit and loss account.

The formula for apportioning the net profit or loss between the partners is normally detailed in the partnership agreement. This formula may take a variety of forms. Thus, a partnership agreement between A, B and C may provide that A is to be paid a salary of £4,000 per annum, that interest at the rate of 10% per annum is to be allowed on capital, and that the balance of net profit is to be divided in the ratio of 2:3:5. It is clear, however, that despite the terms used in this type of agreement, the designation of particular payments as being 'salary' and 'interest on capital' merely represent a formula for dividing the net profit among the partners. Such payments should not be treated as normal expenses in calculating the net profit but should be shown in the appropriation section of the profit and loss account.

Example 1

Ash, Birch and Cedar trading in partnership as timber importers realised a net profit of £24,150 for the year ended 30 June 19X3. The condensed trial balance as at 30 June 19X3 shown below reflects the balances in the books after the calculation of the profit but before its appropriation among the partners.

The partnership agreement provides that the net profit is to be divided in the ratio Ash 4:Birch 4:Cedar 2, after allowing them interest at the rate of 12% per annum on the original capital subscribed and crediting Cedar with salary of £2,500 per annum.

The appropriation section of the profit and loss account for the year ended 30 June 19X3 and the resulting balance sheet as at that date are set out below:

Trial balance as at 30 June 19X3

		£	£
Capital account 1 July 19X2	Ash		10,000
	Birch		8,000
	Cedar		6,000
Current account 1 July 19X2	Ash		800
	Birch		1,000
	Cedar		550
Drawings for year to 30 June 19X3	Ash	4,000	
	Birch	3,500	
	Cedar	3,000	
Fixed assets at cost		35,000	
Provision for depreciation to 30 June 19X3			8,000
Current assets		25,000	
Current liabilities			12,000
Net profit for year ended 30 June 19X3			24,150
		70,500	70,500

Profit and loss appropriation account for the year ended 30 June 19X3

		£	£
Net profit			24,150
Less: Interest on capital:	Ash	1,200	
	Birch	960	
	Cedar	720	2,880
			21,270
Less: Salary—Cedar			2,500
			18,770
Balance to Ash 4/10ths		7,508	
Balance to Birch 4/10ths		7,508	
Balance to Cedar 2/10ths		3,754	18,770
			—

Balance sheet as at 30 June 19X3

	Ash £	Birch £	Cedar £	Total £
Capital accounts	10,000	8,000	6,000	24,000
Current accounts at 1 July 19X2	800	1,000	550	
Add: Interest	1,200	960	720	
Salaries			2,500	
Share of net profit	7,508	7,508	3,754	
	9,508	9,468	7,524	
Less: Drawings	4,000	3,500	3,000	
	5,508	5,968	4,524	16,000
Partners' funds employed				40,000

Represented by:	Cost £	Depreciation £	£
Fixed assets	35,000	8,000	27,000
Current assets		25,000	
Less: Current liabilities		12,000	13,000
			40,000

The undermentioned points should be noted with particular care:

(a) The amount to be apportioned between the partners in accordance with the agreed profit sharing ratio is the residual amount *after* all other appropriations by the way of interest and salary have been made. Thus, in the example above, the residual amount to which the profit sharing ratio is to be applied is £18,770 and *not* £24,150.

(b) The interest to be credited to each partner is a percentage of the capital invested in the partnership and *not* a percentage of net profit.

(c) The salary payable to any partner should be debited to his current account. No separate salary account should be opened for a partner.

Partnership formation

The formation of a partnership by the decision of two or more individuals to carry on business together requires an agreement between them dealing with the following matters:

(1) The profit and loss sharing ratio.
(2) The salary, if any, to be paid to partners.

(3) The capital to be introduced by each partner.
(4) The rate of interest, if any, to be allowed on the capital account of each partner.

Equally, changes in the composition of an existing partnership occurring through the admission of a new partner or the retirement of an existing partner involve the termination of the existing partnership and the formation of a new partnership to carry on the partnership business. In such circumstances, there will be the formation of a new partnership and the need for a partnership agreement to deal with the matters mentioned above.

The accounting implications of a partnership formation revolve around two principal issues:

(1) The manner in which the partnership profits or losses are to be shared between the partners. This matter is dealt with in the appropriation section of the profit and loss account.
(2) The value to be placed on the business transferred to the new partnership in order to determine the 'price' to be paid by the new partner for his share of the business. This 'price' will be the amount he will be required to contribute as capital to the partnership. The termination of an existing partnership by the retirement or death of an existing partner also involves the formation of a new partnership between the on-going partners. In this case, the value to be placed on the business transferred to the on-going partners must be determined with a view to establishing the amount to be paid out to the retiring partner for his share of the business.

Example 2
Miles and Knott decide to enter into partnership contributing the following assets respectively:

	Miles	Knott
	£	£
Cash	5,000	8,000
Stock	14,000	9,000
Fittings	3,000	5,000
Land and buildings	18,000	—
Motor vehicles	—	8,000
	40,000	30,000

The initial accounting entries would be as follows:

Debit the following asset accounts:

	£
Land and buildings	18,000
Fittings	8,000
Motor vehicles	8,000
Stock	23,000
Cash	13,000
	70,000

Credit the following capital accounts:

	£
Miles	40,000
Knott	30,000
	70,000

The profit and loss sharing ratio between the partners is not necessarily dependent upon their respective capital contribution. In this example, although Miles contributes more than Knott, the partnership agreement may well provide for them to share profits and losses equally. If the partnership agreement is silent on this point, the Partnership Act 1890 will assume that the partners intended to share profits and losses equally. The partners themselves may agree that the disproportion in the capital contributed should be dealt with by an agreement to pay interest on the capital contributed.

Some partnership agreements require that the capital accounts should be in the same ratios as the profit and loss sharing ratios. In this event, an agreement by Miles and Knott to share profits and losses equally would require the capital accounts to be adjusted accordingly. Two methods available to this end are:
(1) The bonus method.
(2) The goodwill method.

The bonus method

In the foregoing example, the combined capital accounts amounted to £70,000. For the capital accounts to be equal, Miles and Knott would each have to be credited with £35,000. Under the bonus method, Miles would transfer £5,000 from his capital contribution to the credit of Knott's capital account. Implicitly, Miles recognises the advantage of having Knott as his partner in adjusting the capital accounts in this manner.

The initial balance sheet would appear as follows:

	£		£
Capital accounts		Assets	70,000
Miles	35,000		
Knott	35,000		
	70,000		70,000

The goodwill method

The alternative method of equalising the capital accounts is to assume that, in addition to the tangible assets introduced by Knott, there is some intangible asset that should be recognised. Such intangible asset could be an important business connection, such as a client, from which the partnership stood to gain. In the example given, it would be necessary to attribute a value of £10,000 to that asset—described as Goodwill—to bring the capital accounts into equality, as follows:

	£		£
Capital accounts		Goodwill	10,000
Miles	40,000	Tangible assets	70,000
Knott	40,000		
	80,000		80,000

The admission of a partner

In general, two procedures exist for the admission of a new partner to an existing partnership. The first procedure applies in the case where the new partner introduces new assets into what would then be an expanded business. The second procedure applies in situations where existing partners sell a portion of their share of the business to an incoming partner, without necessarily altering the asset structure. Under both procedures, the existing partners will wish to place a correct valuation on the assets as a whole.

First procedure—introduction of new assets

Under this procedure, the negotiations between the existing partners and the new partner will result in a new partnership agreement which will deal with the share of the business attributed to the incoming partner for the value of the new assets introduced by him.

Example 3

Mason and Lewis are in partnership sharing profits and losses equally.
The balance sheet shows the following:

	£		£
Capital accounts:		Sundry assets	38,000
Mason	20,000		
Lewis	18,000		
	38,000		38,000

Andrews is to be admitted to the partnership on the basis of an investment of £25,000 in cash for a one-third share in the partnership.

In this instance, it may be deduced that if the existing partners
are asking £25,000 for a one third share of the expanded business,
the total value of the business is judged to be £75,000. It follows
that either the existing assets are undervalued, or there are unrecorded
assets, or both. Two methods exist to deal with the problem of *goodwill*, which is the term used to cover situations where accounting
adjustments have to be made for assets transferred at higher values
than those recorded in the books. The admission of a new partner
is typically one such situation. The two methods applied to the treatment of *goodwill* are the following:

(1) The recognition of unrecorded goodwill

The first step is to calculate the value of the goodwill to be recorded
in the books of the new partnership on the admission of a new partner.
In the example given, the value of the goodwill may be calculated
as follows:

	£	£
Implied total value of assets		75,000
Less: Book value of sundry assets	38,000	
Cash to be introduced by Andrews	25,000	
		63,000
Value of goodwill		12,000

The second step is to attribute the goodwill to the existing partners,
as follows:

	Dr	Cr
	£	£
Goodwill account	12,000	
Capital accounts		
Mason		6,000
Lewis		6,000
	12,000	12,000

The opening balance sheet of the partnership Mason, Lewis and Andrews will be:

Capital accounts	£		£
		Goodwill	12,000
Mason	26,000	Sundry assets	38,000
Lewis	24,000	Cash	25,000
Andrews	25,000		
	75,000		75,000

(2) The non-recognition of goodwill

If the partners do not wish to record the goodwill element forming a part of the price paid by the new partner for his share, the accounting entries would be as follows on the basis of the facts given in the example:

	£
Sundry assets	38,000
Cash introduced by Andrews	25,000
Total assets	63,000

Since Andrews has a one-third share in the partnership assets, his capital account will be credited with £21,000, i.e. one-third of £63,000. Nevertheless, he will have paid £25,000 for that one-third share. The difference of £4,000 will be credited to the capital accounts of the other partners, and the journal entries reflecting these transactions will be:

	Dr £	Cr £
Cash	25,000	
Capital accounts		
Mason		2,000
Lewis		2,000
Andrews		21,000
	25,000	25,000

The reasoning behind this treatment is that although goodwill is not recorded on the admission of the new partner, its existence is admitted in the price paid by the new partner for his partnership share. The value of that goodwill may be ascertained as follows:

	£
Cash introduced by Andrews	25,000
One-third share of recorded assets acquired by Andrews	21,000
One-third share of goodwill acquired by Andrews	4,000

As the value of the goodwill surrendered by Mason and Lewis to Andrews amounts to £4,000, they must each be credited with a half share of that amount. Their capital account is credited, therefore, with £2,000 each. This method obviates the need to actually record goodwill in the books of the new partnership, and at the same time disposes of the goodwill element included in the price paid by Andrews for his partnership share.

Second procedure—existing assets structure unchanged

When the existing partners merely wish to sell a share of the partnership to an incoming partner, without requiring him to introduce new assets himself, the accounting entries will be concerned simply with recording the transfer to him of that share. The payment effected by the incoming partner may be made directly to the existing partners personally, without going through the books of the partnership.

Example 4

Simpson and Taylor were in partnership sharing profits and losses in the ratio of 2:1, their respective capital account balances being £17,000 and £10,000. It was decided to admit Marshall as a new partner on the payment of £12,000 for a one-third share. The profit and loss sharing ratio of the new partnership was to be one-third each to the three partners.

Two methods exist for recording the admission of Marshall into the partnership, and for dealing with the goodwill implicit in the price paid by him for his partnership share. In this example, the valuation of the goodwill is as follows:

		£
Total valuation of assets transferred	£12,000 × 3 =	36,000
Valuation of existing assets	(£17,000 + £10,000) =	27,000
Valuation of goodwill		9,000

(1) The recognition of unrecorded goodwill

Under this method, the goodwill is recognised by opening a goodwill account and attributing the goodwill to the existing partners in accordance with their partnership shares as follows:

	Dr £	Cr £
Goodwill account	9,000	
Capital accounts		
Simpson (2/3)		6,000
Taylor (1/3)		3,000
	9,000	9,000

The entries for recording the admission of new partner Marshall reflect the fact that he purchased his partnership share from the existing partners. In this case, Marshall paid £12,000 for a one third share which he purchased from Simpson and Taylor in the ratio of their existing partnership shares, namely 2/3 and 1/3 respectively. Since the asset structure remained unchanged and Marshall did not bring in new assets, the capital accounts are adjusted as follows:

	Dr £	Cr £
Capital accounts		
Simpson	8,000	
Taylor	4,000	
Marshall		12,000
	12,000	12,000

(2) The non-recognition of goodwill

Under this method, goodwill is not recognised, and Marshall acquired a one-third share of the existing assets (£17,000 + £10,000) i.e., £9,000. The accounting entries for recording the admission are:

	Dr £	Cr £
Capital accounts		
Simpson	6,000	
Taylor	3,000	
Marshall		9,000
	9,000	9,000

These entries indicate that Marshall now has a one-third share of the total capital of £27,000, transferred to him by the existing partners in terms of their original partnership shares.

Under both methods, the cash payments made by Marshall to the existing partners, namely £12,000 paid as to £8,000 to Simpson and £4,000 to Taylor would normally be made directly to them, and need not go through the partnership books.

The retirement of a partner

The retirement of a partner involves the same essential problem as the admission of a partner, namely the need to agree on a valuation of the goodwill to be transferred to the new partnership. In effect, both the admission and the retirement of a partner lead to the dissolution of the existing partnership and the formation of a new partnership. The Partnership Act 1890 outlines the circumstances which bring about a dissolution of a partnership. Briefly these are:

(1) At the will of a partner.
(2) By the effluxion of time agreed upon or completion of the particular venture.
(3) Transfer of a partner's interest following death or bankruptcy.
(4) Occurrence of an event which makes the partnership illegal.
(5) Fraud making the original agreement voidable.
(6) By action of the court under certain conditions such as lunacy, incapacity or misconduct of a partner.

Set out below are some of the accounting aspects resulting from these situations.

Example 5
King, Edwards and Harris were in partnership sharing profits and losses 2:1:1. King decided to retire, and Edwards and Harris agreed to remain in partnership sharing profits and losses 6:4. On the date of King's retirement, the capital accounts were:

	£
King	42,000
Edwards	36,000
Harris	30,000
	108,000

King, Edwards and Harris agreed that the tangible assets were correctly valued in the books but that goodwill should be valued at £20,000. Given the partnership ratios, the entries recording the goodwill are:

	Dr	Cr
	£	£
Goodwill	20,000	
Capital accounts		
King		10,000
Edwards		5,000
Harris		5,000
	20,000	20,000

The appropriate entries to record King's retirement from the partnership are:

	Dr £	Cr £
Capital		
King	52,000	
Edwards (0.6 × £52,000)		31,200
Harris (0.4 × £52,000)		20,800
	52,000	52,000

These entries show that the partnership King, Edwards and Harris will be terminated by the payment to King of £52,000, being the value of his invested capital, to be paid to him by Edwards and Harris privately from personal sources in the proportion of £31,200 and £20,800 respectively.

In the event that Edwards and Harris do not wish to retain the goodwill figure in the books of the new partnership, it may be written off against their capital accounts in the revised profit and loss sharing ratio, as follows:

	Dr £	Cr £
Capital accounts		
Edwards (0.6 × £20,000)	12,000	
Harris (0.4 × £20,000)	8,000	
Goodwill		20,000
	20,000	20,000

It will be seen that the net effect of these transactions is to credit King for his share of the goodwill amounting to £10,000 (one half of £20,000), the remaining partners sharing that sum between them as follows:

Capital accounts	Edwards £	Harris £	
Goodwill recorded	+ 5,000	+ 5,000	
Goodwill eliminated	− 12,000	− 8,000	
Net change	− 7,000	− 3,000	= − £10,000

Termination of business and dissolution of partnership

The dissolution of a partnership by the termination of business involves a specific procedure. In particular, there is an order of priority in the settlement of claims against the partnership, in which external creditors have precedence before any loans made by the partners themselves to the partnership. Only when these claims have been met, may the amounts standing to the credit of the capital accounts be repaid.

Example 6

Anne, Helen and Christine trading in partnership under the name 'Perfumes' and sharing profits and losses in the ratios 2 : 1 : 1 received an offer from a chain store for the purchase of the entire business. The partnership balance sheet as at the date of the offer was as follows:

	£	£
Capital accounts		
Anne	13,000	
Helen	9,000	
Christine	7,000	29,000
Loan account—Anne		1,000
Current accounts		
Anne	1,300	
Helen	400	
Christine	200	1,900
		31,900

	£	£
Fixture and fittings	6,500	
Motor vehicles	9,700	16,200
Stock	17,200	
Bank	5,300	
	22,500	
Less: Trade creditors	6,800	15,700
		31,900

The offer was for the purchase of the assets, excluding the balance at the bank for the sum of £40,000. The partners decided to accept the offer, and to dissolve their partnership.

The first stage in the dissolution of a partnership by the termination of business is to open a realisation account for that purpose, transferring to that account all assets and liabilities and calculating the profit or loss arising from the realisation.

Realisation account

	£		£
Fixture and fittings	6,500	Chain store	40,000
Motor vehicles	9,700		
Stock	17,200		
	33,400		
Gain on realisation			
	£		
Anne	3,300		
Helen	1,650		
Christine	1,650	6,600	
	40,000		40,000

The second stage is to settle the obligations outstanding, and repay the amounts due on the capital accounts of the partners. In this case, the balances on the capital accounts will have been calculated as follows:

Capital account	Anne (£)	Helen (£)	Christine (£)
Capital account—balance	13,000	9,000	7,000
Current account—balance	1,300	400	200
Share of gain on realisation	3,300	1,650	1,650
	17,600	11,050	8,850

The distribution of the funds lying in the bank account will be as follows:

Bank account

	£		£
Balance	5,300	Trade creditors	6,800
Chain store	40,000	Loan—Anne	1,000
		Capital accounts	
		Anne	17,600
		Helen	11,050
		Christine	8,850
	45,300		45,300

All the accounts are now closed.

The insolvency of a partner: the rule in *Garner* v. *Murray*

Where losses have occurred on realisation, their allocation to the capital accounts of the partners may result in the appearance of a debit balance on the account of at least one partner. In that event, the partner concerned is required to pay into the partnership a sum equal to the amount of the debit balance, and that sum will be paid to the other partners in the proportion of their respective balances on capital account. In effect, the dissolution of a partnership under such conditions requires a partner to use his personal assets to settle a financial claim against him by the other partners.

Where a partner has a debit balance on capital account at the dissolution of partnership, and has no personal assets as a result of insolvency, that debit balance must be transferred to the solvent partners in accordance with the rule in *Garner* v. *Murray*. This rule states that the debit balance on capital account of the insolvent partner must be shared by the solvent partners in the ratio of their capital accounts, and *not* in accordance with their profit and loss sharing ratio.

Example 7

After disposing of their business following a period of sustained losses, the partnership balance sheet of Jervis & Co. was as follows:

	£	£
Capital accounts		
Jervis	20,000	
Bond	10,000	
Sanderson	3,000	33,000
Current account		
Jervis		1,820
		34,820
Current accounts		
Bond	8,260	
Sanderson	8,400	16,660
Bank		18,160
		34,820

The partners were sharing profits and losses equally.

In this example, the debit balance on Bond's current account would be transferred to his capital account, leaving a credit balance on his capital account of £1,740 (£10,000 − 8,260). However, when the same procedure is applied to Sanderson, his capital account has a debit balance of £5,400 (£3,000 − 8,400). To complete the dissolution of the partnership, Sanderson must pay £5,400 into the partnership from his own personal assets, the final settlement between the partners being as follows:

Bank account

	£		£
Balance	18,160	Capital accounts	
Capital account		Jervis	21,820
Sanderson	5,400	Bond	1,740
	23,560		23,560

In the event of Sanderson being insolvent, the rule in *Garner* v. *Murray* applies to the apportionment of his debt of £5,400 to the partnership, unless that rule is specifically excluded in the partnership agreement. Given that the ratio of the capital accounts between the solvent partners is Jervis 2/3 and Bond 1/3, the debit balance on Sanderson would be transferred to them as follows:

	Dr £	Cr £
Capital accounts		
Jervis 2/3 × £5,400	3,600	
Bond 1/3 × £5,400	1,800	
Sanderson		5,400
	5,400	5,400

The adjusted balances on the capital accounts of Jervis and Bond are now as follows:

	Dr £	Cr £
Capital accounts		
Jervis		
Balance b/d		21,820
Transfer Sanderson a/c	3,600	
Balance c/d	18,220	
	21,820	21,820
Bond		
Balance b/d		1,740
Transfer Sanderson a/c	1,800	
Balance c/d		60
	1,800	1,800

It may be noted that the effect of Sanderson's insolvency, and the application of the rule in *Garner* v. *Murray* to his deficiency of £5,400 is to render the balance on Bond's own capital account into debit to the extent of £60. Bond is now obliged to pay into the partnership the sum of £60, and the settlement between Jervis and Bond is as follows:

<table>
<tr><td colspan="4" align="center">Bank account</td></tr>
<tr><td></td><td align="right">£</td><td></td><td align="right">£</td></tr>
<tr><td>Balance</td><td align="right">18,160</td><td>Capital account Jervis</td><td align="right">18,220</td></tr>
<tr><td>Capital account Bond</td><td align="right">60</td><td></td><td></td></tr>
<tr><td></td><td align="right">18,220</td><td></td><td align="right">18,220</td></tr>
</table>

Piecemeal realisation of partnership assets

When a decision is taken to discontinue the partnership business and to dissolve partnership, there is no certainty that the assets can be sold off in one single transaction. To avoid losses and to obtain the best possible prices, the partners may decide to sell off the assets over a period of time, as and when buyers appear. The piecemeal realisation of partnership assets involves a delay in the dissolution of the partnership and the settlement of the claims of the partners, as the final balances on their capital accounts cannot be established immediately. None the less, the partners will be anxious to obtain as much as possible by way of return on capital in the interim period. There are two methods of dealing with this problem.

First method

Open a realisation account in which initially every unsold asset is treated as a total loss. Transfer the loss to the capital accounts of the partners, thereby establishing the resulting balances on their capital accounts for the purpose of determining their entitlement to a distribution of the available balance in the bank account, if any. Each time an asset is sold, open up a realisation account, credit that account with the proceeds and transfer to the capital accounts of the respective partners the proportion due to them in accordance with their profit and loss sharing ratios, and thereafter effect a settlement by payment out of the bank account. This method is rather clumsy, for it requires successive realisation accounts for dealing with individual asset sales.

Second method

Known as the *safe payment schedule method*, this procedure involves drawing up a schedule of safe payments at the time when the decision to dissolve partnership is made. The safe payments are defined as those which could be made at once and would not involve a potential recall of funds from the partners. It requires a calculation of the potential loss to the partnership which would eliminate any credit balance on each of the individual partners' capital account. For this purpose, their respective capital and current accounts must be merged.

Example 8

Maurice, Norman and Oliver are in partnership sharing profits and losses in the ratio 2:2:1. At the date of their decision to dissolve partnership, the credit balances on their combined capital and current accounts were £60,000, £40,000 and £40,000 respectively. Their loss absorption potentials, being the loss to the partnership itself which would wipe out these credits balances may be calculated as follows:

	Maurice (£)	Norman (£)	Oliver (£)
Credit balance	60,000	40,000	40,000
Profit and loss sharing ratio	÷ 40%	÷ 40%	÷ 20%
Loss absorption potential	150,000	100,000	200,000

The partner with the 'strongest position' is Oliver, for he can sustain the highest partnership loss on realisation. The safe payment schedule involves progressively reducing each partner's loss absorption potential to equality.

First, since Oliver has the highest loss absorption potential, it may be reduced to that of the partner with the next highest loss absorption potential, namely Maurice, by making a payment to Oliver out of the existing partnership bank account of a sum which would reduce his loss absorption potential from £200,000 to £150,000. Since Oliver's share of potential partnership losses is only 20%, Maurice and Oliver may be brought into equality making an initial cash payment to Oliver of £10,000 (20% of £50,000), thereby reducing the credit balance on his capital account to £30,000.

Second, repeat the process by reducing the loss absorption potential of both Maurice and Oliver to that of Norman. This involves reducing their respective loss absorption potential by £50,000 each to £100,000 by making a cash payment of £20,000 (40% of £50,000) to Maurice, and a further payment of £10,000 (20% of £50,000) to Oliver.

It may be seen that the safe payment schedule provides a ranking order for making payments out of partnership funds. Once it has been established it may be applied to the situation existing at the date when the decision to dissolve partnership is taken. In this regard, the balance sheet as at that date is given as follows:

	£	£
Capital and current accounts		
Maurice	60,000	
Norman	40,000	
Oliver	40,000	140,000
		140,000
Sundry Assets	155,000	
Less: Creditors	22,000	133,000
Cash		7,000
		140,000

The safe payment schedule provides the following ranking order for the distribution of cash available to the partnership:

	Cash (£)	Creditors (£)	Maurice (£)	Norman (£)	Oliver (£)
Balance	7,000	22,000	60,000	40,000	40,000
First distribution	7,000	7,000			
Balance	—	15,000			
Next available £15,000		15,000			
Balance		—			
Next available £10,000			—	—	10,000
Balance			60,000	40,000	30,000
Next available £30,000 in the ratio 2 : 1			20,000		10,000
Balance			40,000	40,000	20,000
Further distribution in the ratio 2 : 2 : 1.					

The safe payment schedule allows a piecemeal dissolution to be effected by the making of orderly payments to the partners without fear of overpayment at any one time.

Questions

1. Cabernet, Pinot and Gamay trade in partnership under the name Western Wines. The partnership agreement allows for the payment of 15% per annum on capital, and the payment of a salary of £3,500 per annum to Pinot. The balance of the net profit or loss is to be apportioned in the ratio of Cabernet 5: Pinot 2 and Gamay 3.

Required:
Using the trial balance as at 30 September 19X7 given below, prepare a profit and loss account for the year ended 30 September 19X7 and a balance

sheet as at that date. The additional information which is required for this purpose is as follows:

(a) The closing stock as at 30 September 19X7 is valued at £21,234 at cost.

(b) Bad debts amounting to £625 should be written off.

(c) Depreciation is to be provided as follows:

(1) Racks and fittings at the rate of 25% using the declining balance method.

(2) Delivery vans on the basis of a 5-year life using the straight line method and assuming no scrap value at the end of 5 years.

(3) Cooling equipment on the basis of a 10-year life using the straight line method and assuming no scrap value at the end of 10 years.

(d) Rates are prepaid to the extent of £500.

(e) Telephone charges due and unrecorded amount to £120.

Trial balance as at 30 September 19X7

		£	£
Capital accounts 1 October 19X6	Cabernet		18,000
	Pinot		12,000
	Gamay		10,000
Current accounts 1 October 19X6	Cabernet		4,600
	Pinot		3,760
	Gamay		2,640
Drawings for year to 30 September 19X7	Cabernet	4,800	
	Pinot	5,200	
	Gamay	3,850	
Warehouse and shop at cost		27,500	
Racks and fittings		8,300	
Provision for depreciation			1,100
Delivery vans		7,400	
Provision for depreciation			1,020
Cooling equipment—at cost		4,400	
Provision for depreciation			3,960
Salaries to employees		16,422	
Rates, lighting and heating		3,412	
Advertising		3,685	
Stock		18,347	
Motor expenses		3,210	
Insurances		318	
Repairs and renewals		410	
Telephones and postage		586	
Printing and stationery		214	
Purchases		114,210	
Sales			168,111
Debtors and accounts receivable		8,614	
Creditors and accounts payable			7,197
Balance at bank		1,327	
Cash in hand		183	
		232,388	232,388

2. Jill and Dora run a small clothing boutique in partnership, Jill, having completed a secretarial course some time ago, has prepared the following current account and balance sheet.

	Jill £	Dora £		Jill £	Dora £
Drawings	6,320	7,920	Opening balance	2,280	1,560
Closing balance	1,960	1,440	Interest on capital	1,000	800
			Share of profit	5,000	4,000
			Salary		3,000
	8,280	9,360		8,280	9,360

Balance sheet as at 31 October 19X5

	£	£		£	£
Capital accounts			Shop—at cost	16,000	
Jill	10,000		*Less:* Depreciation	3,120	12,880
Dora	8,000	18,000	Fittings	10,000	
Current accounts			*Less:* Depreciation	4,100	5,900
Jill	1,960				
Dora	1,440	3,400	Stock		4,180
Loan—Jill's uncle		4,000	Debtors		4,220
			Prepayments—Expenses		280
Creditors—Goods		1,660	Cash in hand		320
Accrued expenses		180			
Bank overdraft		540			
		27,780			27,780

Investigating further, you discover the following:
(1) Part of the closing stock which had been included at cost of £440 had badly faded in storage and could only be expected to realise £160.
(2) Dora had introduced £4,000 of her capital on 30 April 19X5 but had been credited with interest for a whole year.
(3) Bank charges had been overlooked and amounted to £140 for the year.
(4) Depreciation of £900 on fittings had been omitted for the year.
(5) A creditor for goods for £740 had been omitted from both purchases and creditors although the goods had been correctly included in closing stock.
(6) A charge of £1,200 for rates was in the profit and loss account but £160 of this applied to the period after 31 October 19X5.
(7) Jill's uncle had made the loan to the business at the concessional interest rate of 7½% per annum but this had not been included in the profit and loss account.
(8) Dora's salary should have been £2,800 and not £3,000 as shown.

Required:
(a) Prepare a statement showing the true net profit before appropriation.
(b) Prepare the revised current accounts of Jill and Dora.
(c) Redraft the balance sheet as at 31 October 19X5.
(d) Explain why, in the case of partnerships, the treatment of (i) interest paid to a partner and interest paid to a third party and (ii) the salary of a partner and the salary of an employee is different.

3. Burton, Brew and Bernstein have been in partnership for many years trading as timber importers. They are considering taking Earnshaw into the partnership as at 1 January 19X6.

The capitals and profit-sharing ratios are as follows as at 31 December 19X5

	Capital £	Profit sharing ratios (%)
Burton	70,000	60
Brew	45,000	20
Bernstein	35,000	20

Earnshaw will introduce £40,000 for a 20% share of the partnership capital and profits.

Required:
(a) Show the bookkeeping entries necessary to record Earnshaw's admission as a partner by both of two alternative methods.
(b) If, instead of contributing to the partnership assets, Earnshaw purchased a 20% share from the existing partners directly, prepare a schedule showing how much cash each partner would receive.

4. Fowles and Johnson are in partnership with capital account balances of £42,000 and £30,000 respectively and sharing profits and losses Fowles 60%; Johnson 40%.

They are considering admitting Moir into the partnership and have asked you to record the consequences of each of the following three *independent* propositions.

(1) Moir will introduce £26,000 into the partnership for a quarter share of capital and profits of the partnership.
(2) Moir will introduce £16,000 into the partnership for a one-fifth share of the capital and profits of the partnership. After admission the partnership total capital should be £88,000.
(3) Moir will purchase one third of the partners existing shares for £30,000. If goodwill is implied it is to be recorded.

5. Henry and Peter were partners in a wholesale and retail paint business. They shard profits three-fifths and two-fifths respectively. From 1 April 19X0 Roger, previously an employee earning £8,000 per annum, became a partner and the new profit sharing ratio was—Henry two-fifths, Peter two-fifths and Roger one-fifth. Roger's salary as an employee ceased but he was to be credited with £6,000 per annum partnership salary. He agreed to bring in £10,000 as capital and it was also mutually agreed that at 1 April 19X0 the book value of the land and buildings should be increased by £30,000 and that of the equipment and vehicles reduced by £4,000. Goodwill was to be valued at the same date by reference to expected future earnings (agreed as £30,000 per annum after allowing for partners' services) and an acceptable yield on capital (agreed as 20% per annum). The capital accounts were to be adjusted to reflect the goodwill valuation, no goodwill account being raised. Roger had paid in the capital sum but the other adjustments had not been made by the year-end, 30 June 19X0, when the books showed:

Trial balance at 30 June 19X0

	Dr £	Cr £
Gross profit (earned evenly over the year)		120,000
Land and buildings (cost)	50,000	
Equipment and vehicles (book value 1 July 19X9)	40,000	
Stock at end of year	12,000	
Administrative expenses (including Roger's salary to 31 March 19X0)	54,000	
Bank		5,000
Capital accounts (H £40,000, P £30,000, R £10,000)		80,000
Drawings (H £30,000, P £20,000, R £2,000)	52,000	
Debtors and creditors	38,000	41,000
	£246,000	£246,000

Depreciation is charged on the equipment and vehicles at 20% of book value per annum. At 1 April 19X0 the net current assets value in the books was £5,000.

Required:
Prepare the profit and loss account for the year ended 30 June 19X0 and a balance sheet at that date.

6. Bull, Cox and Dale have been working in partnership as veterinary surgeons and practitioners for several years. At 1 January 19X0 a summarised balance sheet shows:

Capital accounts:		Surgery	10,000
Bull	16,000	Cars	16,000
Cox	10,000	Equipment	4,000
Dale	8,000	Net current assets	4,000
	£34,000		£34,000

The partnership agreement allows for 10% per annum interest on capital—then profits shared in the ratio of Bull, 5/12; Cox 1/3; and Dale 1/4, with Dale being guaranteed a minimum of £13,000 per annum in addition to his interest on capital.

Bull retired on 30 June 19X0, on which date the goodwill was valued by an agreed method at £24,000. A goodwill account is not to be maintained in the books. Bull took over the car he had been using—its book value at 1 January 19X0 was £6,000, and the agreed valuation at 30 June, £4,600. Cox and Dale continued in partnership, sharing profits equally after allowing interest on capital at 10% per annum as before (Dale not having a guaranteed share).

Fees earned were £36,000 for the first half-year and £28,000 for the second half. The working expenses were £9,000 and £7,000 for the two half-years respectively. Depreciation on the cars is charged at 20% per annum on book values and on the equipment at 10% per annum on book values.

At 30 June Cox agreed to purchase the surgery, which is adjacent to his house, for £22,000 cash, and then to lease it back to the new partnership for £3,000 per annum. The cash was partly used to repay to Bull all but £8,000 of the amount owing to him, interest of 15% per annum being paid on that balance. The profit on the surgery was to be credited to the partners' capital accounts. Cox and Dale withdrew £16,000 and £15,000 respectively during the year.

Required:

Prepare the partners' personal accounts, the profit and loss account for the year and a summary balance sheet at the end of the year.

7. Brown, Green and White are in partnership sharing profits and losses in the ratio of 3:3:2 respectively after allowing interest on capital at 5% p.a. None of the partners get a salary but all are engaged full-time in the business. At 31 March 19X9, the end of the financial year, Brown is to retire, and Green and White will continue together, but are to form a limited company, Green & White Ltd. There is nothing specific in the partnership agreement about the valuation of goodwill but it seems to be mutually understood that any such valuation should be based on the annual profits, and that three years purchase of a profit figure is reasonable. The partners need a recommendation of how this vague understanding should be interpreted.

The position at the end of the financial year is:

Balance sheet, Brown, Green & White, 31 March 19X9

	£
Land and buildings	44,000
Vehicles	6,000
Stock	29,600
Debtors	1,800
Bank	600
	82,000
Less: Creditors	2,000
	£80,000
Capital accounts:	£
Brown	35,000
Green	30,000
White	15,000
	£80,000

The net profit figures (before any appropriations) for the last five years were: 19X9 £30,000; 19X8 £32,000; 19X7 £28,000; 19X6 £14,000; 19X5 £24,000.

It is agreed that the land and buildings should be valued at £60,000 and stock at £28,000. Brown is to take one of the cars at a valuation of £1,200 (book value £2,000). Otherwise the assets and liabilities are to be valued as shown in the balance sheet. Brown is prepared to leave his capital in the new company for the time being, but hopes to withdraw it after a few years.

Required:

Prepare entries to close off the books of the partnership to the point immediately before the partners' final balances are settled by shares (or other consideration) from the company. Decide on a calculation of goodwill, making any assumptions which seem reasonable.

8. Jim and Ken have been trading in partnership for several years, sharing profits or losses equally after allowing for interest on their capitals at 8% p.a. At 1 September 19X7 their manager, Len, was admitted as a partner and was to have a one-fifth share of the profits after interest on capital. Jim and Ken shared the balance equally but guaranteed that Len's share would not fall below £6,000 p.a. Len was not required to introduce any capital at the date of admission but agreed to retain £1,500 of his profit share at the end of each year to be credited to his capital account until the balance reached £7,500. Until that time no interest was to be allowed on his capital. Goodwill, calculated as a percentage of the profits of the last five years was agreed at £15,000 at 1 September 19X7, and Len paid into the business sufficient cash for his share. No goodwill account was to be left in the books. Land and buildings were professionally valued at the same date at £28,400 and this figure was to be brought into the books, whilst the book value of the equipment and vehicles was, by mutual agreement, to be reduced to £15,000 at that date. Len had previously been entitled to a bonus of 5% of the gross profit, payable half-yearly: the bonus together with his manager's salary were to cease when he became a partner. It was agreed to take out a survivorship policy and the first premium of £1,000 was paid on 1 September 19X7.

The trial balance at the end of the 19X7 financial year is given below. No adjustments had yet been made in respect of Len's admission, and the amount he introduced for goodwill had been put to his current account. The drawings of all the partners have been charged to their current accounts.

It can be assumed that the gross profit and trading expenses accrued evenly throughout the year. Depreciation on the equipment and vehicles is to be charged at 20% p.a. on the book value.

Trial balance at 31 December 19X7

	£	£
Capital accounts:		
Jim		30,000
Ken		15,000
Current accounts:		
Jim	7,800	
Ken	7,100	
Len		1,800
Land and buildings	18,000	
Equipment and vehicles	21,000	
Stock	9,200	
Gross profit		42,000
Trading expenses	15,000	
Manager's salary	4,000	
Manager's bonus	1,050	
Debtors and creditors	5,850	3,100
Bank balance	2,900	
	£91,900	£91,900

Required:
Prepare the profit and loss account and the partners' capital and current accounts for the year ended 31 December 19X7, and a balance sheet at that date.

9. Nelson, Edwards and Powell, have been trading for some time as partners in a firm of bookbinders. Following a period of poor trading results the partners have decided to dissolve the partnership. Recognising that the firm cannot be sold as a going concern it has been decided to sell the assets piecemeal in order to obtain the best possible cash returns.

The partners' accounts at 31 March 19X5, the effective date of dissolution, were as follows:

	Nelson	Edwards	Powell
Profit sharing ratios	40%	20%	40%
Capital accounts	£52,000	£82,000	£38,000
Current accounts	£8,000 (Cr)	£12,000 (Dr)	£12,000 (Cr)

In addition to this information the balance in hand at the bank is £8,000 and the external creditors are owed a total of £23,000.

Required:
Draw up a safe cash predistribution plan showing how cash is to be distributed upon realisation of the assets.

12 Company Accounts: Capital Structure

The growth of limited liability companies has been a feature of Western industrialised society. The size of the company sector in the economies of Western countries, the contribution which it makes towards national economic growth, the extent to which it provides for employment and the burden of taxation which it assumes merely underline the economic importance of this form of business organisation.

The Companies Acts of 1948, 1967, 1976, 1980 and 1981 reflect the evolution of the legislation applying in the United Kingdom to limited liability companies, and contain specific rules which apply to their financial accounting procedures. An important consequence of the United Kingdom's entry into the European Economic Community has been the recognition of the requirements of the Fourth Directive issued by the European Economic Commission with regard to financial accounting procedures. They are now contained in the Companies Acts of 1980 and 1981. These Companies Acts stipulate, in detail, not only the content of financial reports but also the manner in which these reports should be presented to shareholders. These Acts were consolidated in the Companies Act of 1985.

The purpose of this chapter is to:
(a) examine the legal framework essential to understanding how a company is set up and capitalised,
(b) examine the accounting procedures for issuing shares,
(c) discuss how a company may be formed to take over a business,
(d) discuss the accounting problems associated with loan capital,
(e) examine the accounting treatment of dividends, and
(f) examine the accounting procedures for the redemption of shares.

Formal requirements for company status

The registration of a company as a company with limited liability under the Companies Act 1948 results in the creation of legal entity which has an independent life from those physical persons who own its capital, who are known as shareholders, and those physical persons who manage its affairs, who are known as directors.

There is a strict procedure for registering a company in this way. It consists of submitting a number of documents to the Office of the Registrar of Companies, prior to the latter issuing a Certificate of Incorporation which marks the 'legal birth' of the company. The Memorandum of Association and the Articles of Association are two of the most important documents to be submitted and they are normally prepared by a solicitor engaged for this purpose.

The Memorandum of Association essentially defines the relationship between the company and external parties. Thus, it contains a definition of the company's objectives. For example, a company established to deal only in wines and spirits would be acting *ultra vires* or illegally if it were to begin operating as electrical engineers. Likewise, the Memorandum of Association contains a capital clause which determines the size of the capital of the company. A company is not legally entitled to raise capital in excess of the amount stated in the capital clause without seeking an amendment to the capital clause. Accordingly, the amount shown on the balance sheet of a company as the authorised share capital is the amount of capital which a company is legally authorised to raise by means of an issue of shares (see below). The balance sheet also shows the issued share capital, and indicates thereby what further margin is left for raising further capital.

The Articles of Association are concerned with the internal regulation of the company's affairs. These include the rights of various classes of shareholders, the manner in which meetings should be held and the rights and duties of members and officers of the company. The Articles of Association are usually lengthy documents. The Companies Act 1948 contains a model form of Articles of Association, which most companies adopt sometimes with minor modifications.

In conformity with the EEC Second Directive, the distinction between private and public companies has been retained and strengthened in the Companies Acts 1980 and 1981. In essence, a private company is one which imposes restrictions on the transfer of its shares, and is particularly useful for privately financed businesses seeking to operate under the cover of limited liability. A public company is one which generally will not impose restrictions on the transfer of its shares, and will seek to be financed by the issue of shares to the public. It is not necessary for a public company to have its shares quoted on a stock exchange to be described as a public company. The distinction between a private and a public company is explained in the Companies Act 1980 which states that a public company is a company limited by shares or limited by guarantee and having a share capital. It is a company the Memorandum of Association of which states that:

(a) the company is to be a public company, and that
(b) the provisions of the Companies Acts as to the registration as a public company have been complied with.

The Companies Act 1980 defines a private company as a company which is not a public company, in terms of the provisions stated above.

A public company is required to bear the suffix 'plc' after its name, which means 'public limited company', and a private company is required simply to carry the suffix 'ltd' after its name, meaning that it is a 'limited company'.

Share capital and shareholders' equity

The capital of the company is divided into separate units known as shares. Thus, the capital of a company may be 100,000 shares of £1 each representing a total of £100,000. A shareholder who has purchased and paid for his share cannot be called upon to contribute further to the company's capital in respect of his shareholding. In effect, his liability to contribute to the company's debts in the case of insolvency is limited to the amount which he has agreed to pay for his shares. This is the strict meaning of limited liability. Accordingly, the most important difference in this context between the owner of a business which is not a limited liability company and the owner of shares in a limited liability company is that the former is liable at law for the debts of his business to the extent of his personal property whereas the latter is liable at law only to the extent of the amount unpaid on the shares which he holds.

Whereas shares are initially purchased from a company at the price stipulated by the company, all subsequent transactions in these shares take place between buyers and sellers usually through the medium of a stock exchange, which is a formalised market for share dealings. Thus, a company may make a public offer of a parcel of 100,000 shares at a price of £1 each, and will receive £100,000 from various buyers. Subsequently, however, the market price of the shares may rise to £2, which is the price which an existing shareholder will obtain if he seeks to sell his shares to another person through the stock exchange.

From the foregoing, the shareholders' equity consists essentially of the total sum which the company has itself received in respect of the shares which have been issued and of the profits of the company which have not been paid out to shareholders as dividends.

Types of shares

The flexibility introduced into the capitalisation of a company by the subdivision of the capital into shares of small denominations is further enhanced by the ability of a company to attach different rights to these shares. As a result, shares having different rights appeal to different classes of investors and broaden the base from which the company may acquire its capital.

The main types of shares are:

(a) Preference shares.
(b) Ordinary shares.
(c) Deferred shares.

In the United Kingdom, shares of whatever class must be stated in terms of a fixed nominal amount, irrespective of the price which the company may have obtained for such shares. The net profit of the company which it is decided to distribute to shareholders as dividends is declared in terms of 'X pence per share'. In the United States, however, shares are not required to have a nominal or par value. They are issued as shares of no par value. As a result, such shares simply represent a unit of ownership and are issued and recorded at whatever price is decided upon by the directors.

Preference shares

Preference shares are preferential over other classes of shares in a company in respect of dividends, and usually as regards the repayment of capital when a company is dissolved. The main feature of preference shares is their entitlement of a fixed rate of dividend before any dividends are declared in favour of other classes of shareholders. When a company is wound up, preference shareholders receive the refund of the capital they have subscribed immediately after preferred, secured and unsecured creditors have been paid, if the preference shares are preferential as to capital as well as income.

Preference shares generally fall into three main classes:

Cumulative preference shares

Where the net profit of a company is insufficient in any year to declare a dividend in favour of holders of cumulative preference shares, the right of such shareholders to receive a dividend in respect of that year is carried over and accumulates until the company has sufficient net profit to pay the accumulated dividend entitlement.

Preference shares are now deemed to be cumulative unless expressly issued by a company as non-cumulative preference shares.

Participating preference shares

In addition to being cumulative, preference shares may also participate in the net profit available for distribution after other shareholders have received a stated dividend percentage. Thus, such preference shareholders receive not only their fixed dividend entitlement which will be cumulative, but in a good year will also receive a further dividend after ordinary and deferred shareholders, as may be, have received a dividend. For example, the conditions of issue attached to participating preferences shares may state that an extra 1% dividend, as well as the fixed dividend, will be paid to participating preference shareholders for every 1% by which a dividend declared for the ordinary shareholders exceeds 12%. In this way, preference shareholders can benefit from their investment in successful companies.

Redeemable preference shares

Business opportunities may arise and induce a company to seek further capital. Where such capital is needed only for a reasonably short period but where it would be disadvantageous to undertake an indefinite commitment to pay dividends, a company may issue redeemable preference shares.

A number of restrictions are attached to the issue of redeemable preference shares, for example, the shares must be stated to be redeemable, the earliest date of redemption must also be stated and the terms of redemption must be clearly given. Moreover, redeemable preferences shares may be redeemed only out of the proceeds of a fresh issue of shares or from a reserve created by the company.

The attraction of preference shares from the viewpoint of an investor is that they offer a less risky investment than ordinary shares, but less opportunity for gains. They do not usually carry voting rights, except when the non-payment of dividend or alteration of class rights entitles them to vote at a meeting of preference shareholders.

Ordinary shares

Ordinary shares are the most important class of shares, for not only do they represent the risk capital invested in a company but they carry voting rights conferring control over the company's affairs through the right to elect its directors.

Ordinary shareholders are also entitled to the balance of the company's net profit after payment of interest on loans, taxation and dividends on preference shares. It is the usual practice for companies to declare only a portion of the net profit as dividends and to retain the balance of undistributed profits to provide further capital for investment purposes. The dividend percentage is recommended by the board of directors to the shareholders at their annual general meeting, and paid after being approved by vote.

As is the practice with other types of shares, ordinary shares issued in the United Kingdom bear a fixed nominal value. The company may, nevertheless, attach any selling price to such shares, save that shares may not be issued at a discount.

It is quite commonplace for shares to be issued at a premium, that is, at a price in excess of the fixed nominal value.

Example 1

Unac plc issued 100,000 ordinary shares having a nominal value of £1 each at a price of £2.50 each. All the shares offered for sale were subscribed for by the public.

The result of this sale is shown in the books of Unac plc as follows:

	£	£
Debit cash	250,000	
Credit ordinary share capital		100,000
Credit share premium account		150,000

It should be noted that the ordinary share capital account is credited only with the nominal value of the shares issued, and that the premium received in excess of this value is credited to a share premium account. Any dividend subsequently paid by the company is declared as a percentage of the nominal value of the shares.

Deferred shares

These are shares which have the opposite characteristics of preference shares, for holders of these shares are not entitled to receive dividends until ordinary shareholders have received a stated dividend percentage. Moreover, in the event of a liquidation, ordinary shareholders usually also have a priority as regards the return of capital.

Deferred shares are now seldom issued. Their original intention was to indicate confidence in the company, and for this reason they tended to be subscribed for by the founder members of the management of the company. For this reason, they are sometimes referred to as 'founders' or 'management' shares. Under conditions of prosperity, holders of deferred shares received considerable benefits in the form of a high dividend rate, and in some cases, the voting rights attached to such shares gave their holders virtual control over the company.

Redeemable shares

Prior to the Companies Act 1981, United Kingdom companies could only issue redeemable shares in the form of redeemable preference shares. The Companies Act 1981 (now the 1985 Act) permits a company to issue redeemable shares of other classes than preference shares provided that:

(a) The company's Articles of Association give the authority.

(b) The company has in issue shares that are not redeemable.

Accounting procedures for the issue of shares

Assuming that shares will be issued for cash only, the double-entry procedure for recording the issue of share capital are:

Dr   Bank account
Cr   Share capital account

the sum being debited and credited to these accounts being the cash received for the shares issued. If a company is issuing shares of a particular class, there will be a credit entry in the appropriate share capital account, for example, preference share capital account, ordinary share capital account, etc., as the case may be.

A public company wishing to issue shares to the public has to proceed initially by issuing an advertisement in the form of a prospectus, which generally appears in the press and elsewhere. The Companies Acts and Stock Exchange regulations contain strict provisions regarding the information which must be disclosed in the prospectus, which is a formal offer to the public of shares in the company. It states the number of shares offered, and the price at which they are offered is also usually stated.

The response of the public to the offer of shares in the prospectus may result in an over- or under-subscription of the number of shares on offer. If there is an over-subscription of shares, the number of shares applied for will have to be adjusted by the company to the number of shares offered. The company may insure against the possibility of an under-subscription of shares by entering into an agreement with underwriters, who for a commission, will agree to buy all the shares which are not taken up by the public. As a result, all the shares offered are sold, whether or not they are over- or under-subscribed. The procedure for dealing with issues of shares by way of a prospectus is known as *application and allotment*.

Application and allotment

The company will open a separate bank account for the purpose of receiving the money subscribed for the shares offered. The accounting entries will be:

Dr   Bank (application and allotment) account
Cr   Application and allotment account

the sum debited and credited being the money received by the company with the formal applications for the shares offered in the prospectus.

Once the date limit for applications for shares has passed, the board of directors is able to compare the number of shares applied for against the number offered in the prospectus. In the case of an over-subscription, there will have to be a decision to tailor down the excess number of shares applied for to match the available number offered. Once the decision has been made, the next stage in the process is the allotment of shares to shareholders whose applications have been accepted, in whole or in part. The accounting entries are:

Dr   Application and allotment account
Cr   Share capital account

the sum debited and credited being the money required on application and allotment for the shares allotted. The surplus money subscribed in respect of unsuccessful applications will be refunded at this stage.

Generally, prospective shareholders are required to send with their applications, a cheque covering the total price of the shares for which they are applying. Occasionally, however, the prospectus will require a proportion to be paid on application and the remainder on allotment. In this case, the successful applicants will be advised of the amount payable in respect of the shares allotted to them. The accounting entries are as follows:

Dr   Bank (application and allotment) account
Cr   Application and allotment account

with the additional amount due and paid on allotment.

Example 2

Bluechip plc issued a prospectus offering for sale 1 million £1 ordinary shares at a price of £1 each, 75p being payable on application and 25p being payable on allotment. The number of shares applied for coincided exactly with the number of shares offered, and Bluechip plc proceeded with the allotment of the shares. The accounting entries are as follows:

		£	£
Dr	Bank (application and allotment) account	750,000	
Cr	Application and allotment account		750,000

Following the allotment decision, the accounting entries are:

			£	£
Dr	Application and allotment account		1,000,000	
Cr	Ordinary share capital account			1,000,000

Given that the prospectus stated that the obligation to pay 25p per share was consequential upon the allotment by the company of the shares, the successful applicants are debtors at law for the balance owing to the company on the shares allotted to them. The next stage is to record the receipt of the amount due on allotment as follows:

			£	£
Dr	Bank (application and allotment) account		250,000	
Cr	Application and allotment account			250,000

The application and allotment account having served its purpose is closed as follows:

Application and allotment account

	£		£
Ordinary share capital	1,000,000	Bank (application and allotment)	750,000
		Bank (application and allotment)	250,000
	1,000,000		1,000,000

Calls

As indicated earlier, the practice is to demand the full amount payable for shares upon application and allotment. A practice which is rarely followed is to require the price of the shares to be paid in instalments, there being a proportion of the price payable on application and allotment, leaving the amount unpaid to be called-up by the company at a later date.

Example 3

Oldhat plc has issued a prospectus offering for sale 4,000,000 ordinary shares of 25p nominal value at a price of 75p to be paid as to 55p on application, 10p on allotment and the balance of 10p six months after allotment. According to the prospectus, the closing date for applications to be lodged was 31 March 19X5, allotment to be settled by 30 April 19X5, and the final payment to be made by 31 October 19X5.

6,000,000 applications were received and 2,000,000 were rejected. All monies were subscribed on due date. The accounting entries are as follows:

31 March 19X5

		£	£
Dr	Bank (application and allotment) account	3,300,000	
Cr	Application and allotment account		3,300,000

being the monies due and paid on application.

30 April 19X5

		£	£
Dr	Application and allotment account	1,100,000	
Cr	Bank (application and allotment) account		1,100,000

being monies returned to unsuccessful applicants.

		£	£
Dr	Application and allotment account	2,600,000	
Cr	Ordinary share capital account account		600,000
Cr	Share premium account		2,000,000

being the allotment of 4,000,000 ordinary shares
of nominal value 25p paid as to 15p, and premium of
50p per share.

		£	£
Dr	Bank (application and allotment) account	400,000	
Cr	Application and allotment account		400,000

being the monies due on allotment by successful applicants.

31 October 19X5

		£	£
Dr	Call account	400,000	
Cr	Ordinary share capital account		400,000

being the call of 10p per share.

		£	£
Dr	Bank account	400,000	
Cr	Call account		400,000

being the monies received on call from shareholders.

In this example, the excess number of bids over the number of shares offered was treated as bids rejected. In order that all applicants should be treated fairly, it is normal to scale down the number of shares bid for by individual applicants. In this way, each applicant is alloted some shares, and no bid is completely rejected. The excess monies subscribed by applicants is not returned immediately, but is credited as an advance payment of sums due on allotment.

Example 4

Okier plc received 12,000,000 applications for 10,000,000 shares offered to the public in a prospectus. The nominal value of the shares was 25p per share and the offer price was 60p. The prospectus required 45p per share on application, and the balance of 15p per share on allotment. All applications were scaled down pro rata to the 10,000,000 shares proposed to be issued.
The accounting entries would be as follows:

	£	£
Dr Bank (application and allotment) account	5,400,000	
Cr Application and allotment account		5,400,000

being the monies received on application
(12,000,000 at 45p per share).

	£	£
Dr Application and allotment account	6,000,000	
Cr Ordinary share capital account		3,500,000
Cr Share premium account		2,500,000

being the allotment of 10,000,000 shares of 25p
nominal value at a premium of 35p per share.

	£	£
Dr Bank (application and allotment) account	600,000	
Cr Application and allotment account		600,000

being the balance of monies due on allotment.

Thus, an applicant for 120 shares would have sent in a cheque for £54 (120 × 45p). In the scaling down process, he would have been allotted 100 shares at a price of 60p each, i.e. £60 in total. Having already sent the company £54 with his application for 120 shares, the balance remaining to be paid is only £6. This sum may be checked as follows:

	£
Amount due on allotment of 100 shares (100 × 15p)	15
Less: Excess paid on bid (20 × 45p)	9
Balance payable on allotment	6

Bonus issues

Bonus shares are issued to shareholders without payment. The issue of bonus shares is a means of capitalising retained profits which have been accumulating. In both Examples 3 and 4 it has been assumed, as is usual, that the premium payable is part of the first monies received.

Example 5
The condensed balance sheet of Greylag Ltd as at 31 March 19X5 is as follows:

	£	£
Ordinary share capital		1,000
Retained profits		50,000
		51,000
Fixed assets		48,000
Current assets	7,000	
Less: Current liabilities	4,000	3,000
		51,000

Clearly, the retained profits have been built up for the purpose of investing in fixed assets. There is no likelihood that the company would ever distribute these retained profits as dividends. In recognition of this reality, the company proposes to convert them into capital by the issue of 50 bonus shares of £1 each for every one share of £1 held by shareholders.

The accounting entries recording this decision is as follows:

		£	£
Dr	Retained profit account	50,000	
Cr	Ordinary share capital account		50,000

Note that the bonus shares are issued free of payment to shareholders, and that as a result of the bonus issue, a shareholder previously holding 2 shares now holds 102 shares (2 plus 100 bonus shares).

The balance sheet after issue of the bonus shares is as follows:

	£	£
Ordinary share capital		51,000
Fixed assets		48,000
Current assets	7,000	
less: Current liabilities	4,000	3,000
		51,000

The issue of the bonus shares has not changed the asset structure of the company, and the value of the individual investor's shareholding in the company has not changed. Instead of having say 2 shares in a company having assets amounting to £51,000 at book value, he has 102 shares. Where a company's shares are quoted on a stock exchange, the market's reaction to the issue of bonus shares will depend upon expectations as to future dividends.

The formation of a company by the acquisition of a business

Companies often originate from partnerships or from the business of sole traders. It is common practice for the business of the partnership or of the sole trader to be sold as a going concern to a company formed specifically to take over the business. The arrangement in these cases is for the company to take over the assets and liabilities of the business in return for the issue of shares.

Example 6
Having successfully operated and expanded his business for some years, Ronald Champion has decided to form a limited liability company and to transfer his business to the company. As at the date of transfer the balance sheet of the business is as follows:

Ronald Champion		
Balance sheet as at 1 April 19X7		
	£	£
Capital		27,350
Represented by:		
Fixed assets at written down value		18,400
Current assets	14,600	
Less: Current liabilities	5,650	8,950
		27,350

The new company is to be called Ronchamp Limited. The authorised share capital is to amount to £60,000 consisting of 10,000 12%
preference shares of £1 each and 50,000 ordinary shares of £1 each.

The business it to be transferred to Ronchamp Ltd for £27,350
and Ronald Champion is to receive all the preference shares which
the company is authorised to issue and the balance of the consideration in the form of ordinary shares. In order to conform with the
requirements of the Companies Act 1948 that the minimum number
of shareholders in a company shall be two, he transfers 100 of the
ordinary shares to his wife.

Ronchamp Limited		
Balance sheet as at 1 April 19X7	£	£
Fixed assets at cost		18,400
Current assets	14,600	
Creditors—amounts falling due for payment within one year	5,650	8,950
		27,350

	Authorised	Issued and fully paid
Share capital	£	£
12% preference shares of £1 each	10,000	10,000
Ordinary shares of £1 each	50,000	17,350
	60,000	27,350

It is the usual practice on these occasions to revalue the assets
on their transfer to the company, and to transfer the net result of
the revaluation to the capital account of the proprietor(s) of the business being sold.

Example 7
Suppose that the business of Ronald Champion in the previous example had included under fixed assets premises at cost of £12,000.
Assume that the market value of these premises was £19,500. A
revaluation of these premises immediately prior to transfer of the

business to Ronchamp Ltd would have been effected in the books of Ronald Champion as follows:

	£	£
Dr Premises account	7,500	
Cr Capital account		7,500

being the increased value of the premises on revaluation.

The result of the valuation would have been that the assets sold to the company would have been increased in value by £7,500 and Champion would have received a further 7,500 ordinary shares of £1 each.

Goodwill

It frequently happens that the vendor of a business believes that the value of the business transferred to a company is greater than that shown in his books. In Example 7, this increased value is due to a higher market value than that recorded. However, even after specific assets have been revalued to take account of their current market value, the vendor may still insist that the global value of the business is higher than that shown by a market valuation of its individual assets. This additional value is referred to as goodwill. Goodwill is a extremely complex problem in accounting. The purpose of this section is not to attempt to analyse the different methods of valuing goodwill, but simply to focus on the manner in which it arises.

In accounting, goodwill is treated as an intangible asset associated with the total or global value of all other assets employed by a business. Goodwill often arises as an element of added value which is specific to the business, and is often taken to represent some trading advantages which it enjoys. For this reason, goodwill is often associated with marketing advantages in the form of the goodwill of a clientele, a trade mark or a monopoly or quasi-monopoly position in the market. It is usually recognised when businesses are sold or acquired. Thus, if in the course of negotiating a price at which a business is to be acquired, the company pays a sum which is greater than the market value of the net assets, the difference is referred to as goodwill and is shown as a separate asset.

Example 8
Paul Emmerson, a wholesale clothing merchant, wishes to retire and has been offered the sum of £25,000 for his business by the Handbridge Clothing Co Ltd. Emmerson's balance sheet as at 30 June 19X5 is as follows:

Balance sheet as at 30 June 19X5

	£
Capital	18,320
Represented by:	£
Fixed assets	14,610
Net current assets	3,710
	18,320

All the assets in the balance sheet are deemed to be correctly valued and Emmerson accepts the offer.

Handbridge Clothing Company Ltd had been formed for the purpose of carrying on the business once Emmerson had accepted the offer. The share capital issued was 28,000 ordinary shares of £1 each and so immediately before transfer the balance sheet of the company was as follows:

Handbridge Clothing Company Ltd
Balance sheet as at 30 June 19X5

Current assets		£
Cash at bank		28,000

	Authorised	Issued and fully paid
Share capital	£	£
Ordinary shares of £1 each	28,000	28,000

Immediately after the transfer of the business to the company, the balance sheet of Handbridge Clothing Company Ltd would appear as follows:

Balance sheet as at 30 June 19X5

	£
Fixed assets	
Intangible assets—goodwill	9,680
Tangible assets	14,610
	24,290
Net current assets	3,710
	28,000
Share capital (as shown previously)	28,000

When a partnership is formed into a limited company it must be noted that in deciding how many shares are to be given in exchange for each partner's equity in the partnership, any surplus on valuation, and this includes goodwill, will be credited to the partners' current accounts in proportion to their net profit-sharing ratios. Any partner's equity in the partnership consists of both the capital and the current account as seen in Chapter 11.

Loan capital

So far, it has been assumed that the capital provided to a company is obtained from shareholders in return for shares in the company. However, many firms—particularly large firms—tend to finance a significant proportion of their capital needs by means of long-term borrowing. Such borrowings excluded routine overdraft facilities from banks which are essentially short-term by nature.

Since shareholders have no liability for the debts of the company, except in so far as there may be an unpaid amount on the shares which they hold, safeguards are required to protect the interests of creditors. In this context, it should be stated that it is a rare occurrence to find a company which has outstanding calls in respect of issued shares. The first line of protection afforded to creditors is a limitation on the power to borrow which is found in the Memorandum and Articles of Association. Thus, the power to borrow money must be stated in the Memorandum of Association and the maximum limit of borrowing must be stipulated in the Articles of Association.

Although long-term borrowings may be obtained from financial institutions such as banks, the conventional method of obtaining long-term loan capital is by means of the issue of debentures. A debenture is a fixed interest security issued by a company, and is usually secured on the assets of the company. Unsecured debentures which are often described as unsecured notes, may be successfully issued by large companies.

Debentures are usually issued in larger monetary units than shares, frequently in £100 units. They are normally redeemable at clearly stated dates and on predetermined terms. Occasionally, they are redeemable by a right of conversion into shares, when they are known as convertible debentures.

The security provided is either by creating a fixed charge on specific assets of the company or by creating a floating charge over all its assets. Both charges are the result of a legal process, usually associated with drawing up a trust deed on behalf of the debenture holders. The creation of a fixed charge identifies specific assets which are reserved as security: a floating charge does not identify any particular assets and only crystallises when the company is in breach of a condition of the trust deed. The security granted to debenture holders under either a fixed charge or a floating charge is realisable by the trustees for the debenture holders, and the assets charged as security may be sold on behalf of the debenture holders. This extreme situation would only usually arise in the case of an insolvency.

The conditions attached to the debentures are stated in the trust deed, which provides not only for the rate of interest payable, the date of redemption, etc., but also grants the trustees for the debenture holders power to act on behalf of the body of the debenture holders, even to the extent of calling meetings of the debenture holders, and conducting negotiations with the company on their behalf over any question affecting their interests. The power of the trustees is clearly defined in the trust deed.

It is important to note the difference between the fixed rate of dividend payable in respect of a preference share and the fixed rate of interest payable in respect of debentures. This difference stems from the fact that a preference shareholder is in fact a member of the company and the owner of a share in the company. Hence, the preference dividend is a distribution of profits. By contrast, a debenture holder is not a member of the company but a creditor of the company whose rights against the company are stated in the form of a debenture. The debenture interest is a charge against the company's profits and must be treated as an expense in the process of profit calculation.

The accounting entries recording the issue of loan capital are as follows:

Example 9

Weaklink plc issued a debenture loan of £5,000,000 carrying interest at 12% per annum and redeemable ten years from date of issue. Once the legal matters have been settled and the loan subscribed, the accounting entries are:

		£	£
Dr	Bank account	5,000,000	
Cr	12% Debenture account		5,000,000

It is quite usual to see large public companies proceeding with the issue of loan capital by way of a prospectus. In such cases, the accounting entries are similar to those used for the issue of share capital. They record the monies received with the applications for portions of the loan capital, normally in blocks of £100, and when the allotment process is completed, the accounting entries record the loan capital issued, and the excess applications returned.

Dividends

Dividends are declared at a rate, expressed in pence per share. Companies quoted on the Stock Exchange generally declare two dividends in respect of each accounting period. The first is an interim dividend declared and paid during the accounting period to which it relates. The second is a final dividend declared and paid after the final results are known. The procedure with regard to the final dividend is for the board of directors to propose the final dividend to the shareholders meeting to approve the annual financial report. The final dividend recommended by the board of directors is paid only after it has been approved by the Annual General Meeting of shareholders. Preference shareholders, by contrast, have a preferential right to a dividend prior to ordinary shareholders, and it is the practice for such dividends to be declared by the board of directors themselves, if there is an adequacy of profits to cover such dividends.

Example 10

Browntag plc has prepared its final accounts for the year ended 31 December 19X6 which show a net profit of £85,600 after allowing for tax. The issued share capital was as follows:

100,000 Ordinary shares of £1
  60,000 12% Non-participating preference shares of £1.

In addition to the declaration of the dividend of 12% to preference shareholders, the board of directors has recommended a final dividend of 15% to ordinary shareholders. At this stage, the accounting entries are as follows:

		£	£
Dr	Profit and loss account	22,200	
Cr	Preference share dividend account		7,200
Cr	Ordinary share dividend account		15,000

These entries will be shown separately on the profit and loss account, the dividend proposed in respect of the ordinary shares appearing as 'Dividend proposed on ordinary shares £15,000'. On the balance sheet, the dividend declared to preference shareholders and the dividend recommended in respect of ordinary shareholders will appear under current liabilities. The payment of these dividends will be made after the annual general meeting, at which the ordinary shareholders will have approved the dividend recommended by the board of directors. The payment of these dividends will be recorded as follows:

		£	£
Dr	Preference share dividend account	7,200	
Dr	Ordinary share dividend account	15,000	
Cr	Bank account		22,200

Redemption of shares

The Companies Act 1948 allowed companies to issue only one class of redeemable shares, namely, redeemable preference shares. Moreover, the redemption of such shares could be financed only as follows:

(a) Out of profits otherwise available for distribution, transferred for that purpose to a capital redemption reserve account.

(b) Out of the proceeds of a new share issue effected for the purpose of redeeming the shares in question.

Example 11

Bluecap plc and Greenpack plc, two unrelated companies both had in issue redeemable preference shares due for redemption. Bluecap plc decided to obtain the required fund by the issue of additional ordinary shares at par, whereas Greenpack plc chose to transfer available profits to a capital redemption reserve account, and to redeem the shares by this means.

The issued share capital and reserves of the two companies were as follows:

	Bluecap plc		Greencap plc	
	£	£	£	£
Redeemable preference shares	25,000		30,000	
Issued ordinary shares	60,000		70,000	
Profit and loss account	29,000	114,000	64,000	164,000

After the redemption of the preference shares—at par—the situation was as follows:

	Bluecap plc		Greencap plc	
	£	£	£	£
Issued ordinary shares	85,000		70,000	
Capital redemption reserve	—		30,000	
Profit and loss account	29,000	114,000	34,000	134,000

The accounting procedures relating to these transformations were as follows:

Bluecap plc

		£	£
Dr	Bank account	25,000	
Cr	Ordinary share capital account		25,000
Dr	Redeemable preference share account	25,000	
Cr	Bank account		25,000

Greencap plc

		£	£
Dr	Profit and loss account	30,000	
Cr	Capital redemption reserve account		30,000
Dr	Redeemable preference share account	30,000	
Cr	Bank account		30,000

Redemption of shares at a premium

Where redeemable preference shares have been issued with an obligation upon the company to redeem them at a premium, the premium paid on redemption must be debited either to the profit and loss account or to the share premium account, if the latter is available.

Example 12
Redspot plc wished to redeem £50,000 redeemable preference shares issued in units of £100 at £105. Two procedures are available to the company.

(a) Out of the proceeds of a new issue of ordinary shares at par

		£	£
Dr	Redeemable preference share account	50,000	
Cr	Redemption of shares account		50,000
Dr	Profit and loss account or share premium account (if in existence)	2,500	
Cr	Redemption of shares account		2,500

being the premium of £5 per £100 block of shares

		£	£
Dr	Bank account	50,000	
Cr	Ordinary share capital account		50,000
Dr	Redemption of shares account	52,500	
Cr	Bank account		52,500

(b) By transfer of profits to a capital redemption reserve account

		£	£
Dr	Redeemable preference share account	50,000	
Cr	Redemption of shares account		50,000
Dr	Profit and loss account or share premium account (if in existence)	2,500	
Cr	Redemption of shares account		2,500
Dr	Profit and loss account	50,000	
Cr	Capital redemption reserve account		50,000
Dr	Redemption of shares account	52,500	
Cr	Bank account		52,500

Redemption of shares under the Companies Act 1985

The Companies Act 1981 (now the 1985 Act) extended the right to issue redeemable shares to shares of any class, and removed the limitation on the issue of such shares found in the Companies Act 1948, which restricted the redemption of shares to shares originally issued as redeemable preference shares.

The following conditions must be satisfied however:

(a) The Articles of Association of the company must contain the powers so to do. This may be achieved by an alteration of the Articles of Association, if the company was formed prior to 1981.

(b) The company may issue redeemable shares of any class, so long as there are in issue shares that are non-redeemable.

Redeemable shares may be issued as redeemable on a specified date, or as redeemable at the option of the company or the shareholders. The conditions relating to redemption must be stated in the prospectus or other document in terms of which the shares are issued.

The Companies Act 1985 requires that the following conditions be observed when redemption occurs:

(a) The shares must be fully paid.

(b) Payment must be made by the company at the time of redemption, and cannot be deferred, for example, by leaving a credit balance in respect of a payment not made for the redemption of shares.

(c) The redemption must be financed out of *either*

    (i) the proceeds of a new issue of shares made for that purpose, *or*

    (ii) out of profits available for distribution, transferred for that purpose to a capital redemption reserve account, *or*

    (iii) in the case of private companies, out of capital, if the Articles of Association provide the authority so to do, subject to certain restrictions.

(d) The terms of redemption may be set out in the Articles of Association, but these must not conflict with the provisions of the Companies Act 1985.

(e) The shares once redeemed must be treated as cancelled shares, and as a consequence reduce the issued share capital, though not the authorised share capital.

Redemption of shares at a premium under the Companies Act 1985

If a premium is payable on the redemption of shares of any class, generally such premium should be paid out of distributable profits. However, if the shares themselves were originally issued at a premium, a proportion of any premium payable on redemption may be paid out of the proceeds of an issue of shares made for that purpose. The Companies Act 1985 determines that proportion as the lower of:

(a) the aggregate of the premiums that the company received at the time when the shares now redeemed were issued, *or*

(b) the amount of the company's share premium account, after transferring in the premium, if any, payable on the fresh issue of shares.

The limit to the proportion of the premium on redemption on shares which may be financed out of the proceeds of a new issue of shares may not be exceeded. Once that proportion has been calculated in accordance with the rule specified above, that proportion is to be debited to the share premium account. The effect of this rule is to place a restriction on the use of the share premium account for the purpose of paying premiums on the redemption of shares. Where the premium payable on redemption is greater than the proportion which may be debited to the share premium account, the balance must be found from profits available for distribution and charged, therefore, to the balance remaining on the profit and loss account.

The Companies Act 1948 made it possible for any premium payable on the redemption of redeemable preference shares to be paid out of the share premium account. The rule contained in the Companies Act 1985 prohibits the use of the share premium account for that purpose. However, this prohibition does not apply to the redemption of redeemable shares issued prior to the Companies Act 1981.

Example 13

On 1 January 19X4, in addition to having in issue 1,000,000 non-redeemable shares of £1 each, Blackjack plc had issued 2,000,000 £1 redeemable ordinary shares at a price of £1.50. The conditions of issue provided that these shares would be redeemed on 1 January 19X8 at a premium of 75p per share. When the time for redemption arrived, Blackjack plc issued 2,000,000 £1 ordinary shares at a premium of 40p per shares, to finance the cost of redeeming the shares.

The acounting entries in time sequence are as follows:

	£000	£000
1 January 19X4		
Dr Bank account	3,000	
Cr Redeemable ordinary share capital account		2,000
Cr Share premium account		1,000
1 January 19X8		
Dr Bank account	2,800	
Cr Ordinary share capital account		2,000
Cr Share premium account		800

The proportion of the proceeds of the new issue of shares which may be used to pay the premium on redemption may be calculated as follows:

(a) Premium received by the company on the issue of the shares now to be redeemed: £1,000,000

(b) Share premium account after the inclusion of the premium received on the issue of the new issue of shares (£1,000,000 + £800,000): £1,800,000

Applying the rule provided in the Companies Act 1985, since (a) above is less than (b), the proportion of the proceeds of the new issue which may be used to pay the premium on redemption is £1,000,000. Accordingly, the accounting entries recording the redemption of the redeemable ordinary shares are as follows:

		£000	£000
Dr	Redeemable ordinary share capital account	2,000	
Cr	Redemption of shares account		2,000
Dr	Premium on redemption account	1,500	
Cr	Redemption of shares account		1,500
Dr	Redemption of shares account	3,500	
Cr	Bank account		3,500

The accounting entries relating to the treatment of the redemption premium are as follows:

		£000	£000
Dr	Share premium account	1,000	
Dr	Profit and loss account	500	
Cr	Premium on redemption account		1,500

It should be noted that the sum of £5,000,000, representing the proportion of the premium on redemption which *may not* be paid out of the share premium account, must be paid out of profits available for distribution and charged, therefore, against the balance of undistributed profits shown on the profit and loss account.

In the event that the company may have utilised a portion of the share premium account between 1 January 19X4 and 1 January 19X8, the consequences would be as shown below.

Example 14
Suppose that Blackjack plc had utilised the share premium account to effect a bonus issue of 950,000 £1 ordinary shares at par value, the proportion of the proceeds of the new issue of shares which could be used to pay the premium on the redemption of the shares is as follows:

(a) Premium received by the company of the issue of the shares now to be redeemed: £1,000,000.

(b) Share premium account, after inclusion of the premium received on the issue of the new shares, and deduction of the balance used to issue bonus shares (£1,000,000 + £800,000 − £950,000): £850,000.

Applying the rule provided in the Companies Act 1985, since (b) is less than (a), the proportion of the proceeds of the new issue which may be used to pay the premium on redemption is only £850,000. The accounting entries relating to the treatment of the redemption premium are as follows:

		£000	£000
Dr	Share premium account	850	
Dr	Profit and loss account	650	
Cr	Premium of redemption account		1,500

Purchase by a company of its own shares

Unlike companies in Europe and in the USA, United Kingdom companies did not have the right to purchase their own shares from other shareholders. The Companies Act 1985 confers this right upon United Kingdom companies, subject to certain restrictions.

The right to purchase their own shares removed a number of problems which faced companies prior to the Companies Act 1981. For example, the restriction on transferability of shares applying to private companies meant that circumstances could arise when a shareholder could not sell his shares and realise the capital which he had invested, and other difficulties could arise when the holder of a substantial block of shares died. The right to purchase their own shares now makes it possible for these types of problems to be eliminated. For public companies, this new provision may be seen as an opportunity to review the capital structure in the light of current economic events.

The following conditions must be observed in the event of a company purchasing its own shares:

(a) The Articles of Association must contain powers to purchase the shares.

(b) After purchase, the company must have other unredeemable shares in issue.

(c) After purchase, the company shall have at least two shareholders.

(d) After purchase, a public company must satisfy the legislation in respect of the issued share capital, which should not be less than the minimum authorised capital (currently £50,000).

(e) The rules applying to the redemption of shares apply also to the purchase of its own shares by a company, namely:

(1) Payment must be made at the time of purchase.
(2) Generally, purchases must be made out of *either* the proceeds of a new issue of shares made for that purpose, *or* out of distributable profits.
A private company may make a purchase out of capital.
(3) Any premium paid must be funded out of distributable profits. Where the purchase of shares is financed out of a new issue of shares issued at a premium, the proportion of the premium payable on purchase which may be financed from the proceeds of the new issue is limited to the lower of:
  (i) The aggregate of the premiums received when the shares were issued originally, or
  (ii) the amount of the share premium account after crediting the premium, if any, payable on the fresh issue of shares.
The balance of the premium which exceeds this proportion must be financed out of distributable profits. Furthermore, the share premium account must be debited with an amount equivalent to the proportion calculated as above.

It will be noted that the rules applying to the purchase of its own shares by a company are similar to those applying to the redemption of shares in terms of the Companies Act 1985.

The Companies Act 1985 also lays down the procedures which must be followed for the purchase of its own shares by a company. Where the shares themselves are not quoted on a stock exchange, the company must obtain the permission from its shareholders for each purchase of its own shares. This safeguard is necessary to prevent a company offering particularly favourable terms to a shareholder wishing to sell his shares to the company. Where the shares are quoted on a stock exchange, the company needs to have only a general authority from its shareholders to purchase its shares, and does not require to have each separate share purchase authorised.

Once shares have been purchased by a company, such shares must be cancelled. They cannot be resold. This rule is similar to the rule applying to the redemption of shares. There is no restriction on the right of a company to make a simultaneous issue of new shares.

Questions

1. Magellan plc has the following capital structure:

	£000
Ordinary shares	4,000
£1 redeemable preference shares	1,000
Distributable reserves	3,000
Other reserves	1,500
	9,500
Net assets	9,500

The company wishes to redeem the preference shares at a premium of 20p per share without a fresh issue.

Required:
Show the entries necessary to give effect to the redemption and the balance sheet after the event.

2. Preserve plc proposes to issue 200,000 12½% preference shares of £1 each at £1.30 per share. This is being undertaken to partially finance the purchase of a block of 600,000 of its own £0.50 ordinary shares. These ordinary shares were originally issued at £0.75 per share and are being bought now by the company at an agreed price of £0.80 per share. Before any of these transactions were started the balance on the share premium account was £100,000.

The company has adequate distributable profits to meet any necessary transfers.

Required:
(a) prepare a statement showing what transfers (if any) are necessary to capital redemption reserve and
(b) prepare a statement showing how much of the share premium (if any) can be used to offset the premium being paid by the company on the purchase of its own shares.

3. Frank Graine, a seed merchant, has received an offer for his business from a large agricultural supply company. His balance sheet as at 31 December 19X0 is as follows:

Balance sheet as at 31 December 19X0

	£
Capital—F. Graine	85,556

Represented by:	£
Freehold warehouse at cost	16,420
Warehouse fittings—written-down value	3,000
Motor vans—written-down value	12,700
	32,120

Current assets	£	
Stock	37,242	
Debtors	24,380	
Bank balance	7,094	
	68,716	
Less: Current liabilities	15,280	53,436
		85,556

After details had been examined, the following terms were decided upon: (1) Morgain plc, the buying company, would issue 30,000 ordinary shares of £1 each to Graine. The ordinary shares of Morgain plc are presently quoted on the stock exchange at £3 each; (2) Morgain plc would take over all assets and liabilities except the bank balance; (3) The value of the warehouse was to be taken as £27,000; (4) Fittings were only valued at £2,500 and the vans at £12,000; (5) Inspection revealed that of the stock, seeds costing £1,780 had deteriorated and were worthless; (6) Experience led Morgain plc to believe that £2,000 of the debts would not be recoverable; (7) A creditor for £620 had been omitted.

Required:
(a) Calculate the value of goodwill in the business as a result of the purchase.
(b) Show how much will appear in the share premium account of Morgain plc as a result of this purchase.
(c) Prepare a schedule of the assets and liabilities taken over by Morgain plc at the new values.
(d) Prepare a statement for Frank Graine showing the value to him of the business as a consequence of the offer.

4. Grevin plc made an issue of 1,000,000 ordinary shares for £1.25 each. The nominal value of these shares was £1.00. The terms of the issue required that the cash payments were made as follows:

19X4
1 March   On application (inclusive of 15p of the premium)   40p per share
1 April   On allotment   60p per share
1 May   Balance due per share.

The applications were received and the following analysis was made, ranked by the size of the individual application.

	Number of shares	
Number of applicants in class	Applied for by each applicant	Allotted to each applicant
125	5,000	4,000
40	10,000	5,000
20	100,000	10,000
1	400,000	100,000

In the terms of the issue it was stated that any amounts overpaid as a result of a smaller allotment than application would be retained in reduction of further sums due on shares allotted. All surplus monies were to be returned on 15 April 19X4.

Required:
(a) Prepare a cash statement showing the amount of monies received and repaid for each class of applicant and
(b) Record the above transactions in the books of the company.

5. Nurncor plc had an authorised share capital of 500,000 ordinary shares of £1 each. On 1 September 19X5, the company offered for sale 300,000

shares of £1 each at £2.50 per share. The terms were that £2.00 was payable on application and the balance on allotment. The premium was included in the application money.

By 15 October, the closing date for applications, there had been some 480,000 applicants. Applications for 80,000 of the shares were rejected and monies returned. All other applications were reduced proportionately. The terms of the issue had indicated that excess money on application would be applied to allotment.

Required:
(*a*) Show the cash account that would have resulted in the books of Nurncor plc.
(*b*) Record all the transactions in the issue of the shares upon conclusion of the event.

6. Set out below is the balance sheet of Bridgeton plc as at 31 March 19X5:

	£
7% Redeemable preference shares of £1 each—fully paid	195,000
1,350,000 Ordinary shares of 50p each—fully paid	675,000
Profit and loss account	138,000
	1,008,000
Sundry assets	1,038,000
Investments	52,500
Balance in hand at bank	90,000
	1,180,500
Less: Current liabilities	172,500
	1,008,000

The preference shares are redeemable at a premium of 7½p per share on the 1 April 19X5 and the company has decided to undertake this by the following:

(*a*) to sell the investments for the current market price of £45,000.
(*b*) to use the retained profits in the redemption sufficient to leave a balance on the profit and loss account of £30,000.
(*c*) to offer ordinary shares to the public at a premium of 12½p per share to make up any difference as required by the Companies Acts.
   Note: The authorised ordinary share capital was 2,500,000 shares of 50p each.

Required:
(a) Show the entries necessary to record the above scheme assuming that all was completed according to plan.
(b) Show the balance sheet after the redemption transactions were completed.

7. Clinkers Ltd had decided to exercise their right under the debenture trust deed to redeem the debentures any time before 19X5. The terms were that a premium of 5% was to be paid if the option was exercised. The company had further decided that the date at which they would exercise this was to be 1 January 19X1. The balance sheet as at 30 June 19X0, the financial year end, is set out overleaf.

	£000	£000
Share capital	Authorised	Issued
7% Preference shares of £1 each	300	300
Ordinary shares of £1 each	450	240
	750	540
Profit and loss account		150
		690
7½% Debentures (19X5)		90
		780
Fixed assets		660
Net current assets (after deducting bank overdraft of £60,000)		120
		780

In order to raise the necessary cash for the redemption, the company decided to issue the balance of its ordinary shares at a premium of 10p per share. 50p was demanded on application and the balance on allotment. All the shares were subscribed and the debentures were redeemed. The shares were offered on 1 September 19X0 and the redemption took place on the date decided.

Required:
(a) Show the entries necessary to record the above transactions.
(b) Assuming that the company had no trading profits or losses between 30 June 19X0 and 1 January 19X1, prepare a summarised balance sheet.

13 Company Accounts: Disclosure Requirements

Company accounts are prepared primarily providing information to persons who are not directly involved in operating the business. These include existing and potential shareholders; existing and potential holders of debentures and loan stock; employees; analyst advisers; customers, trade creditors and suppliers; the government and the public. The information contained in financial reports is used for two major purposes:

(a) Reporting on the stewardship of resources. Control over resources rests with professional managers acting on behalf of owners who expect to be provided with periodic reports by which managerial performance can be evaluated;

(b) Making decisions concerning the use of scarce resources. Investors must decide whether to buy, sell or retain their ownership interests in a business entity. Loan creditors must decide whether to make loans and in what amounts and on what terms. Government agencies decide whom to tax and whom to subsidise. Labour unions make decisions on bargaining tactics. Company accounts are a main source of information for parties making such decisions.

Legal requirements

The Companies Act 1985 lays down minimum statutory requirements for the preparation of the accounts of companies. Successive Acts have added to the level of disclosure required from companies. The impetus for this movement came from the changing economic and social conditions which brought demands for better protection for investors and creditors and a wider, social role for the financial reporting function.

The Companies Act 1985 requires every company to maintain adequate accounting records, and to prepare financial statements in respect of each accounting year, known as the accounting reference period. The following documents must be presented to the annual general meeting of shareholders:

(a) a profit and loss account,
(b) a balance sheet,
(c) a directors' report,
(d) an auditors' report.

The auditors' report is a formal attestation of the verification of the accounts kept by the company and of the financial reports extracted from these accounts. In effect, the auditors are required to attest that the provisions of the Companies Act 1985 have been met with regard to the obligation that 'every balance sheet shall give a true and fair view of the state of affairs of the company as at the end of its financial year, and every profit and loss account shall give a true and fair view of the profit or loss of the company for the financial year'. The true and fair view rule requires that the information contained in the financial statements is sufficient in quantity and quality to satisfy the reasonable expectations of users. By and large, these expectations will be determined by generally accepted accounting practices, and this implies that accounting standards will be observed. Consequently, financial statements which deviate from accounting standards without adequate justification or explanation may not be deemed to give a true and fair view in a court of law.

The financial affairs of a company become publicly known to the extent that it is required to lodge a copy of the financial statements made available to shareholders with the Registrar of Companies. Any member of the public may examine the financial statements filed with the Registrar of Companies upon payment of a fee. Small or medium-sized companies are exempted from the obligation to file with the Registrar of Companies the same financial statements as are presented to their shareholders, and need only file modified financial reports.

Large companies, defined as companies having a turnover of over £5.75 m, gross assets over £2.8 m and average weekly employees over 250, are required to file full financial statements with the Registrar of Companies. To be classified as a large company in terms of the foregoing conditions, it is sufficient that two out of the three conditions are fulfilled.

The 1985 Companies Act implements the EEC's Fourth Directive on the Harmonisation of Company Law, which sets out requirements relating to the preparation and publication of company accounts throughout the European Economic Community. The EEC Fourth Directive not only stipulated the form and the content of company financial statements, but also defined the fundamental accounting concepts upon which financial accounts should be based.

The Companies Act 1985 requires that the four fundamental accounting concepts contained in SSAP 2: *Disclosure of Accounting Policies* (see Chapter 6) are followed. These are:

(a) a presumption that the company is a going concern,
(b) consistency in accounting policies from year to year,
(c) that prudence has been exercised in accounting judgements, and

in particular that the profit and loss account includes only profits which have been realized at balance sheet date,

(d) that revenues and expenses have been accounted for on an accrual basis.

The Companies Act 1985 defines the term 'realised profits' as those realised in accordance with the best accounting practice at the time. SSAP 2 states that 'realised' means 'realised in the form either of cash or of other assets, the ultimate cash realisation of which can be assessed with reasonable certainty'. Consequently, profits on long-term contracts, such as those discussed in Chapter 8, normally would be regarded as realised profits.

Accounting bases have been developed for applying fundamental accounting concepts to financial transactions and accounting data. By their very nature, accounting bases are more diverse and numerous than fundamental concepts since they relate to the details of accounting practice. Significant matters for which different accounting bases exist and which may have a material effect on the computation of the profit or loss, as well as the representation of the financial status of the company, include bases for the depreciation of fixed assets and stocks and work in progress, discussed in Chapter 7 and 8 respectively.

For this reason, companies are also required to state which specific accounting bases have been adopted in the treatment of particular items. The selection of accounting bases constitutes the accounting policy of the company and must be stated in the notes appended to the accounts.

The balance sheet

The Companies Act 1985 provides two formats for the balance sheet presentation, one being vertical and the other being horizontal. Once a company has chosen which format it intends to adopt, it may not alter that choice without giving an explanation to shareholders in a note to the accounts.

It will be noted from the vertical format shown hereunder that the Companies Act 1985 provides for the classification of broad headings by a letter prefix. Major subdivisions are identified by roman numerals and minor subdivisions are referred to by arabic numerals. These prefixes do not have to be shown on the published balance sheet, but are used in the Companies Act to set out the manner in which accounting items have to be aggregated on the balance sheet, and the extent to which information has to be disclosed. In this regard, it should be noted particularly that any item shown on the format which is preceded by a letter or roman numeral prefix must be disclosed in a company's published balance sheet.

A company's balance sheet may include an item not otherwise shown on the proposed format, and indeed, may show any item in greater detail than is required by the Companies Act 1985. The following items may not, however, be treated as assets in any company's balance sheet:

(a) preliminary expenses,
(b) expenses and commissions relating to the issue of shares or debentures,
(c) research costs.

With regard to the arrangement of items, it is provided that items preceded by arabic numerals on the format may be amalgamated, if they are not material or if the amalgamation facilitates the assessment of the company's state of affairs. In the latter case, the individual items which have been amalgamated must be disclosed by note. Furthermore, these items may be shown in a different order or may have their title adapted where the special nature of the company's business requries such alteration.

The Companies Act 1985 also provides further general disclosure rules for establishing the comparability of accounting numbers. Thus, corresponding amounts for the previous year must be shown for all balance sheet items, and where, for example, because of a change of accounting policy the numbers are not comparable, adjustments must be made to the previous year to establish comparability. Equally, corresponding amounts must be given, and they must likewise be adjusted if necessary, in respect of every item stated in the notes to the balance sheet (other than amounts relating to the movements on fixed assets, reserves and provisions). Full amounts must be disclosed, and there should be no set off of items representing assets against items representing liabilities.

With regard to particular items disclosed on the balance sheet format, the Companies Act 1985 introduces a number of requirements. Some of these are listed hereunder.

(a) Fixed assets

Subject to any provision for depreciation or diminution in value, fixed assets are to be shown at the purchase price or production cost, as the case may be. Fixed assets with limited useful economic life must be depreciated.

Companies Act 1985: Format for Vertical Balance Sheet

			£	£	£
A.	**Called up share capital not paid***				X
B.	**Fixed assets**				
	I	*Intangible assets*			
		1 Development costs	X		
		2 Concessions, patents, licences, trade marks and similar rights and assets	X		
		3 Goodwill	X		
		4 Payments on account	X		
				X	
	II	*Tangible assets*			
		1 Land and buildings	X		
		2 Plant and machinery	X		
		3 Fixtures, fittings, tools and equipment	X		
		4 Payments on account and assets in course of construction	X	X	
	III	*Investments*			
		1 Shares in group companies	X		
		2 Loans to group companies	X		
		3 Shares in related companies	X		
		4 Loans to related companies	X		
		5 Other investments other than loans	X		
		6 Other loans	X		
		7 Own shares	X		
				X	
					X
C.	**Current assets**				
	I	**Stocks**			
		1 Raw materials and consumables	X		
		2 Work in progress	X		
		3 Finished goods and goods for resale	X		
		4 Payments on account	X		
				X	
	II	*Debtors*			
		1 Trade debtors	X		
		2 Amounts owed by group companies	X		
		3 Amounts owed by related companies	X		
		4 Other debtors	X		
		5 Called up share capital not paid*	X		
		6 Prepayments and accrued income*	X		
				X	

* These items may be shown in either of the positions indicated.

			£	£	£
III	*Investments*				
	1	Shares in group companies	X		
	2	Own shares	X		
	3	Other investments	X		
				X	
IV	*Cash at bank and in hand*			X	
				X	
D.	**Prepayments and accrued income***			X	
E.	**Creditors: amounts falling due**				
	within one year				
	1	Debenture loans	X		
	2	Bank loans and overdrafts	X		
	3	Payment received on account	X		
	4	Trade creditors	X		
	5	Bills of exchange payable	X		
	6	Amounts owed to group companies	X		
	7	Amounts owed to related companies	X		
	8	Other creditors including taxation and social security	X		
	9	Accruals and deferred income*	X		
				(X)	
F.	**Net current assets (liabilities)**				X
G.	**Total assets less current liabilities**				X
H.	**Creditors: amounts falling due after**				
	more than one year				
	1	Debenture loans	X		
	2	Bank loans and overdrafts	X		
	3	Payments received on account	X		
	4	Trade creditors	X		
	5	Bills of exchange payable	X		
	6	Amounts owed to group companies	X		
	7	Amounts owed to related companies	X		
	8	Other creditors including taxation and social security	X		
	9	Accruals and deferred income*	X	X	
I.	**Provisions for liabilities and charges**				
	1	Pensions and similar obligations	X		
	2	Taxation, including deferred taxation	X		
	3	Other provisions	X	X	

* These items may be shown in either of the positions indicated.

		£	£	£
J.	**Accruals and deferred income***		X	X
				X

K. Capital and reserves

			£	£
I	Called up share capital			X
II	Share premium account			X
III	Revaluation reserve			X
IV	Other reserves:			
	1 Capital redemption reserve		X	
	2 Reserve for own shares		X	
	3 Reserves provided for by the articles of association		X	X
	4 Other reserves		X	
V	Profit and loss account			X
				£X

* These items may be shown in either of the positions indicated.

A provision for the diminution in value of a fixed asset investment may be made, and must be made in respect of any fixed asset where the reduction in value is expected to be permanent. The fixed assets so reduced are shown at their reduced amount on the balance sheet, and the provision for reduction in value disclosed in a note to the accounts or shown on the profit and loss account.

Whilst maintaining historic cost valuations as the normal basis for balance sheet purposes, the Companies Act 1985 allows alternative valuation bases provided that the items affected and the basis of valuation is shown in a note to the accounts. This permits companies to revalue assets or to use current cost valuations. The amount of profit or loss arising from the adoption of an alternative accounting valuation must be credited, or debited as the case may be, to the revaluation reserve.

The Companies Act 1985 requires the following information to be disclosed in respect of each fixed asset item:

(a) the aggregate purchase price, production cost or alternative accounting valuation at the beginning and end of the accounting reference period, showing the effect of acquisitions, disposals or transfers or any revaluation during this period,

(b) the cumulative provision for depreciation, or diminution in value as at the beginning and end of the accounting reference period, showing the annual provision for depreciation, any adjustment to that provision arising from the disposal of any asset and any other adjustment to the provision.

Illustration: The requirements of the Companies Act 1985 would be satisfied by the following presentation:

	Freehold land and buildings £000	Plant and machinery £000	Total £000
Cost:			
At 1 January	1,000	200	1,200
Additions	30	40	70
Disposals	—	(20)	(20)
At 31 December	1,030	220	1,250
Accumulated depreciation:			
At 1 January	200	50	250
Depreciation for the year	20	24	44
Disposals	—	(19)	(19)
At 31 December	220	55	275
Net book value:			
At 1 January	800	150	950
At 31 December	810	165	975

With regard to intangible assets, the Companies Act 1985 makes the following provisions:

Development costs (but not research costs) may be capitalised, but only in 'special circumstances'. In practice, this treatment must be read in conjunction with SSAP 13: *Accounting for Research and Development* discussed in Chapter 7, which defines the special circumstances that must exist before development costs may be capitalised. Where development costs are capitalised and shown on the balance sheet, the Companies Act 1985 requires that notes must be appended disclosing (a) the period over which the costs are being written off and (b) the reason for capitalising the development costs.

Concessions, patents, licences, trade marks, etc. may be shown on the balance sheet only if they have been acquired by purchase and are not required to be shown under goodwill, or if they were created by the company itself.

Goodwill may be shown as an asset on the balance sheet only if it was acquired by purchase. In such a case, it must be written off over a period that does not exceed its useful economic life.

(b) Investments

Investments must be classified as under:

(1) Shares held in group companies, where the company is a member company in a group of companies. Group companies exist where

a company (called a holding company) controls another company (called a subsidiary company).
(2) Loans to group companies.
(3) Shares in related companies, where the company is related to another company in which the relationship involves at least a 20% shareholding by one company in another.
(4) Loans to related companies.
(5) Other investments other than loans, for example, shares in companies which are neither group nor related companies.
(6) Other loans.
(7) Own shares, where—as allowed by the Companies Act 1985—the company is allowed to purchase its own shares.

The valuation of investments poses particular problems, where there is not a stock exchange quotation for shares or debentures. The Companies Act 1985 does not require unquoted investments to be valued, and the requirements would be satisfied by the conventional historic cost of such investments. Where investments are listed on a recognised Stock Exchange, the aggregate market value must be disclosed, if this value differs from the value at which they are stated on the balance sheet.

(c) Current assets

The value to be placed on any current asset is the lower of the purchase price or production cost and the net realisable value. With regard to stocks, the Companies Act 1985 requires stocks to be subdivided into the following categories:

(1) Raw materials and consumables.
(2) Work in progress.
(3) Finished goods and goods for resale.
(4) Payments on account.

Stocks may be valued using any of the recognised valuation methods, namely, FIFO (first in first out), LIFO (last in first out), or weighted average cost. As noted in Chapter 8, SSAP 9: *Stocks and Work in Progress* (1975) does not permit the use of LIFO. Any material difference between the value of the stock shown on the balance sheet and its replacement cost, or if more appropriate the most recent purchase price, must be disclosed for each category of stocks.

As regards debtors, the Companies Act 1985 requires amounts falling due for more than a year to be shown separately for each item included under debtors. This would include amounts owing in respect of share capital not paid as well as amounts owing by group companies.

(d) Called up share capital

The share capital issued and the amount called up must be shown separately. Where the company has issued shares of different classes, the number and aggregate nominal value of each class must be given by note to the balance sheet. Where redeemable shares have been issued, the following information must be given:

(1) the earliest and latest dates on which the company has power to redeem the shares,
(2) whether those shares must be redeemed in any event or are liable to be reeemed at the option of the company,
(3) whether any (and if so, what) premium is payable on redemption.

Moreover, if there has been an issue of shares during the financial year, the following information must be given:

(1) the reason for the issue,
(2) the class of shares issued,
(3) in respect of each class of shares issued, the number issued, their aggregate nominal value and the consideration received by the company.

(e) Reserves

The Companies Act 1985 does not give a general definition of a 'reserve', but it is generally accepted that the term 'reserve' does not include the following:

(1) a provision for depreciation, renewal or diminution in value of assets,
(2) a provision for a known liability,
(3) a provision for undue fluctuations in charges for taxation.

Any share premium account and any revaluation reserve must be shown separately under 'Reserves', and any other reserve built up by the company must be shown under an appropriate heading. The profit and loss account balance must be shown separately.

In the event that there has been any transfer to or from the reserves shown as separate items during the accounting period, there must be shown by way of note to the balance sheet the following information:

(1) the amount of reserves at the beginning of the year,

(2) the amounts transferred either in or out, and the source and application of such amounts,

(3) the amount of reserves at the end of the year.

(f) Other disclosure requirements

Among other disclosure requirements to be noted are the following:

(1) there must be disclosed in a note to the accounts the accounting policies used by the company in determining the amounts shown as items in these accounts,

(2) the basis of translation of any item originally denominated in foreign currencies and translated into sterling must be shown.

The modified balance sheet

A small-sized company, defined as one which satisfies at least two of the following three conditions, may submit a modified balance sheet (shown below) to the Registrar of Companies. The conditions are that it

(1) has a turnover up to £1.4 million,

(2) has gross assets up to £0.7 million,

(3) has average employees per week up to 50 employees.

A medium-sized company, defined as one which satisfies at least two of the following three conditions, may also submit a modified balance sheet to the Registrar of Companies. In this case the conditions are that it

(1) has a turnover up to £5.75 million,

(2) has gross assets up ot £2.8 million,

(3) has average employees per week up to 250 employees.

However, if such a company adopts the modified balance sheet format, the details required by the full balance sheet format be disclosed in notes to the accounts.

It should be noted that a large company may also adopt the modified balance sheet format, and in such a case, the notes to the accounts must disclose all the details required by the full balance sheet format.

The right to submit a modified balance sheet relates only to the accounts which must be delivered to the Registrar of Companies. Small- and medium-sized companies are obliged to prepare full sets of accounts for presentation to their shareholders.

PUBLISHED ACCOUNTS: FORMAT FOR MODIFIED BALANCE SHEET

		£	£
A.	**Called up share capital not paid**		X
B.	**Fixed assets**		
	I Intangible assets	X	
	II Tangible assets	X	
	III Investments	X	
			X
C.	**Current assets**		
	I Stocks	X	
	II Debtors	X	
	III Investments	X	
	IV Cash at bank and in hand	X	
		X	
D.	**Accruals and deferred income**	X	
		X	
E.	**Creditors:** Amounts becoming due and payable within one year	(X)	
F.	**Net current assets (liabilities)**		X
G.	**Total assets less current liabilities**		X
H.	**Creditors:** Amounts becoming due and payable after more than one year	X	
I.	**Provisions for liabilities and charges**	X	
J.	**Accruals and deferred income**	X	
			(X)
			£X
K.	**Capital and reserves**		
	I Called up share capital		X
	II Share premium account		X
	III Revaluation reserve		X
	IV Other reserves		X
	V Profit and loss account		X
			£X

The profit and loss account

The Companies Act 1985 provides two horizontal and two vertical formats for the presentation of the profit and loss account. Essentially, the two formats may be distinguished by the way in which costs are analysed. Format 1 analyses costs by type of operation, while format 2 analyses costs by type of expenditure. The vertical formats of these two different types of analyses are given below.

Format 1: Operational Format	£	£
1 Turnover		X
2 Cost of sales		(X)
3 Gross profit (or loss)		X̄
4 Distribution costs	X	
5 Administrative expenses	X	
		(X)
		X̄
6 Other operating income		X
		X̄
7 Income from shares in group companies	X	
8 Income from shares in related companies	X	
9 Income from other fixed asset investments	X	
10 Other interest receivable and similar income	X	
		X
		X̄
11 Amounts written off investments	X	
12 Interest payable and similar charges	X	
		(X)
Profit on ordinary activities		X̄
13 Tax on profit (or loss) on ordinary activities		(X)
14 Profit (or loss) on ordinary activities after taxation		X̄
15 Extraordinary income	X	
16 Extraordinary charges	(X)	
17 Extraordinary profit (or loss)	X̄	
18 Tax on extraordinary profit (or loss)	(X)	
		X
		X̄
19 Other taxes not shown under the above items		(X)
20 Profit (or loss) for the financial year		£X̄

	£
Profit (or loss) for the financial year	X
Dividends paid and proposed	(X)
Transfers to (from) reserves	(X)
Retained profit (or loss) for the financial year	£X̄

Format 2: Type of Expenditure Format

	£	£	£
1 Turnover			X
2 Change in stocks of finished goods and work in progress			X
3 Own work capitalised			X
4 Other operating income			X
			X̄
5 (a) Raw materials and consumables	X		
(b) Other external charges	X		
		X	
6 Staff costs:			
(a) Wages and salaries	X		
(b) Social security costs	X		
(c) Other pension costs	X		
		X	
7 (a) Depreciation and other amounts written off tangible and intangible fixed assets	X		
(b) Exceptional amounts written off current assets	X		
		X	
8 Other operating charges		X	
			(X)
			X̄
9 Income from shares in group companies		X	
10 Income from shares in related companies		X	
11 Income from other fixed assets investments		X	
12 Other interest receivable and similar income		X	X
			X̄
13 Amounts written off investments		X	
14 Interest payable and similar charges		X	
			(X)
			X̄
Profit on ordinary activities			X̄
15 Tax on profit (or loss) on ordinary activities			(X)
16 Profit (or loss) on ordinary activities after taxation			X̄
17 Extraordinary income		X	
18 Extraordinary charges		(X)	
19 Extraordinary profit (or loss)		X̄	
20 Tax on extraordinary profit (or loss)		(X)	
			X
			X̄
21 Other taxes not shown under the above items			(X)
22 Profit (or loss) for the financial year			£X̄

	£
Profit (or loss) for the financial year	X
Dividends paid and proposed	(X)
Transfers to (from) reserves	(X)
Retained profit (or loss) for the financial year	£X̄

A company must adhere to the format it has chosen in subsequent accounting years, unless in the opinion of the board of directors there are special reasons for a change. Details of any decision to change the format must be given in the note to the accounts.

The profit and loss account must be prepared in the order and under the headings given in the formats. Each item in the format is prefixed by an arabic number, which need not be shown in the published accounts. It is permissible to amalgamate certain items if the amount involved is not material, or if such an amalgamation facilitates the assessment of the company's affairs. It is also possible to adapt the title or to rearrange the position of certain items where the special nature of the company's business requires such alteration.

As in the case of the balance sheet, the corresponding previous years' figures must be shown, and notes to the profit and loss account must be provided to explain and add to the information disclosed. Thus, if there has been a change in accounting policy affecting one of the items on the profit and loss account, a note must be given allowing an appropriate comparison with the previous year's figure.

(a) Turnover

The turnover means any amount derived by the company from the provision of goods and service in the context of its ordinary activities. The term 'turnover' replaces the term 'sales' previously used. It includes all receipts from these activities after deduction of:

(1) trade discounts, value added tax,
(2) any other taxes on such receipts.

Additionally, there must be disclosed in notes to the accounts the following information relating to the analysis of the turnover:

(1) where the company carries on two or more classes of business which differ substantially from each other, the amount of the turnover attributable to each class,
(2) where the company has traded in different 'markets' (defined as geographical boundaries), the amount of the turnover attributable to each market must be stated.

(b) Expenditure

In calculating the cost of sales, distribution and administrative expenses (format 1), the following must be included:

(1) provisions for depreciation or diminution in value of assets. Amounts written off investments must be shown separately,
(2) directors' and employees' emoluments. When using format 2, the emoluments of employees and executive directors must be shown under 'staff' costs, and directors' fees may be shown under

'other operating charges'. Additionally, notes to the accounts must show the following information:

—in respect of directors, distinguishing between directors' fees and directors' salaries:

(a) aggregate emoluments, including fees and percentages, expenses allowances charged to United Kingdom tax, pension contributions paid in respect of them and benefits in kind,

(b) aggregate of directors' and past directors' pensions, excluding pensions from schemes maintained by contributions,

(c) aggregate of compensation paid to directors or past directors for loss of office,

(d) prior year adjustments arising from expense allowances being disallowed for tax purposes, or a director's retaining emoluments for which he was previously accountable.

—in respect of employees:

(a) the number of employees (other than directors and persons working outside the United Kingdom), whose emoluments fall in each bracket of a scale in multiples of £5,000 commencing at £30,000. These thresholds were fixed as at 31 December 1982, and are likely to be revised every two or three years.

(b) the average number of employees, calculated by dividing up the annual number of employees by the number of weeks in the accounting year. Where format 1 is used, there must be shown in respect of all employees taken into account in determining the relevant annual numbers:

—wages and salaries paid to employees,

—social security costs (being contributions by the company towards any state social security or pension scheme),

—other pensions costs (being contributions to company pension schemes and pensions paid).

(c) the average number of employees for each category of employees, such category being defined by the directors having regard to the manner in which the company's activities are organised.

(3) sums payable for the hire of plant and machinery, the sums so payable being shown in the notes to the accounts,

(4) auditors' renumeration, the total payable being shown in the notes to the accounts,

(5) sums paid in respect of any exceptional transactions, being defined as transactions falling outside the ordinary activities of the company.

(c) Interest payable and similar charges

There must be shown in the notes to the accounts information relating to the interest charged in respect of the following:

(1) bank loans and overdrafts, and other loans made to the company which are:
either repayable otherwise than by instalment and fall due for repayment within five years from the end of the accounting year, or are repayable by instalment, the last of which falls due for payment before the end of that period,
(2) loans of any other kind made to the company, i.e. those repayable wholly or in part after more than five years.

(d) Extraordinary items, exceptional items and prior year adjustments

The required formats for the presentation of the profit and loss account provide headings for extraordinary income, extraordinary charges and tax on extraordinary profit or loss. The Companies Act 1985 does not define extraordinary items. They are interpreted in the light of SSAP 6: *Extraordinary Items and Prior Year Adjustments* (1974) as 'those items which derive from events or transactions outside the ordinary activities of the business and which are both material and expected not to recur frequently or regularly. They do not include items which, though exceptional on account of size or incidence, derive from the ordinary activities of the business'. SSAP 6 defines prior year adjustments as 'those material adjustments applicable to prior years arising from changes in accounting policies and from the correction of fundamental errors. They do not include the normal recurring corrections and adjustments of accounting estimates made in prior years. It should be noted that the definition of extraordinary items includes and defines 'exceptional items'. Details of extraordinary items will be given in notes to the accounts. Exceptional items must be included in the calculation of profit or loss on ordinary activities before taxation, and details given in a note relating to the profit and loss items in which they are included.

Where prior year adjustments, as defined in SSAP 6, have occurred, resulting in any material amount being included in the profit and loss account, separate disclosure of their effect must be shown. The relevant prior year adjustments are those arising from changes in accounting policies or the correction of some fundamental mistake. Such adjustments may de dealt with through reserves.

(e) Taxation

The requirements of the Companies Act 1985 are twofold. First, the profit and loss account must disclose the net profit or loss on ordinary activities before taxation, and the taxation charge on those activities should then be deducted to give the net profit or loss on ordinary activities after taxation. Second, the notes to the accounts must contain the following additional information:

(1) the amount of the charge for United Kingdom corporation tax,
(2) if that amount would have been greater but for double taxation relief, the amount it would have been but for such relief,
(3) the amount of the charge for United Kingdom income tax,
(4) the amount of the charge for taxation imposed outside the United Kingdom profits, income and (so far as charged on revenue) capital gains.

These notes must also specify the base on which the charge to United Kingdom corporation tax and income tax is calculated, and give details of any circumstances affecting the liability to corporation tax, income tax and capital gains in the current and succeeding years. The manner in which this liability is determined is discussed in Chapter 14.

Example

Startop plc has adopted Format 1 of the Companies Act 1985 for preparing both the balances sheet and the profit and loss account for the year ended 31 December 19X4. Accordingly, the information required to be disclosed to shareholders is as follows:

	*Notes	19X4 £000	19X4 £000	19X3 £000
The Startop Company Limited				
Profit and loss account for the year ended 31 December 19X4				
Turnover	2		1,340	1,108
Cost of sales			804	676
Gross profit			536	432
Distribution costs	78		64	
Administrative expenses	214		292 203	267
Operating profit	3		244	165
Interest payable	5		54	41
Profit on ordinary activities before taxation			190	124
Tax on profit on ordinary activities	6		76	58
Profit on ordinary activities after taxation			114	66
Extraordinary loss	7	34		
Tax on extraordinary loss		(17)	17	—
Profit for the financial year			97	66
Dividends paid and proposed	8		32	28
Amount set aside to reserves			65	38

* The notes are not produced here but the numbers are given to indicate how the supplementary information required is provided

	Notes	19X4 £000	19X4 £000	19X3 £000	19X3 £000
The Startop Company Limited					
Balance sheet at 31 December 19X4					
Fixed assets					
Intangible assets	9		31		31
Tangible assets	10		432		441
			463		472
Current assets					
Stocks	11	214		188	
Debtors	12	282		206	
Cash at bank		103		74	
		599		468	
Creditors					
Amounts falling due within one year	13	252		250	
Net current assets			347		218
Total assets *less* Current liabilities			810		690
Creditors amounts falling due after one year					
Debenture loan	14		50		50
			760		640
Provision for liabilities and charges					
Deferred taxation	15		22		22
			738		618
Capital and reserves					
Called up share capital	16		400		350
Share premium account			25		20
Profit and loss account			313		248
			738		618

The directors' report

There is a general requirement that the directors' report should contain a fair review of (i) the development of the business of the company during the year and (ii) its position at the end of the year. The directors' report should deal with the following matters in particular:

(a) future developments, giving an indication of likely future developments in the business,

(b) research and development, giving an indication of activities in this area,

(c) significant changes in fixed assets,

(d) names of directors who have served at any time during the year,
(e) directors' interests in contracts,
(f) directors' interests in the shares or debentures of the company,
(g) post balance sheet events, particulars of important events affecting the company which have occurred since the end of the year,
(h) political and charitable contributions,
(i) a statement of the company's policy on the employment, training and career development of disabled persons,
(j) any other matter which is material to the shareholders' appreciation of the company's state of affairs.

Questions

1. Although the trial balance of BLM Limited appears to be correct because the totals are equal, it contains several errors. You are required to draw up the trial balance correctly.

Trial balance at 30 June 19X6	£	£
Ordinary share capital		100,000
Preliminary expenses	10,000	
Share premium account	3,000	
General reserve		40,000
Goodwill		6,000
Retained profit, at 1 July 19X5		700
Deferred taxation		17,000
10% Debentures (secured on fixed assets)		20,000
Bank overdraft	4,000	
Sundry creditors		30,000
Fixed assets, at cost	100,000	
Depreciation for the year		10,000
Provision for depreciation of fixed assets	30,000	
Provision for bad debts	1,600	
Stock of materials	29,000	
Work-in-progress	7,000	
Stock of finished products	71,000	
Sundry debtors	51,000	
Trade investment	12,000	
Sales		360,000
Purchases	149,000	
Wages and salaries	45,000	
Rent, rates and insurance	33,000	
Discount received	2,900	
Returns outwards	1,400	
Income from investments	800	
Carriage inwards		5,000
Bad debts written off	600	
Discount allowed		7,100
Selling expenses	37,000	
Rent received	1,000	
Returns inwards		5,600
Dividends paid	15,000	

	£	£
Carriage outwards		11,000
Office expenses	5,000	
Lighting and heating	3,100	
	£612,400	£612,400

(Institute of Cost and Management Accountants)

2. Shortly after the end of the accounting year on 30 November 19X9, the following relevant information was obtained from the records of Greystone Limited:

	£
Capital: Authorised	35,000
Issued and fully paid—Ordinary shares of £1 each	25,000
8% Redeemable preference shares of £1 each	6,000
Loan capital—9% Debentures	8,000
Retained earnings at 30 November 19X8	19,900
Land and buildings:	
at 30 November 19X9: at cost	20,000
at 30 November 19X8: provision for depreciation	6,000
Fixtures and fittings:	
at 30 November 19X9: at cost	40,000
at 30 November 19X8: provision for depreciation	8,000
Sales	50,600
Stock in trade—at 30 November 19X8	9,000
Purchases	30,500
Establishment expenses	2,700
Administrative expenses	6,000
Discounts allowed	600
Discounts received	400
Trade debtors	12,900
Provision for doubtful debts	400
Trade creditors	5,000
Balance in hand at bank	7,600

Additional information:
(1) Depreciation is provided at the following annual rates on the cost of fixed assets held at the relevant accounting year end:

Land and buildings	$2\frac{1}{2}$%
Fixtures and fittings	10%

(2) It is now estimated that 5% of the amount due from trade debtors at 30 November 19X9, will never be paid; it is proposed that the provision for doubtful debts should be adjusted accordingly.

(3) The interest on the debentures for the year ended 30 November 19X9, has been paid and recorded correctly in the cash book, but it was debited to various personal accounts in the debtors ledger. In every case, the debenture interest paid was the only entry in the personal account.

(4) The following information is given concerning the value of the company's stock in trade at 30 November 19X9:

	£
At net realisable value it was	13,800
At cost to the company it was	13,000
At selling price it was	19,000

(5) During the year under review, certain fixtures and fittings, which had cost £2,000 and whose written down value at 30 November 19X8, was £1,600, were sold for £600. The only entry concerning the sale of these fixtures and fittings relate to the sale proceeds which had been paid into the company's bank account and credited to sales.

(6) the directors propose to pay the dividend on the preference shares and a dividend on the ordinary shares of 10% for the year ended 30 November 19X9.

Note: Ignore A.C.T.

Required:

(a) The trading and profit and loss account for the year ended 30 November 19X9, and a balance sheet as at that date.

(b) Explain briefly the reasons determining your choice of stock valuation at 30 November 19X9.

(Association of Certified Accountants)

3. The following balances were extracted from the books of Homer Traders Limited at 31 March 19X9:

	£
Ordinary shares of £1 each, fully paid	30,000
8% Preference shares of £1 each, fully paid	5,000
Shares premium account	4,000
6% Loan stock	5,000
Trade creditors	7,400
Trade debtors	16,500
Sales	240,000
Purchases	211,000
Discounts allowed	250
Discounts received	650
Freehold buildings:	
At cost	25,000
Provision for depreciation	2,500
Fixtures and fittings:	
At cost	32,000
Provision for depreciation	12,800
Stock at 1 April 19X8	21,000
Returns outwards	4,000
Establishment expenses	6,500
Administration expenses	2,800
Selling and distribution expenses	8,350
Bad debts written off	200
Provision for doubtful debts	900
Profit and loss account at 1 April 19X8	18,100
Goodwill	8,000
Bank overdraft	1,250

Additional information:

(1) Depreciation is provided annually on the cost of fixed assets held at the end of the financial year at the following rates:

Freehold buildings	2%
Fixtures and fittings	10%

(2) The trade debtors balance included £500 due from K. Smythe who has now been declared bankrupt. In the circumstances, it has been decided

to write the debt off as a bad debt.

(3) The provision for doubtful debts at 31 March 19X9, is to be 5% of trade debtors at that date, after writing off bad debts.

(4) Establishment expenses prepaid at 31 March 19X9 amounted to £200.

(5) Administration expenses accrued due at 31 March 19X9 amounted to £350.

(6) The company paid the interest on the loan stock for the year ended 31 March 19X9, on 30 April 19X9.

(7) Gross profit is at the rate of $16\frac{2}{3}$% of sales.

(8) The company's directors propose that the preference share dividend be paid, and a dividend of 10% on the ordinary shares be paid.

Required:

(a) The trading and profit and loss account for the year ended 31 March 19X9 of Homer Traders Limited and a balance sheet at that date.

(b) Give reasons why a company would not wish to distribute all its profits to its shareholders.

Note: Ignore A.C.T.

(Association of Certified Accountants)

4. The following balances have been extracted from the books of the Nemesis Company Limited as at 30 September 19X7:

	£
Creditors	6,300
Sales	80,000
Land at cost	18,000
Buildings at cost	38,000
Furniture and fittings at cost	22,000
Bank (credit balance)	6,000
Depreciation—buildings	6,000
—furniture and fittings	10,000
Discounts received	1,764
Unappropriated profit at 1 October 19X6	2,000
Provision for doubtful debts	816
Goodwill	16,400
Cash in hand	232
Stock at 1 October 19X6	14,248
Interim dividend on preference shares	600
Rates	2,124
Wages and salaries	8,000
Insurance	1,896
Returns inward	372
General expenses	436
Debtors	12,640
Purchases	43,856
Debenture interest	400
Bad debts	676
5% Debentures	16,000
6% £1 Preference shares	20,000
£1 Ordinary shares	20,000

	£
General reserve	10,000
Share premium	1,000

Additional information:

(1) Stock on hand at 30 September 19X7 was £15,546.

(2) Insurance paid in advance—£100.

(3) Wages owing—£280.

(4) Depreciation is to be provided at 10% on cost of buildings, and at 20% on the written down value of furniture and fittings.

(5) Provision for doubtful debts is to be reduced to 5% of debtors.

(6) Debenture interest outstanding of £400.

(7) The directors propose to pay a 5% ordinary dividend and the final preference dividend, and to transfer £8,000 to general reserve.

Required:

Prepare the trading and profit and loss account for the period ended 30 September 19X7 and a balance sheet as at that date.

(Association of Certified Accountants)

14 Introduction to the Treatment of Taxation in Accounting

Taxation is a very important aspect of the accountant's work, and has become a specialist function in corporate planning activity. This is because of the incidence of taxation on business profits, requiring that attention be given to ensuring that no more tax should be paid than is required under law.

The business firm is exposed to three main forms of taxation:

(a) Value added tax (VAT) which applies to goods and services which the firm acquires and to those that it sells.
(b) Income tax which applies to the profits of business organised as sole traders and partnerships.
(c) Corporation tax which applies to the profits of corporate bodies.

The accounting responsibility is to ensure that the appropriate amount of taxation is provided for, and to devise appropriate accounting procedures to record transactions with the responsible government departments.

The various forms of taxation applying to business profits have their own rules for determining the liability to tax. These rules are initially contained in the tax laws approved by Parliament. Such rules are general in nature, and responsibility for applying them rests with the Inland Revenue, as regards income and corporation tax, and with the Customs and Excise, as regards value added tax. The accountant needs to be familiar with the tax legislation approved by Parliament, as a matter of basic knowledge in dealing with the Inland Revenue and the Customs and Excise.

Two additional sources of knowledge are contained in the Guidelines and Directives issued by the Board of Inland Revenue and the Customs and Excise Board to their officers. These rules provide an official interpretation of the legislation in particular matters with procedures to be applied in respect thereof. It is important for the accountant to know how Government officials are required to apply the law.

This chapter is concerned with the accounting responsibility of devising appropriate procedures for creating the required provisions for taxation and for recording transactions with the tax authorities.

Value added tax

The concept of the value added as a basis of levying taxes on business firms was introduced into the United Kingdom as a consequence of entry into the Common Market. The value added is an economic concept of the output of a business firm, which is stated as the value which enterprise activity has added to a product or service in the course of processing inputs of factors of production.

The value added is computed by deducting from the value realised by the sale of goods and services the cost of goods and services acquired by the firm. Example 1 below shows the computation of value added.

Example 1: Computation of value added
Manufacture and sale of a briefcase

	Selling price £	Value added £
From rancher—for hide	10	10
From tanner and processor	12	2
From manufacturer	20	8
From leather goods wholesaler	23	3
From retail shop	30	7
		30

The rate(s) of value added tax is determined annually by Parliament. For example, the basic VAT rate applicable for the year 1985 was 15% on goods and services, with certain exemptions.

The appropriate rate of value added tax is added by the firm to the invoiced cost of goods and services sold. Responsibility for collecting the VAT rests on the firm, which has to account to the Customs and Excise on a quarterly basis. This involves accounting procedures for:

(a) recording transactions attracting VAT,
(b) recording the amount of VAT collected,
(c) recording payments made to the Customs and Excise of VAT collected.

Example 2
During the quarter ended 31 March 19X5, Nagger & Co. Ltd sold goods to the value of £300,000, which were subject to VAT at a rate of 15%. Sales invoices for the quarter showed the following:

Sales net of VAT	£300,000
VAT at 15%	£45,000
Total invoiced	£345,000

Payment of the VAT at the due date to the Customs and Excise was eventually made.

The accounting entries are as follows:

	£	£
Dr Debtors ledger accounts with sales as invoiced	345,000	
Cr Sales account with sales as invoiced		345,000

Since the firm merely acts as collecting agents for VAT, it would be incorrect to show in the profit and loss account the gross sales invoiced, as this would falsify the sales revenues accruing to the firm. Accordingly, it is necessary to transfer from the sales account the VAT collected, and to record the VAT as accruing to the Customs and Excise.

The entries are as follows:

	£	£
Dr Sales account with the VAT collected	45,000	
Cr Customs and Excise account with VAT collected		45,000

On payment of the VAT collected to the Customs and Excise, the entries are:

	£	£
Dr Customs and Excise account with VAT paid	45,000	
Cr Cash with the VAT paid		45,000

An important feature of the VAT system, noted earlier, is that the firm is taxed only on the value added. Consequently, where the firm has acquired goods and services on which it has itself paid VAT, it is allowed to set off against the VAT payable to the Customs and Excise, the VAT which it has paid itself on the goods and services acquired.

Accordingly, the firm has to set up accounting procedures to record the VAT charged on invoices which it has received and paid. This involves establishing procedures for:

(a) recording transactions on which VAT is payable,
(b) recording the VAT paid,
(c) debiting against the Customs and Excise the VAT which has been included on the invoices charged to the firm.

Example 3
During the quarter ending 31 March 19X5, Nagger and Co. Ltd had paid the following invoices on which VAT at the rate of 15% had been included:

		£	£	£
Purchases	25,000 plus VAT at 15%	(3,750) =	28,750	
Telephone	1,000 plus VAT at 15%	(150) =	1,150	
Advertising	1,500 plus VAT at 15%	(225) =	1,725	

The accounting entries are:

		£	£
Dr	Purchases account with gross amount paid	28,750	
Dr	Telephone account with gross amount paid	1,150	
Dr	Advertising account with gross amount paid	1,725	
Cr	Cash book with gross amount paid		31,625

Since the firm is entitled to a credit for the VAT which it has paid under invoice, it is necessary to eliminate the VAT included on these invoices from the amounts, which in due course will be transferred to the profit and loss account. The VAT is therefore transferred from these accounts to the Customs and Excise account as follows:

		£	£
Dr	Customs and Excise account with VAT paid on invoices	4,125	
Cr	Purchases account with VAT paid		3,750
Cr	Telephone account with VAT paid		150
Cr	Advertising account with VAT paid		225

As a result of these various transactions, the balance appearing on the Customs and Excise account at 31 March 19X5, the date on which the quarter ended, is as follows (taking account of the amount of VAT charged on sales per Example 1).

Customs and Excise account

	£		£
Purchases account	3,750	Sales account	45,000
Telephone account	150		
Advertising account	225		
Balance c/d	40,875		
	45,000		45,000
		Balance b/d	40,875

The net amount payable to the Customs and Excise is, therefore, £40,875. The official VAT forms which the firm has to complete and return to the Customs and Excise will summarise the information contained in the accounting records. These are subject to inspection by Customs and Excise from time to time.

Income tax

The income derived by individuals from business activities is subjected to income tax. Therefore, the business profits of individuals trading as sole traders or in partnerships are assessed to income tax.

In the case of the sole trader having business profits, the formal statement of his tax liability for any particular fiscal year will be stated in the Income Tax Assessment sent to him by the Inland Revenue authorities. No provision for tax on business profits is normally included in the financial statements of the business. The net profit is credited to his capital account, and the tax which he has to pay will be treated as drawings, if paid out of the business. The accounting entries will be as follows:

Dr   Drawings account with tax paid
Cr   Cash with tax paid

In the case of a partnership, the treatment of taxation in the business account is similar. The accountant will prepare a computation of taxable profits for the partnership, and will apportion the taxable profits to the partners on the basis of their respective profit and loss sharing ratios.

Should individual partners wish the partnership to pay income tax on their behalf, this will be effected by debiting their drawings accounts as follows:

Dr   Drawings of individual partner ⎫
Cr   Cash   ⎬ with tax paid
                                    ⎭

Corporation tax

Four significant features characterise the different treatment of taxation in company accounts.

First, unlike sole traders and partnerships, companies are regarded at law as separate and distinct legal persons from those persons who, as shareholders, are the owners of the business. For this reason, the Inland Revenue authorities treat companies as 'taxpayers' accountable for the payment of tax on company profits. Accordingly, companies are required to create adequate provisions for the payment of tax.

Second, unlike sole traders and partnerships, companies are exposed to corporation tax instead of income tax. The main difference is that corporation tax is levied at a standard rate, whereas income tax is levied on a graduated scale. This means that, whatever the size of the profits realised by a company, it will be subject to the same rate of tax. At the present time, the rate of corporation tax applied to public companies is 52%, and that applied to small companies is 38%. Like income tax, corporation tax is an annual tax which is authorised by Parliament with respect to a fiscal year.

Third, the net profits of businesses run by sole traders and partnerships are credited to the capital account or current accounts, as the case may be, of the owners of the business, leaving them to withdraw as drawings whatever sums of money lie available for withdrawal. Companies have to distribute profits to shareholders by the deliberate act of declaring a dividend. At that stage only does the shareholder receive a share of profits. However, as an individual, the shareholder is liable to income tax on dividends paid to him. At first sight this would seem to result in business profits being taxed twice—first, at the appropriate corporation tax rate (52% or 38% as may be), and second, at the appropriate rate of income tax to which the individual shareholder is taxable.

In the case of the public company paying a dividend to shareholders being taxed at 30% (the standard rate of income tax), the total tax paid on business profits flowing to the shareholder—if wholly distributed—would be (taking a tax rate of 50% for simplification):

		£
Company—	Net profit before tax	100
	Corporation tax at 50%	50
	Net profit after tax	50

Shareholders—assuming net profits after tax are wholly distributed	
Gross dividend	50
Income tax at 30%	15
Net dividend received	35

From this illustration, it is apparent that in the circumstances described, the total tax burden on the same business profit would amount to 65%. To avoid this problem, and to arrive at a more equitable distribution of the tax burden on shareholders as a whole, the *imputation system* has been developed.

Under the imputation system, income tax at the rate of 30% is deemed to have been paid on the dividends declared to shareholders by the company. In this treatment, the business profits are deemed to accrue to shareholders. Accordingly, the company profits are allocated as follows:

	£
Net profits before tax	100
Income tax at 30%	30
Net profits accruing to shareholders	70

Whenever dividends are declared, therefore, there is imputed to the net dividend paid to the shareholders a tax credit which implies that income tax has already been paid on their behalf by the company.

The income tax imputed to dividends declared is 3/7th of the net dividend paid. This fraction represents the allocation of company profits explained above—30% income tax and 70% profit after tax accruing to shareholders.

Example 4
Using the illustration given above of a corporation earning net profits before corporation tax of £100, and paying corporation tax at the rate of 50%, it distributes the entire profit after tax to its shareholders. Under the imputation system, the following will be the resulting dividends accruing to shareholders:

	Company £		Share-holders £
Net profits before corporation tax	100		
Corporation tax at 50%	50		
Net profits after corporation tax	50		
Net dividend paid	50	Net dividend received	50.00
Retained profits	0	Income tax imputed 3/7ths × £50	21.43
		Gross dividend	71.43

As individuals, the shareholders will be treated as having already 'paid' standard rate of income tax on their dividend and if their tax rate is 30%, they will be deemed to have settled their liability. If they are taxable at a higher rate, credit for income tax paid at 30% will be given. If they are not taxable, they will be entitled to claim a refund of income tax credit.

Provision for corporation tax

In determining the actual liability for corporation tax it must be made clear that the profit arrived at by acceptable accounting procedures is not the same as that required for taxation purposes. Certain expenses are not regarded as deductible and certain items of income are likewise excluded from the calculation. (In particular, depreciation has to be 'added back' and the statutorily fixed capital allowances substituted.)

The origin of this is that the rules governing the nature and source of profits of a business under corporation tax were originally framed for Schedule D of the income tax system which, before the Finance Act of 1965, was the basis for all business income whether the organisational structure was that of sole trader, partnership or limited company. These rules and any relevant current legislation have simply been employed in service of the corporation tax system.

Accounting dates and corporation tax

Under the corporation tax legislation in the United Kingdom the basis of assessment for the tax is on the actual results of an accounting period. However the actual tax rates are fixed by the Government to relate to the financial year which for this purpose starts on 1 April and ends on 31 March of the following year. The financial year is always referred to by the year in which it starts. This would mean that the financial year starting 1 April 1985 to 31 March 1986 would be identified as 'the financial year 1985'.

Obviously all companies do not have a 31 March year end so that there is a complication in that, if the corporation tax rates differ for consecutive financial years, two rates will be applicable to one year's results of a company.

An additional point that has an impact on the provision for corporation tax in a company's accounts is the fact that the Government's budget proposal wherein the rate is set for a financial year is announced at the end of the year, although a recent announcement by a Chancellor of the Exchequer indicated that rates of corporation tax may be set for several years in advance.

Example 5

The Bartlett Co. Ltd regularly prepares its year-end accounts to the 30 September. Accounts were prepared to 30 September 1984 which gave rise to an agreed taxable profit of £128,000.

The accounting period is from 1 October 1983 to 30 September 1984 which falls into the financial years of 1983 and 1984. If the corporation tax rates were 50% for 1983 and 40% for 1984 then the calculation of the liability would be as follows:

6/12th × £128,000 × 50% = £64,000
6/12th × £128,000 × 40% =   51,200
                           _____
                           £115,200

The ensuing accounting entries would be:

Dr Profit and loss account } with £115,200
Cr Corporation tax

(Remember that the 1984 rate would not be known until March 1985 so that adjustments may well have to be made.)

Payment of corporation tax

(a) Post-1965 companies

For companies formed after 5 April 1965, the payment date for corporation tax is nine months after the closure date of their annual accounts. It follows therefore, that any provision for corporation tax will be a current liability and must be disclosed under the classification in the balance sheet of those items due for payment within one year.

Example 6

Courtbridge Ltd was formed in 1972 and drew its accounts up regularly on 30 June each year. For the year ended 30 June 19X8, it was calculated that a provision of £86,000 was necessary for corporation tax. This, of course, had been calculated by reference to the two financial years into which the company's trading period had fallen which were:

Financial Year 19X7
1 July 19X7 to 31 March 19X8   9 months
Financial Year 19X8
1 April to 30 June 19X8   3 months

The appropriate entries in the books of Courtbridge Ltd were:

Dr   Profit and loss account
Cr   Corporation tax provision   } with £86,000

At 30 June 19X8, the actual rate may not have been known as the Budget date of 19X9 would be the Chancellor of the Exchequer's usual announcement date. However, some Chancellors have announced rates for several years in advance; so some degree of certainty as to the amount can be assumed.

The £86,000 is then disclosed under the balance sheet heading 'Amounts due to be paid within one year'.

(b) Pre-1965 companies

Companies which were in existence before 5 April 1965 are allowed to maintain the same interval between their accounting year end and the payment date for corporation tax as they were allowed under the previous tax regime.

This interval is determined by the 'prior year' rule.

The tax year in the United Kingdom starts on 6 April in one year and ends on 5 April in the next.

Any business is deemed to have the same tax year as that in which the accounting period ends. Thus a business which regularly prepares its accounts to 30 June each year will, for the accounting year end 30 June 1984, be deemed to fall in the tax year 1984/85. So would year endings of 30 April 1984, 31 December 1984, 28 February 1985, etc.

The previous tax system (which still prevails for unincorporated businesses) operated on the previous year assessment basis. Results of businesses with year endings falling in the tax year 1984/85 are used to assess the tax charge for 1985/86. Tax was payable by companies under this system on 1 January of the assessed year.

In the above example the company drawing up its accounts to 30 June 1984 would have had those results used as the basis for 1985/86 and would have been called upon to pay the tax on 1 January 1986, a gap of eighteen months from the accounting year end to payment of the tax related to those results. Had the company regularly prepared its accounts to 31 March, then the accounts to 31 March 1985 are still in the same tax year as the June year ending, and the company would also be called to pay tax on 1 January 1986, a gap of only nine months, but a company using a 30 April year end would have a twenty-month gap.

The significance of this from an accounting standpoint is that it can be seen that in some cases another accounting period will elapse before the tax is paid on the earlier one and hence the balance sheet will reveal two provisions, one a current liability (payable in less than one year) and one a future provision classified as payable after an interval longer than one year.

Applying the payment rules to companies in existence before 5 April 1965 it is possible to identify those accounting dates which will normally give rise to the need for two provisions for corporation tax. These dates are set out below:

Year endings	Payment interval
30 April	20 months
31 May	19 months
30 June	18 months
31 July	17 months
31 August	16 months
30 September	15 months
31 October	14 months
30 November	13 months
31 December	12 months

To illustrate the calculation of the above intervals the example of 31 May will be used for 19X4.

Example 7: Accounting year end 31 May 19X4

Under the previously applied taxation system this is deemed to be concurrent with the tax year 19X4/19X5. In turn, profits for the period 19X4/19X5 are used as the basis for taxation for 19X5/19X6 for which 1 January 19X6 is the payment date. Thus nineteen months elapse between 31 May 19X4 and 1 January 19X6 and may be portrayed:

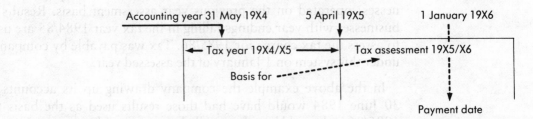

Obviously, two provisions need to be in any balance sheet as there are two tax liabilities still to be settled. One due to be paid within one year and another one year later.

Advance corporation tax

It can be seen from the pattern of tax payment dates that certain anomalies exist in the system. To some extent this is modified by the requirement that if a company makes a 'qualifying distribution' to its shareholders then the company must pay advance corporation tax (ACT). For the purposes of this chapter, the only 'qualifying distribution' to be considered will be that of the most common form— dividends.

From the outset it must be stressed that ACT is not an additional tax but a requirement to make an earlier payment of corporation tax than would otherwise be necessary. The amount to be paid is related to the dividend in the following way. When a dividend is paid, the Finance Act 1972 requires that a company should pay ACT as a fraction of that dividend (the fraction being determined by Parliament from time to time). The payment date is fixed by reference to calendar quarters—31 March, 30 June, 30 September and 31 December. The amount is paid by reference to the rate in force at the end of the quarter in which the dividend was paid and payment is made 14 days after the end of the quarter. (Variations occur depending upon accounting year ends, but this aspect will not be pursued here.)

The fraction referred to above is not determined in isolation from other aspects of taxation. It is governed by the current rate of income tax. The amount of tax payable is calculated as being that amount which when paid would leave the dividend as an amount net of tax. Therefore, from the fiscal year 1979/80 when the standard rate of income tax was 30%, the amount of ACT has been 3/7th of the dividend (i.e., a dividend of £70 would equal £100 'gross').

The impact of this legislation can be seen by comparing two companies with identical profits and year endings—Madison plc and Athens plc. Both reported profits of £200,000 for the year ended 30 June 19X3, and both were subjected to corporation tax at the rate of 52% of assessable profits. Madison paid a dividend of £35,000 on 31 August 19X3. The consequences are as follows:

	Madison plc £	Athens plc £
Profit	200,000	200,000
Corporation tax	104,000	104,000
	96,000	96,000
Dividend	35,000	—
Retained earnings	£61,000	£96,000
Payment of tax		
ACT paid 14 October 19X3	15,000	—
Balance of corporation tax paid 1 January 19X5	89,000	104,000
	£104,000	£104,000

The only difference is the earlier payment of tax of £15,000 paid by Madison plc.

Accounting entries

When the dividend is paid, an obligation is incurred to pay the Inland Revenue the ACT. This is acknowledged thus:

| Dr | Dividends paid | £35,000 | |
| Cr | Bank | | £35,000 |

| Dr | ACT recoverable | £15,000 | |
| Cr | ACT liability | | £15,000 |

This amount is calculated as 3/7ths of £35,000 and is termed 'recoverable' because it can be offset against the corporation tax total due, as assessed on profits. When the balance of the tax is paid (termed 'mainstream'), the ACT may be offset against the total tax payable. The sequence of accounting entries is now:

| Dr | ACT liability | £15,000 | |
| Cr | Bank | | £15,000 |

Payment takes place 14 days after the end of the quarter in which the dividend is paid. The accounting entries are:

Dr	Profit and loss account	£104,000	
Cr	Corporation tax		£104,000

and eventually

Dr	Corporation tax	£89,000	
Cr	Bank		£89,000

with 'mainstream' payment and

Dr	Corporation tax	£15,000	
Cr	ACT recoverable		£15,000

to close off the corporation tax account.

There are practical considerations concerning dividends received from investments, the extent to which ACT is recoverable, and timing of payments and receipts, but these are beyond the scope of this book.

Question

From the information given below, you are required to write up a company's corporation tax account and value added tax account for each of the two years ending 31 March 1982 and 1983:

	£
Corporation tax liability in company's balance sheet at 31 March 1981 for that year	100,000
VAT liability in company's balance sheet at 31 March 1981	37,000
26 September 1981. Paid company's final corporation tax account for the year to 31 March 1981	101,000
2 December 1981. Paid advance corporation tax (ACT) amounting to 30/70 of a dividend of £35,000	
Purchase of goods and services during the year to 31 March 1982, including VAT	1,210,000
Sales during the year to 31 March 1982, including VAT	2,970,000
Payments to Customs and Excise during the year to 31 March 1982, being VAT due	156,000
Taxable profit for the year ended 31 March 1982, on which corporation tax will eventually be payable, subject to any ACT paid on account	270,000
23 September, 1982. Paid company's final net corporation tax account for the year to 31 March 1982	118,000
4 December 1982. Paid ACT amounting to 30/70 of a dividend of £42,000	
Purchases of goods and services during the year to 31 March 1983 including VAT	1,540,000
Sales during the year to 31 March 1983 inclusive VAT	3,850,000

	£
Payments on account of VAT to the Customs and Excise during the year to 31 March 1983	201,000
Taxable profit for the year ended 31 March 1983	350,000

Show clearly the balance carried down on each account at the end of each year and, in the case of the corporation tax account, the charge to the profit and loss account for each year.

The rate of corporation tax is 50%.

The rate of value added tax is 10%, and there were no zero-rated or exempt transactions.

(*Institute of Cost and Management Accountants*)

15 Departmental and Manufacturing Accounts

The way in which the enterprise is organised and the type of business in which it is engaged will affect the nature of the accounting system and the manner in which financial statements will be presented to users.

In this chapter, two special aspects of enterprise organisation and activity which have this impact on the accounting system are considered. First, the enterprise may have been structured around the activities of more than one department. In this case, there is the need to provide information to management which will make it possible to evaluate and compare departments as business units. Second, manufacturing firms as distinct from trading firms have the special problem of establishing the cost of goods manufactured. For the purpose of establishing the periodic profit or loss, it will be necessary for the manufacturing firm to prepare a manufacturing account, in addition to the profit and loss account. The purpose of the manufacturing account is to establish the cost of the goods manufactured and entering into the stock of finished goods.

Departmental and manufacturing accounts may be prepared by sole traders, partnerships or companies. There are no required formats for these accounts, although certain principles should be applied in their presentation.

Departmental accounts

Departmental accounts are prepared for internal use only. The availability of such accounts enables management to make informed decisions for the allocation of resources to different departments and activities. Such decisions include, for example, providing additional resources to one department rather than another, evaluating the performance of the departmental manager and making a decision as to retain him in that position or moving him to another department, examining the cost structure of a department with a view to making pricing decisions for its products.

The preparation of departmental accounts requires that purchases, sales and expenses records be analysed in such a way as to permit separate profit and loss accounts to be prepared for different departments. The procedure used in a manual accounting system would involve analysed purchases and sales journals. With a computerised accounting system, the coding of transactions would perform the same function. Regardless of the sophistication of the accounting system used, the basic procedure in all cases involves classifying operating data by departments and accumulating information for each department in ledger accounts.

Illustration 1 below shows a profit and loss account in which net profit is analysed on a departmental basis. Direct expenses are those expenses defined as relating clearly to the activities of a department, and would not be incurred if that department did not exist. Illustration 1 shows that direct expenses are deducted from gross profits to highlight the contribution of the department to overall profits. The contribution margin in this case is the amount by which departmental revenues exceed direct expenses associated with the department. Indirect expenses cannot be clearly identified with one particular department. They are regarded as associated with the firm as a whole. Indirect expenses are assigned to the individual departments by a

	Furniture Department £	Clothing Department £	Total £
Illustration 1: Departmental Profit and Loss Account for the year ended 31 December 19X5			
Sales	64,000	32,000	96,000
Opening stock	40,000	20,000	60,000
Purchases	24,000	12,000	36,000
	64,000	32,000	96,000
Closing stock	45,000	15,000	60,000
Cost of goods sold	19,000	17,000	36,000
Gross profit	45,000	15,000	60,000
Direct expenses:			
Wages	10,000	5,000	15,000
Advertising	4,000	1,000	5,000
Other	6,000	2,000	8,000
Total direct expenses	20,000	8,000	28,000
Contribution margin	25,000	7,000	32,000
Indirect expenses:			
Administration	8,000	4,000	12,000
Rates	3,000	3,000	6,000
Heat and light	1,000	1,000	2,000
Total indirect expenses	12,000	8,000	20,000
Net profit (loss)	13,000	(1,000)	12,000

process of apportionment, which attempts to place a burden on departments equivalent to the benefit received by departments from these expenses.

The problem of apportioning indirect expenses to departments involves the selection of an apportionment base which reflects the benefits received by individual departments. A variety of bases exist for this purpose reflecting, for example, the value of merchandise sold, the number of employees, the value of fixed assets or the floor space associated with the department as a proportion of the corresponding enterprise total. In Illustration 1, for example, administration has been apportioned to the two departments on the basis of sales value. Therefore, because the sales value of the Furniture Department is twice that of the Clothing Department, it attracts double the charge for administration. In Illustration 1, rate and heat and light expenses have been apportioned on the basis of floor space occupied. Because calculations show that the floor space occupied by the two departments is the same, they have been charged with an equal amount of the total enterprise cost.

It should be observed that it is dangerous to carry the departmental analysis of transactions beyond the stage where the transactions can be clearly or directly associated with the activities of particular departments. Arbitrary apportionment of these costs can interfere with the usefulness of accounting in its task of providing information for managerial control and decision making. There are two reasons why the results of such apportionments may be misleading. Firstly, they have the effect of charging departmental managers with expenses over which they have no control. Secondly, they may provide misleading information for decision making purposes. In Illustration 1 above, the Clothing Department is shown as losing £1,000. A persistent loss in that department may suggest to management that the department should be closed. But such an action would reduce the firm's net profit from £12,000 to £5,000. It may be more useful, therefore, to view the contribution margin as the more obvious measure of financial performance, and in this case, it is seen that closing the Clothing Department would involve the loss of a contribution of £7,000 to total indirect expenses.

Manufacturing accounts

Unlike a trading company which stocks and resells the same commodity that it originally bought, a manufacturing company purchases raw materials which it transforms through a production process into finished goods, which are subsequently sold. To take account of this activity, a manufacturing firm requires an accounting framework for dealing with (a) manufacturing or factory costs, (b) stocks of raw materials, work in progress and finished goods, and (c) manufacturing plant and equipment.

The manufacturing account

The manufacturing account contains all those expenses associated with the factory cost of production. Although there is no required format for the presentation of a manufacturing account, the order in which factory expenses are listed appears as follows:

	£
(a) Direct (raw) materials	x
(b) Direct labour	x
(c) Direct expenses	x
Prime cost	x
(d) Factory overhead (indirect) expenses	x
Factory cost of goods produced	x

The term 'direct' indicates the relationship of the cost element to the product being produced. Direct materials represent that portion of materials used in the manufacturing process that is clearly traceable to the goods produced. Direct labour includes the wages of all personnel directly engaged in the production process, for example, the machinists, assembly men, paintshop operators, etc. Direct expenses would be other items of cost identified with the making of a particular product, for example, the hire of special equipment for a particular job.

'Prime cost' is the term given to the total cost of all direct expenses.

Factory overhead costs consist of all expenses which cannot be directly identified with a product and, therefore, cannot be included under direct materials, direct labour or direct expenses. Factory overhead costs are all those indirect expenses which need to be apportioned to products. They include depreciation on factory buildings and equipment, the cost of heat, light and power, and the wages of factory supervisors, cleaners, timekeepers, etc.

Illustration 2 shows a typical manufacturing account. Note particularly that a manufacturing company has three types of stock accounts. Raw materials on hand and not committed to the production process are held in a raw materials stock account. The other two stock accounts reflect the costs incurred at different stages of completion of the production process. All units placed into production during the accounting period and which remain uncompleted at the closing date are treated as work in progress. The cost of the work in progress has to be established, taking into account the raw material used, the direct labour and direct expenses incurred to date, as well as the overhead costs that have been apportioned to the work in progress. The cost identified with the completed but unsold units on hand at the end of the accounting period are reported as finished goods stock.

Illustration 2: Manufacturing account for the year ended 31 December 19X5		
	£	£
Direct materials		
Opening stock	2,000	
Purchases	7,000	
Carriage inwards	1,000	
	10,000	
Less: Closing stock	1,500	
Direct materials consumed		8,500
Direct labour		12,000
Direct expenses		500
Prime cost		21,000
Factory overheads		
Depreciation—plant	6,500	
Heat, power and light	1,000	
Indirect wages	1,000	
Rates, insurance, etc.	500	
		9,000
		30,000
Work in progress		
Opening stock	2,000	
Less: Closing stock	1,000	
		1,000
Factory cost of goods produced		31,000

The profit and loss account

The profit and loss account of a manufacturing firm follows a format similar to that of a trading firm, with an important exception that purchases are replaced by the factory cost of goods produced. Illustration 3 shows the transfer from the manufacturing account to the profit and loss account of the factory cost of goods produced, which is deducted from sales in calculating the gross profit.

**Illustration 3: Profit and Loss Account for the year
ended 31 December 19X5**

	£	£
Sales		100,000
Cost of goods sold		
Opening stock of finished goods	5,000	
Factory cost of goods produced	31,000	
	36,000	
Less: Closing stock of finished goods	4,000	
		32,000
Gross profit		68,000
Less: Selling and distribution expenses	6,000	
Administrative expenses	30,000	
Financial expenses	8,000	
		44,000
Net profit		24,000

It is possible to integrate the manufacturing account with the profit and loss account into one combined account. In this case, the entry 'factory cost of goods produced' shown in the profit and loss account above is simply replaced by the manufacturing account itself.

The balance sheet

The balance sheet of a manufacturing company will show under current assets the three different classes of stocks, namely, raw materials stocks, work in progress stocks and finished goods stocks.

Example 1
From the information given below you are required to prepare, for internal circulation only, the manufacturing and profit and loss account of W. Wright plc for the year ended 31 December 19X5 and a balance sheet on that date.

Balances at 31 December 19X4	£
Authorised and issued share capital:	
Ordinary shares of £1 each, fully paid	100,000
Profit and loss account	1,000
Creditors	57,400
Fixed assets (cost £60,000)	39,000
Stocks: Raw materials	25,000
Work-in-progress, valued at prime cost	5,800
Finished goods	51,000
Debtors	35,000
Cash at bank	2,000
Administration expenses prepaid	600

The following transactions occurred during 19X5:

Invoiced sales, *less* Returns	243,000
Cash received from debtors	234,700
Discount allowed	5,400
Bad debt written off	1,100
Invoiced purchases of raw materials, *less* Returns	80,000
Payments to creditors	82,500
Discount received	1,700
Factory wages paid	33,300
Factory expenses paid	61,900
Administration expenses paid	16,200
Selling and distribution expenses paid	16,800
Payment for purchase of fixed assets	30,000

Balances at 31 December 19X5:

Fixed assets (cost £90,000)	60,000
Stocks: Raw materials	24,000
Work-in-progress	5,000
Finished goods	52,000
Administration expenses accrued	1,100
Factory wages accrued	700
Selling and distribution expenses prepaid	1,200

The following information is given:

(1) Depreciation of fixed assets is to be apportioned between manufacturing, administration, and selling and distribution in the proportions of 7:2:1.

(2) Discount allowed and bad debt written off are to be regarded as selling and distribution expenses.

(3) Discount received is to be credited to administration expenses.

(4) Taxation is to be ignored.

Accounts for the year ended 31 December 19X5
Manufacturing account

Materials consumed:	£	£
Opening stock	25,000	
Purchases	80,000	
	105,000	
Less: Closing stock	24,000	
		81,000
Factory wages		34,000
Factory expenses		61,900
Depreciation attributed to manufacturing		6,300
Total manufacturing costs		183,200
Change in work-in-progress:		
Add: Opening stock	5,800	
Less: Closing stock	5,000	
		800
Factory cost of finished goods transferred		£184,000

Profit and Loss account

	£	£	£
Sales			243,000
Cost of goods sold			
Opening stock of finished goods		51,000	
Factory cost transferred		184,000	
		235,000	
Less: Closing stocks of finished goods		52,000	
			183,000
Gross profit			60,000
Less:			
Selling and distribution expenses			
Expenses	22,100		
Depreciation	900		
		23,000	
Administration expenses			
Expenses	16,200		
Depreciation	1,800		
		18,000	
			41,000
Profit for the financial year			£19,000

Balance Sheet
as at 31 December 19X5

	£	£	£
Fixed assets:			
Cost			90,000
Less: Depreciation			30,000
			60,000
Current assets:			
Stocks: Materials		24,000	
Work in progress		5,000	
Finished goods		52,000	81,000
Debtors and prepayments			38,000
			119,000
Creditors—amounts falling due within one year:			
Creditors and accrued expenses		55,000	
Bank overdraft		4,000	
		59,000	
			60,000
			£120,000
Capital and reserves:			
Called up share capital			100,000
Profit and loss account			20,000
			£120,000

Manufacturing profit

A manufacturer may be viewed as operating two businesses jointly: that of a producer and that of a trader. A profit from manufacturing may be shown by transferring the goods produced to the profit and loss account at market price, i.e., the price at which they could have been purchased from outside. The manufacturing profit shows the advantage gained from producing the goods rather than buying direct.

Assume, in the example above, that the market value for the goods produced is £200,000. The final three lines of the manufacturing account would read:

	£
Factory cost of finished goods produced	184,000
Add: Manufacturing profit	16,000
Market value of goods transferred	£200,000

The profit and loss account would disclose a trading profit of £44,000:

	£	£
Sales		132,000
Opening stock of finished goods	51,000	
Market value of goods complete	200,000	
	251,000	
Less: Closing stocks of finished goods	52,000	199,000
Trading profit		44,000
Manufacturing profit		16,000
Gross profit		£60,000

Questions

1. The profit and loss account for the year ended 31 December 19X8 of DQ Holidays Ltd, a company which provides holidays at several resorts in Spain, is as follows:

	£		£
Agents' commission	90,600	Sales of holidays	906,000
Hire of aeroplanes	105,000	Net loss for the year	10,000
Coaches from airport to resorts	7,000		
Hotel accommodation	581,400		
Salary and expenses of resort representatives	32,000		
Brochures, advertising head office and other common costs	100,000		
	916,000		916,000

The managing director has complained to you, as chief accountant, that the form of presentation of this profit and loss account does not tell him where or why the net loss has been incurred and is of little use for management purposes.

You are required to redesign the profit and loss account, using also the information given below, so that it will overcome the complaints of the managing director.

You are given the following information:

(1) The public book their holidays with the company through local travel agents who were paid a commission of 10% of the gross price of the holiday.

(2) Holidays were offered at six resorts in Spain, namely P, Q, R, S, T and U.

(3) Only one hotel was used in each resort.

(4) Flights were from Luton Airport to three airports in Spain, as follows:

Airport	For resorts	Annual cost £
X	P and Q	30,000
Y	R and S	30,000
Z	T and U	35,000

(5) Separate coaches were used for the journey from the Spanish airport to each resort hotel. The annual costs of these were:

To resort	£
P	1,100
Q	900
R	1,400
S	1,100
T	1,700
U	800

(6) The annual costs of hotel accommodation at each resort were:

Resort	£
P	305,900
Q	153,200
R	22,600
S	45,400
T	10,200
U	44,100

(7) A separate representative was employed at each resort, and the annual costs were:

Resort	£
P	5,000
Q	4,500
R	6,000
S	5,500
T	5,700
U	5,300

(8) Sales of holidays at the various resorts were:

Resort	£
P	480,000
Q	244,000
R	30,000
S	60,000
T	24,000
U	68,000

(*Institute of Cost and Management Accountants*)

2. John Dell commenced trading on 1 April 19X8 as Highway Stores, retail stationers and confectioners, with an initial capital of £3,000 which was utilised in the opening of a business bank account.

All receipts and payments are passed through the bank account. The following is a summary of the items credited in the business cash book during the year ended 31 March 19X9:

	£
Purchase of fixtures and fittings:	
Stationery department	2,600
Confectionery department	1,500
Staff wages:	
Stationery department	2,200
Confectionery department	1,540
Rent for the period 1 April 19X8 to 30 April 19X9	1,300
Rates for the year ended 31 March 19X9	570
Electricity	370
Advertising	1,100
Payments to suppliers	53,550
Drawings	5,000

The purchases during the year under review were:

	£
Stationery department	26,000
Confectionery department	29,250

The above purchases do not include goods costing £500 bought by the business and then taken by Mr Dell for his own domestic use. The figure of £500 is included in payments to suppliers.

The gross profit in the stationery department is at the rate of 20% of sales whilst in the confectionery department it is 25% of sales. In both departments, sales each month are always at a uniform level. The policy of Mr Dell is to have the month end stocks in each department just sufficient for the following month's sales. The prices of all goods bought by Highway Stores have not changed since the business began.

Total trade debtors at 31 March 19X9 amounted to £9,000.

In August 19X8 Mr Dell and his sister, Mrs Beck, benefited from legacies from their late mother's estate of £5,000 and £4,000 respectively. Both legacies were paid into the bank account of Highway Stores; Mrs Beck has agreed that her legacy should be an interest free loan to the business.

At 31 March 19X9 electricity charges accrued due, amounted to £110.

Mr Dell has decided that expenses not incurred by a specific department should be apportioned to departments as follows:

rent and rates—according to floor area occupied,
electricity—according to consumption,
advertising—according to turnover.

Two-thirds of the business floor space is occupied by the stationery department whilst three-quarters of the electricity is consumed by that department. All the floor space of the business is allocated to a department.

It has been decided that depreciation on fixtures and fittings should be provided at the rate of 10% of the cost of assets held at the year end.

You are required to produce:

(a) a trading and profit and loss account for the year ended 31 March 19X9 for:
    (1) the stationery department, and
    (2) the confectionery department;
(b) a balance sheet at 31 March 19X9.

(Association of Certified Accountants)

3. Brian and Trevor are in partnership managing a small retail store which specialises in sweets and confectionery (managed by Brian), and newspapers and periodicals (managed by Trevor). The partnership agreement provides for Brian to receive 3/5 of the profit, and Trevor 2/5, each partner to be allowed 8% interest on capital, and each to receive a commission of 10% of the profit of their respective sections prior to any other appropriation of profit.

During the year to 31 March 19X8, a trial balance extracted at that date revealed the following financial features.

	£	£
Capital—Brian		14,000
—Trevor		8,000
Current accounts—Brian		2,020
—Trevor	250	
Drawings—Brian	1,100	
—Trevor	900	
Freehold shop premises	10,000	
Equipment (at written down value)		
—Confectionery section	4,500	
—Periodical section	3,500	

	£	£
Purchases—Confectionery section	15,900	
—Periodical section	17,700	
Stock at 1 April 19X7—Confectionery section	2,300	
—Periodical section	3,100	
Sales—Confectionery section		18,500
—Periodical section		21,500
Wages—Confectionery section	1,175	
—Periodical section	1,470	
Miscellaneous expenses	230	
Rates	500	
Light and heat	400	
Advertising	250	
Debtors and creditors	1,800	2,100
Bad debts—Periodical section	95	
Cash in hand	950	
Cash at bank	50	
Provision for doubtful debts—periodical section		50
	66,170	66,170

Additional information available:

(1) Stock at 31 March 19X8 was £3,600 in the confectionery section, and £4,400 in the periodical section.

(2) The partners have agreed that, rates should be apportioned between the confectionery and periodical sections on a 3:2 ratio, advertising on a 1:1 ratio, lighting and heating on a 2:3 ratio, and miscellaneous expenses on a 1:1 ratio.

(3) Wages owing at 31 March 19X8 amounted to £25 for the confectionery section and £30 for the periodical section.

(4) Advertising prepaid at 31 March 19X8 amounted to £100.

(5) The provision for doubtful debts is to be increased to 5% of the debtors of the periodical section, which amount to £1,500 at 31 March 19X8.

(6) Equipment of both sections is to be depreciated at 10% of the written down value at 1 April 19X7.

You are required to:

(a) prepare a trading, and profit and loss account for the Confectionery and the Periodical sections, and also for the business as a whole, for the year ended 31 March 19X8. (*Note:* A balance sheet is not required.)

(b) prepare an appropriation account for the year ended 31 March 19X8;

(c) prepare the partners' current accounts for the year ended 31 March 19X8.

(*Association of Certified Accountants*)

4. Using the information given below, which relates to a manufacturing company VHR Limited, you are required to prepare a statement to show clearly:

(a) cost of raw materials used or consumed;
(b) prime cost;
(c) cost of the finished goods produced;
(d) cost of the finished goods sold (manufactured internally and purchased externally);
(e) gross profit;
(f) net profit before taxation;

for the year ended 31 December 19X5.

		£
Raw materials:	Stock at 1 January 19X6	39,000
	Purchases	152,000
	Stock at 31 December 19X6	41,000
Finished goods:	Stock at 1 January, 19X6	51,000
	Purchases	9,000
	Stock at 31 December 19X6	57,000
Work in progress:	at 1 January 19X6	16,000
	at 31 December 19X6	18,200
Sales		400,000
Manufacturing wages		60,000
Manufacturing expenses		25,300
Repairs and maintenance of plant and machinery		13,500
Depreciation: Factory		38,000
General offices		5,000
Sales warehouse and offices		7,000
Carriage outwards		6,600
Power		10,000
Light and heat: Factory		2,400
General offices		800
Sales warehouse and offices		1,300
Administration expenses		16,200
Selling and distribution expenses		26,100

(*Institute of Cost and Management Accountants*)

5. Using the information given below you are asked to prepare, for internal circulation only, the manufacturing and profit and loss accounts of VBA Limited for the year ended 31 December 19X7 and a balance sheet as at that date.

Trial balance of VBA Limited at 31 December 19X7

	£000	£000
Ordinary share capital		1,000
Reserves		580
10% Debentures		100
Fixed assets, at cost	2,090	
Provision for depreciation of fixed assets		680
Proceeds of sale of fixed assets		15
Stock of materials	220	
Work in progress	40	
Stock of finished goods	230	

	£000	£000
Debtors	420	
Provision for doubtful debts		20
Cash at bank and in hand	20	
Creditors		88
Taxation on 19X6 profits		118
Sales		3,400
Purchases of materials	1,060	
Manufacturing wages	353	
Manufacturing expenses	555	
Administration expenses	292	
Selling and distribution expenses	666	
Debenture interest	5	
Interim dividend	50	
	6,001	6,001

The following information is also given:

(1) The variations in the values of stocks at 31 December 19X7 as compared with the values at 31 December 19X6 were:

		£000
Stock of materials	increase of	30
Work in progress	reduction of	10
Stock and finished goods	increase of	70

(2) Prepaid and accrued expenses at 31 December 19X7 were:

	Prepaid £000	Accrued £000
Manufacturing wages		7
Manufacturing expenses	1	6
Administration expenses	2	5
Selling and distribution expenses	1	1

(3) Debenture interest has been paid to 30 June 19X7 only.

(4) Bad debts of £3,000 are to be written off, and the provision for doubtful debts is to be increased by £1,000. These items are to be regarded as selling and distribution expenses.

(5) Depreciation is to be provided at the rate of 10% per annum on cost on a strict time basis, and is to be allocated to manufacturing, administration, and selling and distribution expenses in the proportion of 8 : 1 : 1.

(6) The item appearing in the trial balance 'Proceeds of sale of fixed assets' refers to items which originally cost £100,000 and which were sold on 30 June 19X7 on which date they had a net book value of £10,000.

(7) Additional fixed assets were purchased for £160,000 on 31 March 19X7. These were included in the figure of £2,090,000 appearing in the trial balance.

(8) A provision of £170,000 is to be made in respect of taxation on the current year's profits.

(9) Provision is to be made for a recommended final dividend of 10% on the ordinary shares.

(Institute of Cost and Management Accountants)

16 Statements of Source and Application of Funds

Financial accounting may be said to be concerned with the control of three types of flows, namely, income flows, funds flows and cash flows. Previous chapters have been concerned with profit flows and their resulting effects on the financial position of an enterprise which is reflected on the balance sheet. The statement of source and application of funds supplements the two conventional statements by reporting changes relating to the financial activities of the firm that are not otherwise readily discernible.

The nature of funds flows

The purpose of the statements of source and application of funds is to supplement the information provided in the year-end accounting statements by summarising significant changes which have occurred in the financial structure of the enterprise, particularly those relating to the source and use of funds. It is addressed to the following types of questions:

'How were fixed assets purchased?'
'How were loans repaid?'
'How were the proceeds of newly issued shares utilised?'
'How was the increase in working capital financed?'
'What changes took place in the composition of current assets and current liabilities?'
'What explanations can be offered for the manner in which profits were applied?'

In many senses, the statement of sources and application of funds may be seen as an essential link between the profit and loss account and the balance sheet, and between successive balance sheets by providing explanations for the changes which have occurred in the final structure of the business.

Figure 16.1 gives a diagrammatic representation of the sources and applications of funds statement. To most people, the term 'funds' means 'cash'. In a general accounting usage, this is often taken to mean working capital which is the difference between current assets and current liabilities. A Statement of Standard Accounting Practice (No. 10) issued by the Accounting Standards Committee of the professional accountancy bodies, whilst not defining funds, does suggest that the focus of such statements should be 'liquid funds'. The process of generating funds may be seen in the circular flow of working capital. Thus, changes in the level of current assets in the form of stock, debtors and cash, and changes in the form of trade and other creditors, may be seen as circular flows in which continual changes are occurring.

Fig. 16.1 Statement of sources and application of liquid funds

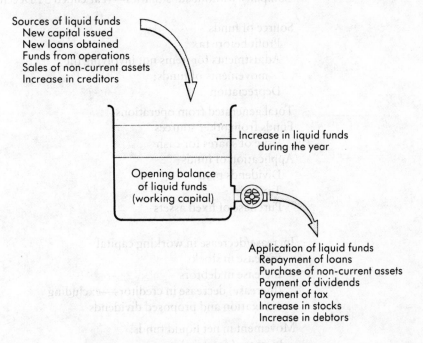

In the United Kingdom, SSAP No. 10: *Statements of Source and Application of Funds*, requires the following items to appear:

(a) The profit or loss for the period.
(b) An adjustment for items charged in the profit and loss account which do not involve a movement of funds, for example, depreciation and other provisions.
(c) Dividends paid.
(d) Acquisitions and disposals of fixed and other non-current assets.
(e) Funds raised or expended in increasing or redeeming issued share capital, long-term or medium-term loans.
(f) Increases or decreases in working capital, subdivided into its components.
(g) Movements in net liquid funds, defined as cash at bank and in hand, as well as cash equivalents (investments held as current assets). Included under this heading are bank overdrafts and other borrowings repayable within one year of the accounting date.

SSAP 10 applies to all enterprises having a turnover greater than £25,000 per annum. It does not prescribe a format which must be followed, but offers a specimen presentation, which is adopted in the example shown below. In practice, companies have produced a variety of presentations. The appendix to SSAP 10 offers the following layout as an example for general guidance.

Company without subsidiaries—year ended 31 December 19X6

	£000	£000	£000
Source of funds			
Profit before tax			xxxxx
Adjustments for items not involving the movements of funds:			
Depreciation			xxxx
Total generated from operations			xxxxx
Funds from other sources			
Issue of shares for cash			xxxxx
Application of funds			
Dividends paid		(xxxx)	
Tax paid		(xxxx)	
Purchase of fixed assets		(xxxx)	(xxxx)
			A
Increase/decrease in working capital			
Increase in stocks		xx	
Increase in debtors		xxx	
(Increase) decrease in creditors—excluding taxation and proposed dividends		xxx	
Movement in net liquid funds:			
Increase (decrease) in:			
Cash balances	(x)		
Short term investments	xx	xx	A

Note: Previous year's figures to be shown. Omitted here.

Preparation of the statement of source and application of funds

The preparation of the statement of source and application of funds requires an analysis of changes in the items on the balance sheet for the purpose of identifying sources and application of funds. It is usual to start with a calculation of the funds from operations, derived from information contained in the profit and loss accounts. Thereafter, attention is given to balance sheet items. Before considering companies, the general approach is described below. If the case of a small business is considered, the distinction between the flows can be established.

Case 1
C. Armitage conducts all his business, that of a small fishmonger, for cash. Having a modest private income he does not withdraw

any cash for his personal drawings until the end of his financial year. His shop is rented with all fittings.

At the start of the year 19X5 his balance sheet was as follows:

Capital as at 1 January 19X5	£5,000
Cash at bank	£5,000

At the end of the year his records showed that a profit had been earned:

Trading and profit and loss account for the year ended 31 December 19X5

	£
Sales	120,000
Purchases (no stocks carried)	85,000
Gross profit for the year	35,000
Less: Expenses	18,000
Net profit for the year	17,000

If we define 'funds' as current assets minus current liabilities, it can be seen that

$$\text{Net profit} = \text{Change in funds} = \text{Change in cash}$$

In other words the three flows—profit, funds and cash—are identical. The balance sheet at 31 December 19X5 will be as follows:

Capital	£22,000
Represented by:	
Cash	£22,000

Case 2

We assume the same data as in Case 1, but with one variation. Some customers buy on credit account terms, and £1,400 is owed to the business at the end of the year. The profit and loss account will be the same as in Case 1, but the balance sheet will now show:

Capital		£22,000
	£	
Debtors	1,400	
Cash	20,600	£22,000

Although profit equals the flow of funds, net cash flow is different. In both cases a flow of funds statement would show for the years:

	£
Funds at start of year	5,000
Arising from operations	17,000
Funds at close of year	£22,000

A statement of net flows of cash would show:

	Case 1	Case 2
Cash at start of year	5,000	5,000
Cash from operations	17,000	15,600
Cash at end of year	22,000	20,600

This reflects the effect on cash, but a better understanding of the position of Case 2 may be yielded by the following statement:

	£	£
Working capital (funds) at start		5,000
Funds arising from operations	17,000	
Increase in debtors	1,400	
Increase in liquid funds		15,600
Liquid funds at close		20,000

Case 3

Assume the same basic data except that:

(1) Freezer equipment of £4,000 is purchased at the start of the year.
(2) Depreciation of £800 is charged as expense in the year.
(3) Stock valued at £2,300 was on hand at 31 December 19X5.
(4) Purchases of an additional £2,100 had been made, but not paid for, at 31 December 19X5.

The profit and loss account and the balance sheet would now show:

Profit and loss account for year ended 31 December 19X5

	£	£
Sales		120,000
Purchases (£85,000 and £2,100)	87,100	
Less: Stock	2,300	84,800
		35,200
Less: Expenses	18,000	
Depreciation	800	18,800
Net profit for the year		£16,400

Balance sheet as at 31 December 19X5

	£
Capital as at 1 January 1985	5,000
Add: Profit for the year	16,400
	£21,400

Represented by:	£	£
Freezer at cost		4,000
Less depreciation		800
		3,200
Current assets		
Stock	2,300	
Debtors	1,400	
Cash	16,600	
	20,300	
Less: Creditors	2,100	18,200
		£21,400

First, in preparing a statement of source and application of funds, a general summary of the changes between the opening and the closing balance sheets is made:

Balance sheets	Opening	Closing	Change
Capital	£5,000	£21,400	£16,400
Freezer	—	4,000	4,000
Depreciation	—	(800)	(800)
		3,200	3,200
Stock	—	2,300	2,300
Debtors	—	1,400	1,400
Cash	5,000	16,600	11,600
	5,000	20,300	15,300
Creditors		(2,100)	(2,100)
		18,200	13,200
	5,000	21,400	16,400

Secondly, the funds arising from the business operations have to be identified. These are:

	£
Net profit per the accounts	16,400
Add: Item not involving movement of funds, i.e. depreciation	800
	£17,200

Depreciation does not involve funds. This is merely a book-entry which reduces the profit and recorded value of an asset by the same amount. Care must be taken not to refer to depreciation as a 'source of funds'. The process of adding back depreciation gives rise to this misconception. The funds arise from trading.

Thirdly, acquisition and disposal of fixed assets must be detailed. Here there is one acquisition for £4,000.

Fourthly, changes in the components of working capital must be itemised. These are not flows, but net changes in the amount of each component. They show that all the funds arising would have been in cash form had not some gone into:

(1) financing debtors where that item has increased,
(2) financing increases in stock, and
(3) partial offsets to (a) and (b) by increase in creditors.

Each of these components can, of course, be decreases with the opposite effect.

The threads of these matters can now be pulled together to produce a statement.

Statement of source and applications of funds

	£	£
Source of funds		
Arising from operations	16,400	
Add: Item not involving movement		
of funds, i.e. depreciation	800	17,200
Increase in creditors		2,100
		19,300
Application of funds		
Fixed asset acquired	4,000	
Increase in stock	2,300	
Increase in debtors	1,400	7,700
Net inflow—increase in liquid funds		£11,600
Cash at end of year		16,600
Cash at start of year		5,000
Net increase		£11,600

This final statement acts as a supplement to the profit and loss account and balance sheets and should allow the reader to better understand the liquid financial consequences of the year's activities.

Turning now to limited companies, consider the following.

Example 1

Set out below are the condensed balance sheets for Repco plc for the years ended 31 December 19X5 and 19X6, and a note of the changes during 19X6. Also given is a condensed profit and loss account for the year ended 31 December 19X6. The following information is given for the purpose of preparing a statement of source and application of funds for the year ended 31 December 19X6:

(a) Assets costing £13,000 were sold for £7,000. These assets had been depreciated down to £3,000 in the books.
(b) Tax paid during the year amounted to £12,000.
(c) Dividends paid during the year amounted to £8,000.

Repco plc			
Balance sheets at 31 December			
	19X5	19X6	Changes
	£000	£000	£000
Tangible assets			
Fixed assets at cost	123	145	22
(depreciation)	(38)	(49)	(11)
	85	96	11
Investment in local authority	26	18	(8)
	111	114	3
Current assets			
Stock	27	41	14
Debtors	39	36	(3)
Bank	8	17	9
	74	94	20
Current liabilities			
Trade creditors	22	28	(6)
Proposed dividends	8	12	(4)
Provision for taxation	12	14	(2)
	42	54	(12)
Net current assets	32	40	8
Total assets *less* current liabilities	143	154	11
10% debentures	30	15	(15)
Ordinary share capital	75	80	5
Profit and loss account	38	59	21
	143	154	11

Condensed profit and loss account for the year ended 31 December 19X6		
		£000
Operating profit		67
Less: Debenture interest	3	
Depreciation	21	24
		43
Add: Gain on disposal of fixed assets		4
Profit before tax		47
Less: Provision for taxation		14
Profit after tax		33
Proposed dividend		12
Undistributed profit		21
Balance brought forward		38
Balance carried forward		59

The statement of sources and application of funds is prepared from the analysis of the 'Changes' column shown above.

Stage 1: Calculation of funds from operations

The calculation of funds from operations is effected by adding back to the undistributed profit all items not involving payments or receipts during the year. For example, depreciation, transfers to reserves, gains and losses on asset disposal are book entries which do not imply any liquid funds flow. Moreover, SSAP 10 requires that dividends and taxation actually paid be shown in the statement of source and application of funds. Since the provision for taxation and the proposed dividend shown in the profit and loss account for the year ended 31 December 19X6 represent amounts which will only be paid in the following year, these provisions must also be added back. The calculation of funds from operations is as follows:

	£000
Undistributed profit	21
Add: Depreciation	21
Provision for taxation	14
Proposed dividend	12
	68
Less: Gain on asset disposal	4
Funds from operations	64

Stage 2: Identification of other funds flows

The following sources of funds during the year ended 31 December 19X6 may be noted:

(a) *Investments*
   The change of £8,000 is a sale which realised exactly £8,000.
(b) *10% debentures*
   Clearly, the change of £15,000 was a repayment of debentures and accordingly a funds flow.
(c) *Ordinary share capital*
   The increase in the ordinary share capital may be assumed to have been an issue of additional ordinary share for cash. (Note that the issue of bonus shares not involving the receipt of cash by the company would have necessitated a transfer from a reserve account.)
(d) *Sale of assets*
   The amount of £7,000 realised from the sale of assets is a source of funds. Note in this respect that the gain on the disposal of

assets of £4,000 recorded in the income statement is not a source of funds, but purely an accounting profit which has been calculated as follows:

	£
Fixed asset at cost	13,000
Less: Depreciation	10,000
Book value	3,000
Sales proceeds	7,000
Gain on disposal	4,000

The following application of funds are given in the information provided:

(e) *Dividend paid*
The dividend actually paid was £8,000.

(f) *Tax paid*
The tax actually paid was £12,000. This was the provision made the previous year on the basis of an estimate of the tax payable on the profit for the year ended 31 December 19X5. It was paid in the year ended 31 December 19X6.

Stage 3: Analysis of changes in the fixed asset and depreciation accounts

From the information given above, the fixed assets account, the provision for depreciation account and the asset disposal account may be reconstituted as follows:

Fixed assets account

	£		£
Balance b/d	123,000	Asset disposal	13,000
Asset purchases	35,000	Balance c/d	145,000
	158,000		158,000
Balance b/d	45,000		

Provision for depreciation account

	£		£
Asset disposal	10,000	Balance b/d	38,000
Balance c/d	49,000	Income statement	21,000
	59,000		59,000
		Balance b/d	49,000

Asset disposal account

	£		£
Fixed assets	13,000	Provision for depreciation	10,000
Gain on disposal	4,000	Bank	7,000
	17,000		17,000

This analysis allows the net change in the fixed asset account of £22,000 to be decomposed as between asset disposals at cost of £13,000 and new asset purchases during the year of £35,000. These new asset purchases constitute an application of funds during the year ended 31 December 19X6.

Stage 4: Preparation of the statement of source and application of funds in accordance with SSAP 10

SSAP 10 requires the statement of source and application of funds to be in the form of an explanation of movements in net liquid funds, defined as cash in hand and at bank, as well as cash equivalent. Applying this requirement to the information given above, the format is in effect a reconciliation of the net liquid funds at the beginning of the year with the net liquid funds at the end of the year, as follows:

Repco plc
Statement of sources and applications of funds for the year ended 31 December 19X6

	Sources	Applications	£000
Liquid funds at 1 January 19X6 (here, cash balance)			8
	£000	£000	
Funds from operations	64		
Taxation paid		12	
New issue of shares	5		
Dividend paid		8	
Debentures redeemed		15	
Disposals—Investments	8		
—Fixed assets	7		
Acquisitions—Fixed assets		35	
	84	70	
Working capital changes			
Net sources as above	14		
Stock		14	
Debtors	3		
Creditors	6		
	23	14	
Net increase in liquid funds (here, cash balance)			9
Liquid funds at 31 December 19X6			17

Questions

1. A friend of yours who owns a newsagent's and confectionery business has asked for your help. He is very worried because he suspects that a shop assistant is stealing money from his till. He comments as follows:
'For the year to 31 March 19X2 my shop made a profit of £8,600 and yet I have had to ask the bank for an overdraft', then adds 'Will you check the figures for me please?' You agree to help and he supplies the following information

Nick's Newsmart
Balance sheets as at 31 March

	19X1			19X2	
£	£	*Fixed assets*		£	£
16,000		Premises, at cost	16,000		
3,600		*Less:* Depreciation	3,900		
	12,400				12,100
3,000		Fixtures and fittings, at cost	8,200		
1,000		*Less:* Depreciation	1,300		
	2,000				6,900
	14,400				19,000
		Current assets			
		Stocks—magazines,			
5,400		periodicals etc.	8,060		
		—sweets,			
1,480		tobacco etc.	3,240		
2,200		Debtors—trade	4,900		
140		—other	420		
6,400		Bank	—		
280		Cash	500		
15,900			17,120		
		Less:			
		Current liabilities			
4,200		Creditors—trade	3,600		
100		—other	120		
—		Bank overdraft	4,000		
4,300			7,720		
	11,600	*Working capital*			9,400
	26,000	*Net assets employed*			28,400
24,600		Opening capital	26,000		
6,800		*Add:* Net profit	8,600		
31,400			34,600		
5,400		*Less:* Drawings	6,200		
	£26,000	Closing capital			£28,400

You confirm that he has not disposed of any fixed assets during the year.

Required:
Prepare a statement of source and application of funds to show Nick where his profit has gone.

(Association of Certified Accountants)

2. The balance sheets for Schurig Co. Ltd for the years ended 19X1, 19X2 and 19X3 are as follows:

Schurig Co. Limited
Balance sheets as at 31 December

	19X1 £000	19X2 £000	19X3 £000
Plant and equipment	13,200	16,110	16,410
Temporary investment	4,200	1,800	1,290
Stock	2,190	2,280	2,490
Debtors	2,040	2,100	2,430
Bank	1,920	2,010	2,580
	23,550	24,300	25,200
Financed by:			
Share capital	4,500	4,500	4,500
Share premium	9,000	9,000	9,000
Retained earnings (profit and loss account)	4,950	5,610	6,480
Creditors	2,760	2,610	2,670
Short-term loans	2,340	2,580	2,550
	23,550	24,300	25,200
Other data			
Profit after tax	960	1,020	1,230
Annual depreciation	645	780	900
Dividends declared and paid	360	360	360

In 19X2, equipment was sold at a loss of £210,000. New plant in 19X2 cost £5,100,000 and in 19X3 cost £1,200,000.

Required:
Prepare a statement of sources and applications of funds for 19X2 and 19X3 in compliance with SSAP 10.

3. Set out below are the condensed balance sheets for Glazings Ltd for 19X1 and 19X2 and a profit and loss account for the year ended 31 December 19X2.

Glazings Limited
Balance sheet as at 31 December

	19X1 £000	19X1 £000	19X2 £000	19X2 £000
Freehold land and buildings	240		240	
Depreciation	30	210	40	200
Plant and machinery	262		694	
Depreciation	42	220	84	610
Motor vehicles	60		60	
Depreciation	30	30	34	26
Stock		204		234
Debtors		360		432
Bank		276		10
		1,300		1,512

Ordinary share capital	600	600
Share premium account	100	100
General reserve	80	100
Retained earnings		
(profit and loss account)	160	220
7% debentures	140	200
Current taxation	60	80
Proposed dividend	16	20
Creditors	144	192
	1,300	1,512

Summarised profit and loss account for the year ended 31 December 19X2

	£000	£000
Trading profit		388
Less: Expenses	130.8	
Depreciation	68	
Loss on sale of assets	9.2	208
		180
Taxation		80
		100
Ordinary dividend proposed	20	
Transfer to general reserve	20	40
		60
Retained earnings brought forward		160
Retained earnings carried forward		220

Plant which cost £28,000 and which was in the books at a written down value of £16,000, was sold for £6,800.

Required:
Prepare a statement of sources and applications of funds for the year ended 31 December 19X2 in compliance with SSAP 10.

4. Set out below are the balance sheets and other details of Notchup plc relating to the years ended 31 March 19X3 and 19X4.

Balance sheets as at 31 March

	19X3	19X4
	£000	£000
Fixed assets		
Land and buildings	240	300
Plant and machinery	396	510
Motor vehicles	114	156
	750	966
Investments		
Shares in subsidiary	162	162
Current assets		
Stocks	86	102
Debtors	104	119
Cash at bank and in hand	86	34
	276	255

Creditors: Amounts falling due within one year

Bank loan	50	42
Trade creditors	72	76
Taxation	38	54
Proposed dividend	50	63
	210	235
Net current assets	66	20

Total assets *Less:*

Current liabilities	978	1,148

Creditors: Amounts falling due after more than one year

12% debenture loan	80	100
	898	1,048

Capital and reserves

Called up share capital

Ordinary share of £1 each fully paid	400	450
Share premium account	150	200
Revaluation reserve	—	20
Profit and loss account	348	378
	898	1,048

Notes:

(a) The fixed assets detailed for the year ended 31 March 19X4 are:

	Cost or valuation £000	Depreciation £000	Net £000
Land and buildings	352	52	300
Plant and machinery	844	334	510
Motor vehicles	326	170	156
	1,522	556	966

(1) During the year, additional land had been acquired. Part of another piece of land had been revalued from £82,000 to £102,000 the differences being placed in 'revaluation reserve'. Depreciation had been written off buildings amounting to £12,000.

(2) Plant, originally costing £85,000 and written down to £15,000, was scrapped during the year. The sum of £2,000 was realised from the sale of the metal content. Depreciation has been written off plant during the year amounting to £110,000.

(3) There had been additions to motor vehicles during the year which cost £75,000. There were no disposals of vehicles during the year.

(b) Details of the profit and loss account for the year ended 31 March 19X4 were:

	£000
Profit before taxation	160
Corporation tax	54
	106
Loss on disposal of plant	13
	93
Dividend proposed on ordinary shares @ 14%	63
	30
Balance brought forward	348
Balance carried forward	378

Required:

(*a*) Prepare a statement of sources and applications of funds for the year ended 31 March 19X4.

(*b*) Comment, briefly, on the purpose and uses of such statements.

17 Interpretation of Accounts

The purpose of previous chapters has been to analyse the functions which may be properly attributed to financial accounting. These have been stated as being as follows:

(1) To provide a methodical system of recording financial accounting data.
(2) To use the financial accounting data to determine periodic income and to ascertain the financial status of an enterprise at the end of the accounting period.
(3) To provide an information basis for the control of financial assets and liabilities.

The notion of financial control lies at the root of conventional accounting. It is concerned with the use and allocation of resources with a view to profit. Financial control is emphatically addressed to the problem of profitability, and may be seen as having two dimensions. First, internal financial control may be defined as the process of rationing funds within the firm to projects and activities which will be most profitable. Thus, a firm is concerned with seeking the most profitable employment of its resources for two reasons: (a) to provide a sufficient return on the capital invested by shareholders, and (b) to provide a sufficient level of internally generated funds to allow the firm to finance its own expenditure plans. Second, external financial control may be viewed as the process by which scarce financial resources are rationed between competing firms on the basis of their profitability.

Investors (both present and potential shareholders) must decide whether to buy, sell, or retain their ownership interests in a business entity. Loan creditors must decide whether to make loans and in what amounts and on what terms. Government agencies decide whom to tax and whom to subsidise. Labour unions make decisions on wage bargaining tactics.

Irrespective of the particular decision-maker, there are three fundamental purposes for using financial data:

(1) Appraisal of past performance. The decision-maker assesses the success of the business and the effectiveness of the management by considering information such as: the return on investment earned, sales volume, and working capital and cash flows. It also helps him compare one business with another.

(2) Evaluation of present condition. The decision-maker requires information such as: the cash position, the stock position, the types of assets owned and the debt/equity ratio.

(3) Prediction of future potential. This necessitates the provision of information which provides the decision-maker with a base from which to predict the future, and supplies insights as to how the firm may respond to future economic developments.

Interpretation

Users of financial statements generally desire information about the profitability, efficiency and financial soundness of the business under study, whatever their time perspectives. Within these three areas, however, the type of financial analysis that takes place depends on the particular interest that the user has in the enterprise. For example, short-term creditors, such as banks, are primarily interested in the ability of the firm to pay its currently maturing obligations. The composition of the current assets and their relation to short-term liabilities are examined closely to evaluate the short-term solvency of the firm. Debenture holders, on the other hand, look to more long-term indicators, such as the enterprise's capital structure, past and projected profits and changes in financial position. In the long run, a firm that continually operates unprofitably will inevitably encounter difficulty in acquiring financial capital to remain solvent. Shareholders, present or prospective, are also interested in many of the features considered by a long-term creditor. They are interested in profitability because this affects the market price of their investment. Nevertheless, they are also interested in the financial stability of the firm. Management, to make internal operating decisions, is interested in all three areas.

Limitations of conventional financial analysis

The major limitations to conventional methods of interpreting financial statements are to be found in the problems inherent in accounting practice. These are:

(a) Limitation stemming from conventions associated with the measurement of periodic profit and the representation of balance sheet values. These limitations undermine the usefulness of accounting numbers for the valuation of the enterprise. In this connection, the Institute of Chartered Accountants in England and Wales has been at pains to stress on repeated occasions that financial reports are not intended to be used for the purpose of valuing the enterprise.

(b) Limitations stemming from the restrictions on the disclosure of information to shareholders and investors. This problem has been examined earlier, and it may be mentioned that as a result of the restrictions on information disclosures allowed by the Companies Act financial statements are not generally regarded as providing the only source of information of immediate relevance to investors. By and large, financial statements have a temporary impact when they are published, but they form a very small part of the total information flow used, for example, on the Stock Exchange.

Interpretation by ratio analysis

The object of financial analysis is to establish the pattern of key variables which are otherwise concealed in the information aggregated in the profit and loss account and balance sheet. The usefulness of ratio analysis in this context is twofold. First, aggregate numbers are reduced into numbers which may provide a basis for comparing the results of the current year with those of previous years, and for comparing the results of different companies for the same year. Second, flexibility is given to financial analysis by allowing information reported in the profit and loss accounts to be integrated with information disclosed on the balance sheet, thereby giving a broader dimension to the analysis of results.

Ratio analysis is the application of a complex number of different ratios which focus on the several aspects of a firm's financial performance and financial status. These ratios fall into two broad categories. The first group consists of accounting ratios which rely upon the information disclosed in the financial statements themselves. The second group consists of market ratios with integrate the information contained in the financial statements of a company with information relating to the Stock Exchange valuation of the company's shares. Accordingly, they apply only to companies whose shares are quoted on a stock exchange.

Accounting ratios

Accounting ratios may be grouped into four categories as follows:

(a) *Profitability ratios* which attempt to measure the efficiency of the enterprise in the generation of profit.

(b) *Activity ratios* which attempt to indicate the relative efficiency with which the firm's resources have been employed.

(c) *Solvency ratios* which attempt to predict the firm's ability to meet its financial obligations and so prevent the possibility of insolvency.

(d) *Gearing ratios* which attempt to determine the financial implications of the firm's capital structure.

Profitability ratios

Profitability ratios are classified into two categories: ratios which express profit as a percentage of sales, and ratios which express profit as a yield associated with the employment of resources. For the purpose of the analysis of profitability, profit is generally expressed as *profit before interest and tax* (PBIT). The reason for excluding interest paid on borrowing from profitability ratios lies in the intention that they should focus on the result of operating decisions rather than financing decisions. The capital structure of different firms will generally reflect a different mix of equity and debt capital. Hence, it would not be possible to compare the profitability of different firms unless their results are calculated on the same basis. Profitability ratios are also generally based on profit before taxation in order to exclude the distortion which would result from the application of taxation rules in the computation of the taxable income of different companies. In this regard, it should be noted that taxation is not neutral when comparing different companies. Indeed, it is often used to encourage companies to follow certain policies, in particular those relating to investments. Companies engaged in the expansion of capital expenditure often may lay claim to accelerated depreciation allowances which have the effect of reducing their taxable profits and the tax payable. As a result, such companies would show comparatively higher after-tax earnings than similar companies not engaged in heavy capital expenditure. For these various reasons, therefore, taxation is also excluded from the profit figures used in profitability ratios.

Ratios of profit as a percentage of sales

Two important profitability ratios are the gross profit ratio and the net profit ratio.

(1) *Gross profit ratio:* This ratio is also commonly known as the gross margin ratio. It expresses the gross profit as a percentage of sales and is calculated as follows:

$$\frac{\text{Gross profit}}{\text{Sales}} \times 100 = \dots \%$$

The gross profit ratio is widely used to check the stability of market conditions for the only two operative factors are sales and the cost of sales. Under normal conditions, the gross profit ratio should show little change from year to year.

(2) *Net profit ratio:* This ratio shows the net profit resulting from sales. It is calculated as follows:

$$\frac{\text{PBIT}}{\text{Sales}} \times 100 = \dots \%$$

It is usual to express the net profit ratio in terms of each £100 of sales. This ratio tends to fluctuate as between different companies operating in the same market owing to the variations in overhead expenses such as advertising, depreciation and management costs. Since companies are required to disclose their total sales revenue, the net profit ratio may be used as a significant ratio of profitability.

Ratios of return on resources employed

The essential purpose of these ratios is to measure profitability as a return or yield on the resources employed by an enterprise. These resources have alternative interpretations as follows:

Net asset value (NAV).
Total assets.
Gross assets.

These alternative interpretations give rise to three ratios, the most commonly used of which is the return on capital employed (ROCE).

(3) *Return on capital employed* (ROCE): This ratio interprets the capital employed as being the net asset value which is found by adding the value of fixed assets to that of current assets and deducting the total of current liabilities. In effect, it interprets the resources employed as being equivalent to the shareholders' equity *plus* long-term borrowings. It is calculated as follows:

$$\frac{\text{PBIT}}{\text{NAV}} \times 100 = \dots \%$$

The return on capital employed (net asset value) may show that the company is using its assets efficiently when compared with the industry average. This could be due to a lower expenditure on fixed assets or, perhaps, using assets over a longer life than the average.

(4) *Return on total assets:* This ratio interprets the value of the resources employed as the total assets employed in the business to give a view of the efficiency with which assets are employed by management. It is calculated as follows:

$$\frac{\text{PBIT}}{\text{Fixed + Current assets}} \times 100 = \dots \%$$

(5) *Return on gross assets:* This ratio requires a modification to the calculation of PBIT by adding back the depreciation charges against assets in the period under review. The reason for this adjustment is to exclude the distortion introduced into profit measurement by different methods of computing depreciation. Hence, its purpose is to obtain a more reliable basis of comparison between companies. It is calculated as follows:

$$\frac{\text{PBIT + Depreciation for the period}}{\text{Fixed assets at cost + Current assets}} \times 100 = \dots \%$$

The objection to using this method of calculating the return on assets employed is that depreciation is intended to ensure the maintenance of capital. To exclude depreciation, therefore, leads to erroneous conclusions as regards calculations of the asset base.

The return on capital employed (ROCE) is regarded as being the most significant ratio of profitability, and it is widely used by businessmen and financial analysts. Its limitations are mainly to be found in its reliance upon accounting conventions for measuring profit and the absence of any verifiable basis for assessing the value of net assets.

Activity ratios

Activity ratios are intended to analyse the use made of resources by the enterprise. Four important activity ratios are as follows:

Stock turnover.
Collection period for debtors.
Ratio of net asset value to sales.
Ratio of total asset value to sales.

(6) *Stock turnover:* The rate at which a business converts stock into sales is a critical indicator of business activity. The stock turnover indicates the number of times the stock is completely sold and replaced by purchases during the accounting period. Given complete data about the cost of sales, the stock turnover may be calculated as follows:

$$\frac{\text{Cost of sales}}{\text{Average stock}} = \text{Number of time stock is turned over}$$

Since an external user of financial reports may not be given data relating to the cost of sales, the following formula is commonly used:

(6a) $$\frac{\text{Sales}}{\text{Average stock}} = \text{Number of times stock is turned over}$$

The natural trading cycle for different types of businesses will obviously not be similar. Hence, it must be expected that the stock turnover will be characteristic of the type of trading operations in which a firm is engaged. Moreover, the trading cycle may be cyclical, resulting in peak and low stock levels. Without knowledge of seasonal variations in stock levels, the stock turnover based on the average of opening and closing stock will not provide an accurate analysis of stock levels throughout the period. This is an important consideration when examining the financial implications of stock levels and the need to minimise investments in stock. In this connection, the holding time in the case of engineering products may well be appreciably longer and will require a higher level of net investment than that associated with a supermarket where stock may be sold within the normal credit period allowed.

This ratio may indicate that a company turns over its stock rather more rapidly than the average. They may have secured a more rapid replacement system with suppliers, thereby enabling lower stocks, on average, to be carried. Efficient re-order systems would seek to minimise stock carrying, whilst not risking stock-outs (i.e., not being able to meet customer demand immediately).

(7) *Average debtor collection period:* The careful control of debtor levels is an important aspect of good financial management. The average length of time for the payment of debts owing to the business is an important indicator of the efficiency of management. It is found by dividing the average daily *credit* sales into the total debtors outstanding as follows:

$$\frac{\text{Debtors}}{\text{Cr Sales}/365} = \text{Average number of days for payment}$$

This formula may be restated as follows:

$$\frac{\text{Debtors}}{\text{Cr sales}} \times 365 = \text{Average number of days for payment}$$

The average debtor collection period is only a first indicator to be used in the analysis of debtors. Debt age schedules and other data would be used for further analysis.

The general proportion of cash sales to credit sales would need to be established. If net monthly credit terms are advanced to customers (which is payment at end of the month following that of the delivery of the goods), then 42 days would be very good indeed.

(8) *Ratio of asset values to sales:* This ratio has two alternative expressions based on different interpretations of asset values. These are (i) net asset value (NAV), and (ii) total asset value (FA + CA), as follows:

$$(i) \quad \frac{\text{Sales}}{\text{NAV}} \quad \text{or} \quad (ii) \quad \frac{\text{Sales}}{\text{FA} + \text{CA}}$$

Both ratios are concerned with assessing the rate at which asset values are converted into sales revenue. They are indicative, therefore, of the ability of assets to generate profit. The most commonly used ratio is the ratio of net asset value to sales.

The return on capital employed (ROCE) mentioned earlier is derived by associating the net profit ratio with the ratio of net asset value to sales as follows:

$$\frac{\text{PBIT}}{\text{Sales}} \times \frac{\text{Sales}}{\text{NAV}} \times 100$$

The ROCE links profitability with activity ratios to provide an integrated view of profitability which is based on the profitability of sales and the profitability of assets. Total assets may be substituted for net assets if it is wished to express the rate of return on that basis.

Example 1

The financial statement of Cornerstores Ltd for the year ended 31 December 19X8 showed the following data:

	£
Sales for the year	5,000,000
Net profit for the year	100,000
Net assets employed	500,000

The net profit ratio is as follows:

$$\frac{PBIT}{Sales} \times 100 = \frac{100,000}{5,000,000} \times 100 = 2\%$$

Thus, by itself the rate of profitability on sales would appear to be quite low. The ratio of net assets values to sales, however, is much greater as follows:

$$\frac{Sales}{NAV} = \frac{5,000,000}{500,000} = 10$$

Combining these two ratios, the ROCE shows that the overall profitability expressed as a return on capital employed is:

$$2\% \times 10 = 20\%$$

or, more formally:

$$\frac{PBIT}{Sales} \times \frac{Sales}{NAV} \times 100 = \frac{PBIT}{NAV} \times 100$$

$$= \frac{100,000}{500,000} \times 100 = 20\%$$

Solvency ratios

Solvency ratios are addressed to the analysis of the ability of a business to meet its immediate financial obligations and thus avoid the possibility of insolvency. Two ratios in common use are the current ratio and the quick or acid test ratio.

(9) *The current ratio:* A general indication of a firm's ability to meet its current liabilities is found in the current ratio, which is calculated as follows:

$$\frac{Current\ assets}{Current\ liabilities}$$

This ratio assumes that current assets could be converted into cash to meet current liabilities. There is no general rule as to the dimension of this ratio which may vary from industry to industry, though any ratio less than 1 would indicate that the firm might have a potential problem in meeting creditor's claims. By contrast, a number significantly greater than one would imply that current assets were being underemployed.

(10) *The acid test ratio:* A limitation of the current ratio is the assumption that all current assets could readily be converted into cash. The acid test ratio focuses on this problem by recognis-

ing that stock is not easily converted into immediate cash. It is calculated as follows:

$$\frac{\text{Current assets} - \text{Stock}}{\text{Current liabilities}}$$

It remains true, however, that other current assets, for example prepayments are also not readily convertible into cash and should not be regarded as available to meet current liabilities. When using the acid test ratio, care should be taken to exclude from current liabilities such claims as are not immediately payable.

The concern with the problem of solvency should not hide the fundamental purpose for borrowing money, namely using borrowed funds to generate profits. A ratio which expresses the relationship between profit and borrowed funds is the following:

$$(11) \quad \frac{\text{Long-term debt} + \text{Current liabilities} - \text{Current assets}}{\text{Profit after interest and tax}}$$

This ratio expresses the length of time it would take to repay indebtedness out of net profit after interest and tax. The reason for this formulation of net profit stems from the fact that debt repayments have to be made from the balance of profit after interest and tax obligations have been met.

In conclusion, it must be stressed that the relevance of solvency ratios in the analysis of potential insolvency is controversial. Hence, care should be taken when applying them to the circumstances of particular companies.

Gearing ratios

The proportion of a company's fixed interest capital to total capital is of considerable importance to ordinary shareholders. The gearing or leverage of a company is defined as the ratio of preferred share capital and loan capital to ordinary share equity. Two formulas are used to express gearing and leverage. The first shows long-term debt (D) as a fraction of capital expressed as long-term debt (D) plus ordinary share equity (S) as follows:

$$(12) \quad \text{Gearing or Leverage} = \frac{D}{D + S}$$

The second formula shows long-term debt (D) as a fraction of ordinary share equity (S) as follows:

(13)　　Gearing or Leverage $= \dfrac{D}{S}$

The first formula is generally found to be more useful since it will always produce a result which is less than one, whereas the second formula will produce a much greater range of answers.

Example 2

Compoost plc has a capital structure which includes £2,000,000 of 11% debenture and 250,000 ordinary shares of £1 each fully paid and £150,000 reserves. Accordingly, the gearing or leverage is:

$$\frac{D}{D+S} = \frac{2,000,000}{6,000,000} = 0.33$$

The values expressed in the gearing ratio of 0.33 have been obtained directly from the balance sheet. In the case of a company whose shares are quoted on the Stock Exchange, it would be more useful to investors to use the market values of the debentures and shares. These market values would be significantly different from those based on accounting procedures.

The capital structure of a company reflects the financial strategy adopted for financing the company's activities. The analysis of the optimal financial structure is the subject of considerable literature and debate. In simple terms, the advantage to be gained from borrowing capital rather than raising capital by the issue of ordinary shares is found in the difference between the company's internal rate of return and the cost of borrowed money. Thus, if the company's rate of return on capital employed is 12% and the interest payable on borrowing is, say 9%, there is a distinct advantage to the ordinary shareholders of borrowing money rather than raising further equity capital. However, the introduction of debt capital into the capital structure increases the degree of risk attached to the expectations of ordinary shareholders. This is because the payment of interest on borrowed money is a prior charge on the company's assets. The more obvious effects of debt capital on the income of shareholders from the company are seen when the company's profit is fluctuating. Thus, when the company's profit falls, the dividends payable to ordinary shareholders is restricted by the amount of interest payable on debt capital. When the company's profits are expanding, the proportional burden of debt is considerably reduced, and the dividends payable to ordinary shareholders increases correspondingly.

An additional ratio which is quite useful is to express the total liabilities of a company as a percentage of total assets is as follows:

$$(14) \quad \frac{\text{Long-term debt capital} + \text{Current liabilities}}{\text{Fixed assets} + \text{Current assets}} \times 100$$

Moreover, gearing or leverage can be used as a profit ratio to indicate the extent to which the company's profit covers its interest obligations. The following ratio expresses the interest coverage:

$$(15) \quad \text{Interest coverage} = \frac{\text{PBIT}}{\text{Debt interest}}$$

Finally, the leasing of plant and machinery can produce misleading ratios in so far as lease payments are written off as expenses against profits and there is no asset base against which to measure profitability. Ratio [16] may be expanded to cover this problem by including the fixed charges incurred under leasing and hiring agreements as follows:

$$(16) \quad \text{Interest and fixed charges coverage} = \frac{\text{PBIT} + \text{Fixed charges}}{\text{Debt interest} + \text{Fixed charges}}$$

Ratio analysis and public quoted companies

A number of additional ratios are applied to the analysis of the results of public quoted companies. The following ratios are frequently used in this respect:

Dividend yield.
Dividend coverage.
Earnings yield.
Earnings per share.
Price/earnings.

(17) *Dividend yield:* The practice in the United Kingdom is to declare dividends by reference to the nominal value of shares. The dividend yield expresses the dividend as a return on the current share price, as follows:

Dividend yield =

$$\text{Declared dividend rate} \times \frac{\text{Nominal value of share}}{\text{Market price of share}}$$

(18) *Dividend coverage:* As a guide to the company's ability to sustain dividend payments, the dividend coverage indicates the ratio of distributable earnings to actual dividends as follows:

$$\text{Dividend coverage} = \frac{\text{Net profit after interest and tax}}{\text{Dividend payable}}$$

(19) *Earnings yield:* This ratio simply expresses the earnings of the company (net profit after interest and tax) as a percentage of the market price of the share. It can be derived by two alternative methods:

(i)   Dividend yield × Dividend cover

or

(ii) $\dfrac{\text{Net profit after interest and tax}}{\text{Market price of share} \times \text{Number of shares issued}} \times 100$

(20) *Earnings per share* (EPS): This ratio is the most commonly used ratio for valuing shares. It represents the earnings of the company, *whether or not they are declared as dividends*, as earnings derived from each ordinary share held in the company. It is calculated as follows:

$$\text{Earnings per share} = \frac{\text{Net profit after interest and tax}}{\text{Number of ordinary shares issued}}$$

Some complications arise in the calculation of this ratio in the treatment of extraordinary items which may have affected the company's earnings for one year only, as well as the impact of corporation tax on earnings. These complexities are examined in Statement of Standard Accounting Practice 3.

(21) *Price/Earnings ratio:* This ratio is widely used by financial analysts and journalists as a capitalisation factor for use in establishing the market value of a company. A capitalisation factor may be defined as a number which is applied to periodic profit for arriving at a capital sum representing the value of a company or other asset. The market value so derived represents the price which the market would be prepared to pay for a company.

Example 3

A company having in issue 200,000 ordinary shares with a nominal value of £1 each and a market price of £3.20 per share on the basis of earnings per share of 40p on the last reported results would be valued as follows:

$$\text{Price/Earnings ratio} = \frac{\text{Price per share}}{\text{Earnings per share}}$$

$$= \frac{£3.20}{40p}$$

$$= 8$$

$$\begin{aligned}\text{Value of the company} &= \text{Capitalisation factor} \times \text{Net income after interest and tax}\end{aligned}$$

$$= 8 \times (40p \times 200,000)$$

$$= £640,000$$

This valuation is exactly the same as would be derived directly from the market price of the company's shares as follows:

$$\begin{aligned}\text{Value of the company} &= \text{Market price of shares} \times \text{Number of shares in issue}\end{aligned}$$

$$= £3.20 \times 200,000$$

$$= £640,000$$

The importance of the P/E ratio lies in its association with expectations about a company's prospects. Changes in the company's earnings generally result in corresponding changes in the share price.

The following example is a comprehensive ratio analysis applied to a quoted company.

Example 4

The following ratio analysis is based on the profit and loss accounts of Edbark plc for the years ended 31 December 19X7 and 19X8, the balance sheets as at those dates, and market data available on 31 January 19X9.

Edbark plc
Profit and loss account for years to 31 December

	19X7 £000s	19X8 £000s
Sales	1,270	1,480
Gross profit	644	760
Net profit for year before tax	120	164
Corporation tax	60	80
Net profit after tax	60	84
Dividend proposed	16	40
Retained profit	44	44

Notes

(1) 90% of all sales were on credit.

(2) The accounts are truncated and are not meant to show conformity with standards or legal disclosure requirements.

(3) The only interest paid was debenture interest.

At the end of January 19X9 the following information was available from the market:

Quoted price of ordinary shares of Edbark (ex div) £3.20 each.

Quoted price of £100 units of debenture £105 (for the sake of simplicity these are treated as irredeemable).

Edbark plc
Balance sheets as at 31 December

	19X7			19X8		
	£000s	£000s	£000s	£000s	£000s	£000s
Fixed assets	Cost	Depn		Cost	Depn	
Freehold property	60	—	60	210	—	210
Fixtures and fittings	240	56	184	300	70	230
Motor vehicles	70	34	36	70	40	30
	370	90	280	580	110	470
Current assets						
Stock		90			164	
Debtors		130			188	
Bank		136			24	
		356			376	
Creditors—amounts falling due within one year						
Trade creditors	70			142		
Proposed dividend	16	86		40	182	
Net current assets			270			194
Total assets *Less:* Current liabilities			550			664
Creditors—amounts falling due after more than one year						
12% debentures			120			120
			430			544
Capital and reserves						
Called up share capital		150			200	
Share premium account		—			20	
Profit and loss account		280			324	
			430			544

Edbark plc
Ratio analysis 19X7 and 19X8

Profitability ratios	Formula	Year 1	Year 2	Ratio Year 1	Ratio Year 2	Industry average	Comment
(1) Gross profit ratio	$\dfrac{\text{Gross profit}}{\text{Sales}} \times 100$	$\dfrac{644}{1,270} \times 100$	$\dfrac{760}{1,480} \times 100$	51%	51%	—	This ratio is not available to shareholders as the gross margin is not disclosed
(2) Net profit ratio	$\dfrac{\text{PBIT}}{\text{Sales}} \times 100$	$\dfrac{120 + 14.4}{1,270} \times 100$	$\dfrac{164 + 14.4}{1,480} \times 100$	10.5%	12%	—	
(3) Return on capital employed	$\dfrac{\text{PBIT}}{\text{NAV}} \times 100$	$\dfrac{134.4}{550} \times 100$	$\dfrac{178.4}{664} \times 100$	24%	27%	—	Only the version based on NAV is given
Activity ratios							
(6A) Stock turnover	$\dfrac{\text{Sales}}{\text{Average inventory}}$	$\dfrac{1,270}{90}$	$\dfrac{1,480}{(90 + 164)/2}$	14 times	12 times	—	
(7) Debtors collection period	$\dfrac{\text{Debtors} \times 365}{\text{Credit sales}}$	$\dfrac{30 \times 365}{0.9 \times 1,270}$	$\dfrac{188 \times 365}{0.9 \times 1,480}$	42 days	51 days	—	
(8) Sales value to NAV Number of times covered	$\dfrac{\text{Sales}}{\text{NAV}}$	$\dfrac{1,270}{550}$	$\dfrac{1,480}{664}$	2.3 times	2.2 times	—	Only the version based on NAV is given
Note: ROCE = Net profit ratio × Sales Value to NAV	$\dfrac{\text{PBIT}}{\text{Sales}} \times \dfrac{\text{Sales}}{\text{NAV}}$	$\dfrac{134.4}{1,270} \times \dfrac{1,270}{550} \times 100$	$\dfrac{178.4}{1,480} \times \dfrac{1,480}{664} \times 100$	24%	27%	—	

Continued overleaf

Edbark plc
Ratio analysis 19X7 and 19X8 (continued)

Profitability ratios	Formula	Year 1	Year 2	Ratio Year 1	Ratio Year 2	Industry average	Comment
(9) Current ratio	$\dfrac{\text{Current assets}}{\text{Current liabilities}}$	$\dfrac{356}{86}$	$\dfrac{376}{182}$	4.1	2.1	—	
(10) Acid test ratio	$\dfrac{\text{Current assets less stock}}{\text{Current liabilities}}$	$\dfrac{356 - 90}{86}$	$\dfrac{376 - 164}{182}$	3.1	1.2	—	
(11) Time to repay liabilities from profit	$\dfrac{\text{Long-term debt plus current liabilities minus current assets}}{\text{Profit after interest and tax}}$	$\dfrac{120 + 86 - 356}{60}$	$\dfrac{120 + 182 - 376}{84}$	−2.5	−0.9	—	

The solvency ratios indicate that the company is able to meet its forthcoming payments with little difficulty. The current and acid test ratios have slipped somewhat from year to year two but still seem good. The recovery of indebtedness by income shows a very wide safety margin.

Gearing ratios

	Formula	Year 1	Year 2	Ratio Year 1	Ratio Year 2	Industry average	Comment
(12) Basic gearing ratio	$\dfrac{\text{Long-term debt}}{\text{Equity}}$	$\dfrac{120}{430}$	$\dfrac{120}{544}$	1:3.6	1:4.5	—	
Ratio of borrowed funds to total funds	$\dfrac{\text{Long-term debt}}{\text{Long-term debt plus equity}}$	$\dfrac{120}{550}$	$\dfrac{126}{664}$	1:4.6	1:5.3	—	
(14) Percentage claims against business	$\dfrac{\text{Long-term debt plus current liabilities}}{\text{Total assets}} \times 100$	$\dfrac{120 + 86}{280 + 356} \times 100$	$\dfrac{120 + 182}{470 + 376} \times 100$	32%	36%	—	
(15) Times interest covered	$\dfrac{\text{PBIT}}{\text{Interest}}$	$\dfrac{134.4}{14.4}$	$\dfrac{178.4}{14.4}$	9x	12x	—	

The gearing ratios of Edbank plc indicate that the company is not heavily financed by debt.

Valuation

Valuation is a controversial, complex and problematical issue in accounting theory and practice. *It is controversial* because many accountants would argue that they are not concerned with valuation but with cost allocation. Others would argue, however, that accounting representations which attach financial measurements to assets and liabilities revenue and expense cannot avoid the implication that such representations have the characteristic of valuation. *It is complex* because valuation itself is a complex subject. Valuation is essentially a subjective process. The value of an object to oneself may be greater than its value in exchange for a variety of reasons. Once it is decided to attempt to make an objective valuation of an object, the valuation process inevitably appears as a price determined between a willing buyer and a willing seller. *It is problematical* because any representation of value should be specific to the needs to users of that information. Hence, a number of important issues are found in the accounting debate in this respect. Accountants would assert that the values represented on the balance sheet cannot be used to derive the value of a business. The cost allocation process results in balances which cannot be used to represent either the value in use of the assets represented, their realisable value or their replacement cost. Hence, there is no obvious mechanism in the accounting process which would permit any valuation of assets to be derived. Accountants would hold that they are not concerned with providing valuations which would be relevant to the most important and fundamental need of investors and other users of accounting information, namely a valuation of the firm. A government committee report in 1975 went only so far as to state that assets should be represented at their value to the business, but limited this interpretation to their current cost.

In view of the foregoing introduction to this topic, it is evident that valuation cannot be dealt with satisfactorily at an elementary level of argument. Certainly, it is beyond the scope of this text to do more than introduce a few of the salient points in issue.

The objectives of valuation

The fundamental objective of any representation of value is to provide information for decison-making. Applying the proprietorship concept of the firm, shareholders may be assumed to be interested basically in the value of the firm to them. On this basis of the going-concern convention, the value may be derived as follows:

(1) By using the reported income for the purpose of calculating the value of the firm as an income-yielding asset. That value would

be derived in the same way as any other asset would be valued, namely by establishing the present value of the stream of future income flowing from that asset.

Example 5

A property yields an annual rent of £1,000. Given that the current rate of interest is 10%, the capitalised value of the rent is:

$$\frac{£1,000}{0.10} = \underline{\underline{£10,000}}$$

Similarly, if the net profit of a business is £1,000 and is expected to continue at that level in perpetuity, and given that the current rate of interest is 10%, the capitalised value of the firm is:

$$\frac{£1,000}{0.10} = \underline{\underline{£10,000}}$$

(2) By using the reported net asset values to calculate the capitalised value of the firm. In this context, it is evident that—if it is accepted that the value of assets is related to the net profit which they produce—then the net asset value should be equal to the capitalised value of net profits.

It should be noted that all references here to discounting 'profits' to arrive at capital value should really refer to net cash flows generated. Profit is used as a shorthand term for this although technically this is incorrect.

Investors attempt to establish the value of a business by reference to the income yield rather than by reference to any accounting representation of asset value. Thus, the objective of ratio analysis in the case of quoted companies is to use such ratios as earnings per share and price earnings ratio to calculate the value of the company's shares and hence the value of the company. No reference is made to the value of assets shown on the balance sheet, except where the company might be in liquidation or might hold valuable assets which are currently considerably undervalued or unused. In such a case, the market price of the shares would reflect an adjustment to the valuation which would be derived more directly from reported earnings.

Given that investors are able to establish a value for a company, the decision which they have to make is typically an investment decision, namely to buy or hold shares in the company or to sell the shares which they currently hold.

Seen in the context of a society having broader social objectives than satisfying the needs of investors for a rational system for investment decision-making, the objectives of valuation may be interpreted again in terms of establishing the value of any enterprise to society. In this sense, the use of scarce national resources in the form of human skills, government and private funds and other resources should be allocated to those firms which are most efficient in utilising such resources. It is true that profitability remains the key success factor in judging the performance of business enterprises. Therefore, it may be argued that the basic objective of valuation is to provide a value of the business as a going concern in terms of the present value of future net income flows. The objective of the balance sheet may be interpreted in this context as providing a verification of the valuation so derived.

The valuation of assets

The accounting process does not attempt to value the business as a going concern. Nevertheless, considerable attention is given to the valuation of individual assets without relating the problems involved to the valuation of the business. In strict terms, a rational theory of asset valuation cannot escape the conclusion that the sum of the value of the net assets of a business should be equal to the present value of the future stream of its net profit. The reasoning for this statement is in itself unexceptional, and may be found in the decision to invest and hold individual assets. Given that a firm has to finance the acquisition of assets, the cost of finance to the firm is equivalent to a given rate of interest. Hence, unless the stream of future income associated with the purchase of any asset has a present value which is *at least equal* to the current acquisition cost, the firm should not acquire that asset.

Example 6

Suppose that a company's cost of capital is 10%, and that the purchase of an asset costing £1,000 is contemplated. In deciding whether or not to purchase that asset, the company is required to assess if the present value of the future net income generated by means of that asset is worth at least £1,000. This means evaluating that stream of future net income as being at least £100 per annum, for the present value of £100 per annum discounted at 10% is £1,000.

From the foregoing example, the generalised proposition which may be advanced is that the sum of the value of the net assets of the company should be equal to the present value of its future net income. This proposition provides a rational framework not only for the purpose of management decisions regarding the acquisition of assets but also for the purpose of financial reporting concerned with providing a basis for rationing scarce funds to competing firms.

Most accountants would probably agree that the present value of assets provides the optimal valuation basis if it is assumed that the objective of financial statements is to facilitate decision-making by the users of those statements. The problem lies in estimating the present value of assets, for this involves forecasting future income. Moreover, it would be well-nigh impossible in practice to forecast the incremental net future income associated with the purchase of most assets.

Alternative valuation methods

Controversy in accounting circles has not been addressed to the problem of selecting the optimal valuation basis relevant to the need of investors to formulate informed judgments about the value of a business and the efficiency of its management in allocating and using scarce funds in the process of managing the asset base. On the contrary, the debate has been concerned with the comparative merits of alternative valuation methods. These are as follows:

(1) Historical cost.
(2) Realisable value.
(3) Replacement or current cost.

Historical cost

The most commendable virtue of historical cost valuation from an accounting viewpoint is that it is supported by documentary evidence in the form of invoices and, therefore, has the attribute of being verifiable by audit. It is also sometimes argued that since all valuations are at best reasoned guesses, historical cost values could well be retained in view of their familiarity to accountants.

Historical cost valuation represents the accounting tradition based on conservatism, and the maintenance of capital concept implicitly reflected by historical cost is the original money contribution by shareholders.

The major drawback of historical cost valuation stems from rapid inflation which distorts money values leading to an understatement of the real value of the non-monetary assets of the firm and an overstatement of the net profit.

Realisable value

This concept of valuation is based on the money value of assets if they were sold. Thus, whereas historical cost valuations reflect typically entry values, realisable values represent typically exit values. Realisable values emphasise the liquidation rather than the use of the company's assets. Hence, they are criticised for representing an unrealistic view of the firm. Supporters of realisable value accounting argue as follows:

(a) It does not pre-empt any decision as to whether or not the enterprise should continue.
(b) Economic theories of the firm portray the firm as an adaptive opportunity-seeking organism. Hence a measure of its ability to switch resources and activities is relevant to users of financial reports.
(c) Realisable values are the best indicators of the sacrifice made by the firm in holding assets and, therefore, are the best measures of the opportunity cost involved.
(d) Realisable values are the most easily understood values.
(e) Realisable values do not invoke the future to measure the present.

Replacement cost

This is the cost of replacing the services of the existing asset. Given that changes in technology occur it should not be thought of simply in terms of replacement by a physically identical asset. Rather it should be thought of as the cost of replacing the service potential of the existing asset.

Current cost

This concept combines the realisable and replacement cost methods and adopts a 'value to the business' or 'deprival value' approach to valuation. In order to value any individual asset it is necessary to ask the question: If the firm were to be deprived of the asset what sum of money would this loss represent? The value to the business approach has been adopted by the Accounting Standards Committee and is considered in depth in the following chapter.

Questions

1. What do you understand by 'value'?

2. Suggest different concepts which render meaningful the notion of the 'value of an enterprise'.

3. Discuss the objectives of valuation from an accounting viewpoint.

4. Examine the relationship between the concept of profit and the value of a business derived from balance sheet numbers.

5. Compare and contrast alternative valuation bases and discuss their advantages and disadvantages when used for the purpose of deriving accounting measurements.

6. Using the profit and loss accounts and balance sheets given below of G. E. & R. Main Co. Limited, wholesale fashion clothes distributors, you are required to:

(1) Prepare a statement of sources and application of funds for the year ended 30 September 19X7.
(2) Calculate those ratios which would be helpful in further interpretation of the results and financial position.

Profit and loss accounts for years ended 30 September

	19X6		19X7	
	£000s	£000s	£000s	£000s
Sales		635		740
Less:				
Cost of sales: Opening stock	37		45	
Purchases	321		397	
	358		442	
Closing stock	45	313	82	360
Gross profit		322		380
Less:				
Wages	122		138	
Advertising	25		26	
Printing, post and stationery	12		14	
Motor expenses	20		26	
Audit fees	8		9	
Directors' remuneration	34		38	
Interest payment including debenture	12		18	
Rent and rates	25		7	
Lighting and heating	8		12	
Telephones	6		8	
Depreciation—Motors	4		3	
Depreciation—Fixtures and fittings	14		22	
Insurance	2		3	
Loss on sale of fixtures	—		24	
		292		348
Net profit for the year		30		32
Balance brought forward		118		140
		148		172
Dividend proposed		8		10
Balance carried forward		140		162

G. E. & R. Main Co. Limited
Balance sheets as at 30 September

	19X6			19X7		
	£000s	£000s	£000s	£000s	£000s	£000s
Fixed assets	Cost	Depn		Cost	Depn	
Freehold property	—	—	—	90	—	90
Fixtures and fittings	120	28	92	150	35	115
Motor vehicles	35	17	18	35	20	15
	155	45	110	275	55	220
Current assets						
Stock		45			82	
Debtors		65			94	
Bank		68			2	
		178			178	
Creditors—amounts falling due within one year						
Trade creditors	35			71		
Proposed dividend	8	43		10	81	
Net current assets			135			97
Total assets *Less:* Current liabilities			245			317
Creditors—amounts falling due after more than one year						
12% debentures			30			45
			215			272
Capital and reserves						
Called up share capital		75			100	
Share premium account		—			10	
Profit and loss account		140			162	
			215			272

Note: During the year to 30 September 19X7 some fittings were sold which originally cost £70,000.

7. The following condensed accounting statements for the years ended 31 December 19X2 and 19X3 relate to Domestic Equipment Company Limited, manufacturers of kitchen equipment.

Condensed profit and loss accounts for the years ended 31 December

	19X2	19X3
	£000s	£000s
Sales	2,000	2,400
Cost of sales	1,200	1,400
Gross profit	800	1,000
Expenses	400	440
Profit before taxation	400	560
less Taxation	170	252
Profit after taxation	230	308
Dividends	160	160
Retained profit	70	148

Condensed balance sheet as at 31 December

	19X2 £000s	19X3 £000s		19X2 £000s	19X3 £000s
Share capital—Issued and fully paid ordinary £1 shares	800	800	Fixed assets (net of depreciation)		
Retained earnings	200	348	Plant and equipment	600	800
9% debenture	100	100	Motor vehicles	200	300
	1,100	1,248		800	1,100
Current liabilities			Current assets		
Creditors	270	300	Stock	400	540
Taxation	170	252	Debtors	180	200
Dividends proposed	160	160	Bank	320	120
	1,700	1,960		1,700	1,960

Note: In the expense figures for 19X3 is included depreciation of £60,000 on plant and equipment and £40,000 for motor vehicles.

Required:
Prepare:
(a) A statement of sources and application of funds.
(b) Such ratios as you may be able to calculate and which you believe would aid in the interpretation of these figures.
(c) Present your interpretation of the results obtained from (a) and (b).

8. Set out below are the trading results, balance sheets and certain other data of the Bigdeal Stores plc for the years to 30 September 19X2 and 19X3. The company owns and operates a chain of department stores throughout the country and is quoted on the London Stock Exchange.

		19X2 £000s		19X3 £000s
Turnover		178,392		191,423
Trading profit after charging the following		12,314		9,503
Depreciation	6,211		8,312	
Interest	1,500		2,050	
Directors' remuneration	64		86	
Audit fees	62		70	
Taxation		5,710		6,117
Profit after taxation		6,604		3,386
Dividend on ordinary shares		2,000		2,500
Transfer to retained earnings		4,604		886
Ex div price of £1 share on results declared in October		£4.20		£5.00

Balance sheets as at 30 September

	£000s	£000s	19X2 £000s	£000s	£000s	19X3 £000s
Fixed assets						
Goodwill			27			—
Shop and properties			42,310			68,810
Fixtures and equipment			12,110			16,834
Vehicles			610			582
c/frwd			55,057			86,226

	£000s	£000s	19X2 £000s	£000s	£000s	19X3 £000s
b/frwd			55,057			86,226
Current assets						
Stock		27,142			34,836	
Debtors and prepayments		1,237			2,142	
Bank		8,629			340	
		37,008			37,318	
Creditors—Amounts falling due after more than one year						
Trade creditors	16,927			24,113		
Dividends	2,000			2,500		
Taxation	5,710	24,637		6,117	32,730	
Net current assets			12,371			4,588
Total assets less current liabilities			67,428			90,814
Creditors—Amounts falling due after more than one year						
10% Debentures			15,000			15,000
11% debentures			—			5,000
			52,428			70,814
Capital and reserves						
Called up share capital			20,000			20,000
Share premium account			13,500			13,500
Revaluation reserve			—			17,500
Profit and loss account			18,928			19,814
			52,428			70,814

Required:
Prepare an analysis of the information supplied above by means of appropriate ratios. Comment upon the implications of your analysis.

18   Current Cost Accounting

Until the advent of the rapid inflation of the 1970s, it was assumed that the money standard of measurement had a relatively stable value and that historical cost accounting provided an accurate and objective method for measuring profit and for balance sheet representations.

The accounting approach to profit determination stresses the maintenance of capital concept, which is understood to apply to the original money contribution made by the proprietors or shareholders. Accordingly, the objectives of historical cost accounting are concerned with ensuring that the expenses charged against revenues in the process of determining periodic profit will be adequate to maintain the value of capital intact.

Inflation erodes the value of the original capital in three important respects:

(a) The provision for the depreciation of fixed assets under conditions of inflation is totally inadequate to provide for the replacement of such assets. This is because the replacement cost rises with inflation.

(b) Equally, the cost of replacing the stock sold rises directly with inflation and is greater than the original cost of acquiring the stock. The FIFO method of stock valuation which is generally applied in the United Kingdom results in the *undervaluation* of the cost of goods sold under conditions of increasing replacement costs. As a result the gross profit in correspondingly *overstated*.

(c) Finally, there is need to cover changes in the purchasing power of contractual observations stated in money terms.

The general consequence of inflation as regards the determination of income is to lead to an overstatement of net profit, and the danger that a dividend policy relying on such measurements could result in a repayment of capital. From the viewpoint of management, the replacement of stocks under conditions of ever rising prices could result in the firm having to obtain further capital simply to maintain the same physical volume of business.

The search for the most appropriate method of accounting for inflation took the form of a protracted debate which began officially in the United Kingdom with the publication in 1974 of SSAP 7: *Accounting for Changes in the Purchasing Power of Money*, and led in 1980 to the issue of SSAP 16: *Current Cost Accounting (CCA)*, and in 1984 to the issue of ED 35, *Accounting for the Effects of Changing Prices*. In 1985 ED 35 was withdrawn and SSAP 16 was declared non-mandatory.

SSAP 16 (1980)

SSAP 16 applies to quoted companies and entities with a turnover of £5 million or more. It does not apply to insurance companies, property investment companies, unit trusts, and to entities such as building societies, trade unions and pension funds.

SSAP 16 allows historical cost accounts to be retained, but requires current cost accounts consisting of a profit and loss account and a balance sheet with explanatory notes to be published along with the traditional historical costs reports.

In effect, a company under CCA publishes two profit or loss figures—the first derived from the traditional method based upon historical cost measurements which we have discussed throughout this text. These are extracted from the bookkeeping system which still remains based upon money values determined by business transactions. The second profit or loss figures are derived from adjustments made to historical cost measurements for the purposes of correcting for the impact of inflation upon the entity.

SSAP 16 profit and loss accounts provide adjustments to the following items:

(a) Depreciation.
(b) Cost of sales.
(c) Monetary working capital.
(d) Gearing.

Additionally, CCA accounts should contain explanatory notes dealing with earnings per share calculations and setting out the basis and methods used in preparing these accounts.

Fixed assets and depreciation

Current cost accounting is an adaptation of historical cost accounting. It has the objective of converting the valuation of fixed assets from that based on their acquisition cost to the firm (historical cost) to a valuation of such assets based on their current cost to the firm. SSAP 16 defines the current cost of assets as the net current replacement cost, applying in this manner the concept of 'value to the business' as the basis of asset valuation. Where it is evident that the asset concerned has suffered a permanent diminution in value in the hands of the business below its net current replacement cost, the basis of valuation used is the recoverable amount. For example, if the net replacement cost of an asset is established at £1,000 by reference to official statistics, but it is evident that excessive use or other reason has permanently reduced the value of the asset held by the firm to below that figure and the sum which could be recovered through sale is only £400, then the valuation to be shown on the current cost balance sheet is to be £400 and not £1,000.

For the purpose of CCA accounting, fixed assets have been grouped into three main categories:

(a) Plant and machinery.
(b) Land and buildings.
(c) Wasting assets and intangibles.

The net current replacement cost of plant and machinery is relatively easier to ascertain than is that of the other two categories. Special valuation procedures are adopted for the latter two categories of fixed assets. The most common valuation procedure followed for plant and machinery is a reference to a published index, by means of which a single item of machinery or a whole plant may be revalued at the net current replacement cost. The revaluation is obtained by the application to the historical cost of the asset of a factor derived from the index at the current balance sheet date and the index at the acquisition date. This factor is calculated as follows:

$$\frac{\text{Index at balance sheet date}}{\text{Index at acquisition date}}$$

The revised value of the asset is shown on the current cost (CC) balance sheet. Where the net current replacement cost is higher than the historical cost (HC), as will be usually the case under inflation, the difference will be debited to the CC fixed asset account and a corresponding credit shown on the CC reserve account.

Example 1

A machine purchased in 19X1 for £18,000 is being depreciated on a straight-line basis over 10 years. The Index for Machine Classification at 31 December 19X1 and at 31 December 19X4 is 140 and 180 respectively. Assuming that CCA is applied for the first time in 19X4, the accounting procedure will require the revaluation of the machine account to the current cost value at 19X4, as follows:

(a) Written down value in HC records:

$$£18,000 - (£1,800 \times 4) = £10,800$$

(b) Adjusted CCA value:

$$£10,800 \times \frac{180}{140} = £13,886$$

(c) Accounting entries:

		£	£
Dr	CC Machine account	£3,086	
Cr	Reserve account		£3,086

These entries deal with the difference between the HC and the CC asset values.

It may be expected that most accounting systems will show assets recorded at their historical cost. Accordingly, the provision for depreciation account will also require adjustment, when CCA is introduced. In the case of the figures shown in this example, the net adjustment of £3,086 takes account of the adjustment for CCA depreciation as follows:

(a) Increase in asset value on introduction of CCA:

$$£18,000 \times \frac{180 - 140}{140} = £5,143$$

(b) Increase in provision for depreciation on introduction of CCA:

$$£7,200 \times \frac{180 - 140}{140} = £2,057$$

where £7,200 is the provision for depreciation under HC for the four years 19X1 to 19X4 inclusive.

(c) Accounting entries adjusting both the asset account and the provision for depreciation account would be as follows:

		£	£
Dr	Machine account	5,143	
Cr	Provision for depreciation account		2,057
Cr	Current cost reserve account		3,086
		5,143	5,143

Example 1 shows the accounting adjustments required to be made to HC records on the introduction of CCA. A feature of inflation is that the replacement cost value of assets will continue to increase through time. The adjustments shown above would bring the HC figures up to date as at the end of the year 19X4. In subsequent years, the annual depreciation on a CC basis would be calculated by reference to the actual replacement cost established at the end of each accounting year, on the basis of the Index of Replacement Cost values. Therefore, while the provision for depreciation under CCA for the actual year under review would be correct, the provision for depreciation accumulated for prior years would require to be increased. The amount of this increase would depend on the rate at which the replacement costs themselves are increasing. In addition to the annual provision for depreciation which would be charged in the profit and loss account a further charge—known as backlog depreciation—has to be made. In effect, the backlog depreciation is equal to the difference between current replacement cost of the asset and the total current cost depreciation already charged.

It follows that, under CCA, the adjustment for depreciation has two elements:

(a) An adjustment to bring the HC provision for depreciation account up to the CC provision for depreciation *for the year under review*.
(b) An adjustment required to bring the shortfall of previous years' CCA depreciation up to the required accumulated provision for depreciation as at the beginning of the year under review.

The first element (a) is charged in the profit and loss account for the year under review, thereby reducing the net profit for that year, and the second element (b) is transferred directly to the current cost reserve account.

Example 2

Equipment purchased for £10,000 on 1 January 19X0 is depreciated on a straight line basis over 5 years. The company's financial year ends on 31 December.

After applying the appropriate indices, the following replacement cost values are determined:

	£
At 31 December 19X1	11,000
At 31 December 19X2	12,000
At 31 December 19X3	15,000
At 31 December 19X4	16,000
At 31 December 19X5	17,500

The following table shows the figures which will be involved under CCA. (HC Depreciation = £2,000 per year).

End of year	Replacement cost (£)	Transfer to credit of CC reserve (£)	CCA depreciation (£)	CCA adjustment to P & L a/c (£)	Required accumulation CCA depreciation (£)	Actual accumulation CCA depreciation (£)	Backlog (£)
1	11,000	1,000	2,200	200	2,200	2,200	—
2	12,000	1,000	2,400	400	4,800	4,600	200
3	15,000	3,000	3,000	1,000	9,000	7,800	1,200
4	16,000	1,000	3,200	1,200	12,800	12,200	600
5	17,500	1,500	3,500	1,500	17,500	16,300	1,200
				4,300			3,200

The accounts for CCA would appear as follows (remember—companies would keep these as separate working documents):

Equipment account

		£
19X1	Cash	10,000
19X1	Current cost reserve	1,000
19X2	Current cost reserve	1,000
19X3	Current cost reserve	3,000
19X4	Current cost reserve	1,000
19X5	Current cost reserve	1,500
		17,500

HC provision for depreciation account

		£	Cumulative £
Year 1	Profit and loss account	2,000	2,000
	Profit and loss account	2,000	4,000
	Profit and loss account	2,000	6,000
	Profit and loss account	2,000	8,000
	Profit and loss account	2,000	10,000
		10,000	

Current cost reserve account

		£			£
19X2	Backlog depreciation	200	19X1	Equipment	1,000
19X3	Backlog depreciation	1,200	19X2	Equipment	1,000
19X4	Backlog depreciation	600	19X3	Equipment	3,000
19X5	Backlog depreciation	1,200	19X4	Equipment	1,000
			19X5	Equipment	1,500
		3,200			7,500

CCA depreciation adjustment account

			CC reserve	Cumulative Profit and loss account
		£	£	£
19X1	Profit and loss account	200		200
19X2	Profit and loss account	400		600
19X2	CC reserve account	200	200	
19X3	Profit and loss account	1,000		1,600
19X3	CC reserve account	1,200	1,400	
19X4	Profit and loss account	1,200		2,800
19X4	CC reserve account	600	2,000	
19X5	Profit and loss account	1,500		4,300
19X5	CC reserve account	1,200	3,200	
		7,500		

The cost of sales adjustment (COSA)

The purpose of the COSA is to charge against sales the current cost of the goods sold rather than the original cost of acquisition or manufacture, as would be the case under historical cost accounting and the FIFO assumption which applies to stock valuation in the United Kingdom. In the examples given hereunder, all stock movements are assumed to reflect FIFO.

Example 3

A company purchased goods in January for £2,500 and resold them in the following November for £3,500. In the meantime, the replacement cost of these goods increased by £400 to £2,900, which was the amount incurred by the company in November. Under HC accounting, the profit and loss account reflecting these transactions would be as follows:

	£	£
Sales		3,500
Purchases (£2,500 + 2,900)	5,400	
Less: Closing stock	2,900	2,500
Gross profit		1,000

Once the true effects of price changes on these transactions are admitted, it is evident that the gross profit of £1,000 consists of two separate elements. First, there is a gain associated simply with holding the goods from January to November when their value increased by £400 (£2,900−£2,500). This holding gain should be distinguished from the gain made on the sale itself, namely the realisation gain, amounting to £600 (£3,500−£2,900). The realisation gain is linked to the trading activity. Under CCA, the profit and loss account would be as follows:

	£
Sales	3,500
Cost of sales—at current cost	2,900
Gross profit	600

Analysing these transactions in cash-flow terms, the resulting situation would be:

	£
Cash balance—January	2,500
Goods purchased—January	2,500
	—
Sales of goods—November	3,500
Goods purchased—November	2,900
Cash balance	600

Comparing the gross profit under HC and CCA with the cash balance, it is evident that a distribution of £1,000 as dividends—which HC accounting would permit—could not be made without further funds of £400 being subscribed to the company as capital or as a loan.

The purpose of the COSA is to avoid the overstatement of profit under inflation, and in this sense, prevent the distribution of what would be the capital of the business.

(a) *Identifying the cost of sales*

Normal trading operations prevent firms from systematically relating goods sold with their costs. To overcome this problem, it is necessary to establish an averaging process having two components. First, averaging the acquisition of stock in terms of time, to derive an average quantity and average acquisition cost. Second, by using average index numbers, to determine the average cost of sales in terms of their current cost. As in the case of the depreciation adjustment, it is necessary to use an appropriate index for the industrial sector in which the company is operating and establish:

(i) The index at the start of the accounting period to apply to the opening stock.
(ii) The average index for the entire accounting period.
(iii) The index at the close of the accounting period to apply to the closing stock.

Assuming that the goods are purchased evenly across the accounting period, both opening and closing stock shown in terms of HC can be converted into current costs by the use of the following index numbers:

$$\frac{\text{Average index for the period}}{\text{Index at date of purchase}}$$

Example 4

A company had opening stock at 1 January 19X7 of £2,692,000 and closing stock at 31 December 19X7 of £5,374,000—both figures being stated at HC. The opening stock represented two months' purchases and the closing stock three months' purchases. The related current cost index, all stated at month-end were:

19X6	November	146.3
	December	148.2
19X7	October	162.6
	November	168.4
	December	170.2

The average index for 19X7 on a full year basis is, therefore,

$$\frac{(148.2 + 170.2)}{2} = 159.2$$

The calculation of the cost of sales involves three steps.

First, restate the closing stock at average cost. Since this represented three months supply, the mid-point is found at mid-November 19X7. At this date, the index is—

$$\frac{162.6 \text{ (end October)} + 168.4 \text{ (end November)}}{2} = 165.5$$

Accordingly, the closing stock revalued at average cost is:

$$£5,374,000 \times \frac{159.2}{165.5} = \underline{\underline{£5,169,430}}$$

Second, restate the opening stock at average cost. In this instance, since the opening stock represented two months' purchase, the end of November 19X6 index will represent the mid-point index for the purpose of comparing the index at the close of the year 19X7 with that at the beginning of the year 19X7, and determining thereby the current cost of the opening stock as follows:

$$£2,692,000 \times \frac{159.2}{146.3} = £2,929,367$$

Third, calculate the difference between the opening and closing stock in current cost terms. The stock increase is:

	£
Closing stock at current cost	5,169,430
Opening stock at current cost	2,929,367
	2,240,063

The calculation of the stock variation in current cost terms will reflect a volume change. To establish the cost change associated with inflation, it is necessary to compare the stock variation at HC with that at CC. In the example given above, the price change is as follows:

	£
Stock variation at HC (£5,374,000 − £2,692,000) =	2,682,000
Less: Stock variation at CC	2,240,063
Cost variation	441,937

The figure of £441,937 derived in this manner is the COSA, which in this case is deducted from the HC profit to arrive at the CC profit, this debit being reflected in a credit to the current cost reserve account.

The formula for calculating the COSA is:

$$COSA = (C - O) - I_a \left(\frac{C}{I_c} - \frac{O}{I_o}\right)$$

where C is the closing stock at HC, O is the opening stock at HC, I_a is the average index for the year, I_c is the index at average purchase date of the closing stock and I_o is the index at average purchase date of the opening stock.

(b) *Balance sheet representation of stock under* CCA

The COSA is an adjustment to HC profit which has the purpose of adding cost variations resulting from inflation to the cost of goods sold in calculating CC profit. This cost variation reflects the additional amount which the enterprise has to finance when replacing stock under conditions of inflation.

The principle of restating assets at current cost for balance sheet purposes raises additional problems when dealing with closing stock. In the simplest case, where year-end stocks are low and the stock turnover is high, the difference between the historical cost and the replacement cost of stock is immaterial and no further adjustment to HC stock valuation is really needed. In all other cases, adjustments are required when converting HC stock valuation to CCA figures.

Example 5

Assume, as in Example 4 above, the opening stock at HC at 1 January 19X7 was £2,692,000 and closing stock at HC at 31 December 19X7 was £5,374,000 and that the month-end index numbers were as follows:

19X6	November	146.3
	December	148.2
19X7	October	162.6
	November	168.4
	December	170.2

Assume now that CCA was applied to the year ended 31 December 19X6, as a consequence of which a credit was passed to the current cost reserve account at 31 December 19X6 in respect of the COSA for that year. As it will have been seen in Example 4, the COSA involves the revaluation of both the opening and the closing stock of the accounting period at CC, and comparing the stock variation with that obtained from HC valuations. The closing stock at CC as at 31 December 19X6 was derived from an average index, and not the index at end December 19X6. Therefore, there already exists in the opening stock at 1 January 19X7 an unrealised gain. The

procedure for establishing the balance sheet stock valuation at 31
December 19X7 and adjusting the current cost reserve at that date
is as follows.

First, calculate the unrealised gain included in the opening stock
at CCA valuation:

$$\text{CCA opening stock} \quad 2,692,000 \times \frac{\text{Index at end of period}}{\text{Index at average purchase date}}$$

$$\text{or } 2,692,000 \times \frac{148.2}{146.3}$$

$$= 2,726,960$$

Less: HC opening stock   2,692,000

Unrealised gain   34,960

Second, calculate the unrealised gain included in the closing stock
at CCA valuation:

$$\text{CCA closing stock} = \text{HC} \times \frac{\text{Index at end of period}}{\text{Index at average purchase date}}$$

$$= 5,374,000 \times \frac{170.2}{165.5} \text{ (see Example 4 above)}$$

$$= 5,526,615$$

Less: HC closing stock   5,374,000

Unrealised gain   152,615

Third, the balance sheet stock value under CCA will be as follows:
Current assets—(extract)

	31 December 19X6	31 December 19X7
Stock	£2,726,960	£5,526,615

The adjustments to the balance standing to the credit of the current
cost reserve account are as follows:

	£	£
Debit current cost reserve account	34,960	
Credit opening stock		34,960
being the unrealised gain existing in opening stock at 1 January 19X7		
Debit closing stock	152,615	
Credit current cost reserve account		152,615
being the unrealised gain existing in closing stock at 31 December 19X7		

The net increase in the current cost reserve account is:

	£
Unrealised revaluation surplus as at 1 January 19X7	34,960
Unrealised revaluation surplus as at 31 December 19X7	152,615
Net increase	117,655

The net increase in the current cost reserve account in respect of the year ended 31 December 19X7 will consist of the COSA adjustment calculated in (a) above amounting to £466,006, and the balance sheet adjustment to the closing stock at 31 December 19X7 calculated in (b) above amounting to £117,655:

	£
COSA	466,006
Balance sheet	117,655
Net increase	583,661

The monetary working capital adjustment (MWCA)

SSAP 16 defines monetary working capital as the aggregate of:

(a) trade debtors, prepayments and trade bills receivable, *plus*

(b) stocks not subject to a cost of sales adjustments, *less*

(c) trade creditors, accruals and trade bills payable, in so far as they arise from the day-to-day operating activities of the business, as distinct from transactions of a capital nature. In addition, in certain circumstances where the bank balance and cash float or bank overdraft fluctuates with the level of stock, trade debtors and creditors, a part of that fluctuation, if material, should also be included in the MWCA. Where items of stock have not been subject to the COSA, these too should be included in the MWCA.

Inflation hits the firm by raising the replacement cost of assets used in the business, and requires that extra cost to be financed if the firm is to maintain its operating capacity. The depreciation and the cost of sales adjustments allowed under CCA charge that extra cost against current profits, thereby financing such cost out of profits.

A further financial problem resulting from inflation is that other costs of doing business are also affected by price changes. One important consequence of credit trading is that as credit sales increase in monetary terms (without necessarily increasing in volume terms), firms have to find extra finance to provide this facility. For example if annual sales give rise to average debtor balances of £50,000, and inflation is running at 20% as regards the business, then the annual increase in the average debtor balances—without any increase at all in the volume of sales—will be £10,000. This figure will continue to rise with inflation. Unless the firm can obtain additional finance to continue to maintain its existing credit practices, it will be forced to curtail and ultimately will lose business.

The MWCA has the purpose of allowing a firm to finance the impact of inflation on working capital requirements out of profits. The MWCA takes into account the impact of inflation on both debtors and creditors balances, but excludes the impact of volume changes on these balances. It is calculated by taking the average monetary working capital, defined as above, and multiplying it by the increase in the index of inflation, divided by the average index, as follows:

$$\text{MWCA} = \text{average MWC} \times \frac{\text{Increase in index}}{\text{Average index}}$$

It may be noted that the MWCA requires a strict definition of the items included as trade debtors and trade creditors, and relies also on an averaging process.

The MWCA applies only to items used in the day-to-day operating activities of the business. Trade debtors are defined to include, in addition to those listed as such in the debtors ledger, trade bills receivable, prepayments and VAT recoverable. Trade creditors are defined to include, in addition to those listed as such in the creditors ledger, trade bills payable, accruals, expense creditors and VAT payable. Creditors and debtors associated with fixed assets transactions should not be included.

Example 6

Assume that the opening balance of trade debtors and trade creditors at 1 January 19X7 amounted to £836,420 and £420,140 respectively, and that the closing balances at 31 December 19X7 were £1,568,760 and £736,290 respectively. Assume, too, that included in trade debtors and trade creditors were the totality of items falling to be considered in the MWCA. The average age of all items included in trade debtors and trade creditors is one month.

Assume also that the relevant index numbers that apply to the MWCA items are those which applied to the COSA in Example 5, namely,

Opening MWCA items	30 November 19X6	146.3
Closing MWCA items	30 November 19X7	168.4
Average for the year ended	31 December 19X7	159.2

First, ascertain the relevant monetary working capital:

                                                        £
Opening MWC   (£836,420 − 420,140) = 416,280
Closing MWC   (£1,568,760 − 736,290) = 832,470

Second, calculate the variation in the MWC during the period:

	£
Closing MWC	832,470
Opening MWC	416,280
Increase in MWC	416,190

This increase represents the unadjusted change in the volume of MWC.

Third, restate the closing and opening MWC in terms of average value and thereby identify the *effect* of the change in the volume of MWC in adjusted terms:

$$\text{Adjusted closing MWC} = \frac{\text{Closing MWC at HC}}{\text{Closing index}} \times \text{Average index}$$

$$\text{Adjusted opening MWC} = \frac{\text{Opening MWC at HC}}{\text{Opening index}} \times \text{Average index}$$

Using the above formula, the net effect of the volume change in MWC is:

£

$$\text{Adjusted closing MWC} = \frac{£832,470}{168.4} \times 159.2 = 786,990$$

$$\textit{Less: Adjusted opening MWC} = \frac{£416,280}{146.3} \times 159.2 = 452,985$$

Adjusted increase in MWC	334,005

Fourth, the MWCA may now be calculated by deducting the adjusted increase in MWC from the unadjusted increase, thereby reflecting the impact of inflation on the amount invested in the MWC. On the basis of the above figures, the MWCA is:

	£
Unadjusted increase in MWC	416,190
Adjusted increase in MWC	334,005
MWCA	82,185

The formula used for calculating the MWCA is similar in nature to that used for the COSA, as follows:

$$\text{MWCA} = (C - O) - I_a \left(\frac{C}{I_c} - \frac{O}{I_o} \right)$$

where O is the opening MWC, C is the closing MWC, I_a is the average index for the period, I_o is the index number appropriate to opening MWC and I_c is the index number appropriate to closing MWC.

The gearing adjustment

The capital structure of a company describes the manner in which the cost of assets has been financed: the gearing represents the relative proportion of shareholders' capital to loan capital in the capital structure. A company which is highly geared will have a relatively high proportion of loan capital in its capital structure.

Shareholders tend to gain at the expense of lenders under inflation, since the loan capital is repayable in fixed monetary terms, that is, loan repayments are fixed at the amount originally borrowed, and are not adjusted for inflation. Inflation acts to transfer wealth from lenders to shareholders, and effectively helps shareholders to finance the cost of maintaining the operating capability of the business by replacing assets at the expense of lenders.

The purpose of the gearing adjustment is to calculate the current cost accounting profit attributable to shareholders by *adding* the benefit flowing to them from the extent of gearing to the current cost profit.

The gearing adjustment is calculated in three stages: first, the net borrowings, second, the gearing proportion and third, the gearing adjustment itself.

Net borrowings are defined in SSAP 16 as:

'the aggregate of all liabilities and provisions fixed in monetary terms (including convertible debentures and deferred tax but excluding proposed dividends) other than those included within monetary working capital which are, in substance, equity capital',

over

'the aggregate of all current assets other than those subject to a cost of sales adjustment and those included within monetary working capital'.

This definition is wider than the conventional definitions used for the purpose of establishing the gearing, including as it does such items as deferred taxation—implicitly interpreted as financing by the Government, and hire purchase creditors as well as the more usual long-term loan commitments such as debentures.

Example 7
The following CCA balance sheets as at 31 December 19X6 and 19X7 are used to calculate the gearing adjustment:

	31 December 19X6 £	31 December 19X7 £
Share capital and reserves	16,325,000	21,470,000
Proposed dividends	495,000	650,000
Total shareholders interest (the average of which = S)	16,820,000	22,120,000
Net borrowings:		
Debentures	5,000,000	5,000,000
Deferred taxation	830,000	900,000
Bank overdraft	2,600,000	2,100,000
Taxation	510,000	614,000
Monetary assets	(1,600,000)	(2,100,000)
Total net borrowing (the average of which = L)	7,340,000	6,514,000
Total (the average of which = L + S	24,160,000	28,634,000

Using the figure for net borrowings shown above, the gearing proportion may be calculated as follows:

$$\text{average } S = \frac{(£16,820,000 + 22,120,000)}{2}$$

$$= £19,470,000$$

$$\text{average } L = \frac{(£7,340,000 + 6,514,000)}{2}$$

$$= £6,927,000$$

Using the formula $\frac{L}{(L + S)}$, the gearing proportion is:

$$\frac{£6,927,000}{£6,927,000 + 19,470,000} \times 100\% = 26.2\%$$

To ascertain the gearing adjustment, apply the percentage obtained to the full adjustment made to allow for the effect of price changes made under:

(1) The depreciation adjustment.
(2) The COSA.
(3) The MWCA.

Assume for the purposes of this example that for the period under review the depreciation adjustment was £276,000 and that the COSA and MWCA were as shown above. The calculation is then:

Total adjustments

	£
Depreciation	276,000
COSA	441,937
MWCA	82,185
	800,122

£800,122 × 26.2% = £209,632

This final figure of £209,632 represents the amount of capital maintenance reserve which is effectively freed for the equity shareholders from the overall total of £800,122 and to that extent it limits the amount transferred to current cost reserve account.

Using an assumed HC profit and interest figures, the following sets out the impact of all the adjustments on the profit and loss account.

		£
HC profit before interest		4,638,000
Less: Current cost adjustments		800,122
		3,837,878
Interest payable	285,000	
Gearing adjustment	209,632	75,368
Current cost profit before taxation		3,762,510

Note: Throughout these various calculations there has been a large number of 'averaging' assumptions. Accordingly it is unlikely that, in practice, any attempt to refine the actual figures down to anything less than the nearest thousand in this example would be undertaken.

ED 35 (1984)

The disclosure requirements of ED 35 are that financial statements should show the effects of changing prices on the operating capability of the company by giving the following current cost information:

(a) a depreciation adjustment;
(b) a cost of sales adjustment;
(c) a monetary working capital adjustment;
(d) a gearing adjustment (unlike SSAP 16, three gearing methods are offered including one that simply applies the retail prices index to net borrowing);
(e) any other material adjustments to the profit and loss account consistent with the current cost convention;

(f) the effect of the above current cost adjustments on the profit or loss on ordinary activities;

(g) the current cost adjustment in respect of extraordinary items;

(h) the effect of all the above current cost adjustments on the profit or loss for the financial year;

(i) the gross and net current cost of fixed assets, accumulated current cost depreciation, and the current cost of stocks.

In 1985 ED 35 was withdrawn and SSAP 16 was declared non-mandatory. However, the ASC has reaffirmed its view that, where historical cost accounts are materially affected by changing price levels, information about the effects of changing prices is necessary for an appreciation of a company's results and financial position. The ASC has announced that it intends to develop a new accounting standard on accounting for the effects of changing prices to take the place of SSAP 16 in due course. It is intended that the proposed new standard will allow more choice of method than SSAP 16 and that the SSAP 16 methodology will be one of those that would comply with the new standard.

Questions

1. The Athens Dredging Company purchased a tractor on 1 January 19X3 for £3,000. Up to the year ended 31 December 19X5, the tractor was depreciated on the basis of historical cost using the straight-line method. The life of the tractor was estimated at 5 years, and no residual value was envisaged. On the introduction of current cost accounting on 1 January 19X6, the company discovered that the replacement cost of the tractor at that date was £3,000—equal to the original cost of acquisition. During the next two years, the Index for Tractors was as follows:

at 1 January 19X6	100
at 31 December 19X6	120
at 31 December 19X7	115

Required:
Show the provision for depreciation account for the three years to 31 December 19X5. Show the entries which would be required for the years ended 31 December 19X6 and 19X7 following the introduction of current cost accounting.

2. The Summers Leroy Corporation had an opening stock at 1 January 19X7 of £3,500,000 and a closing stock at 31 December 19X7 of £4,200,000—both stock valued at historical cost. The opening stock represented three months' purchases and the closing stock two months' purchases. Current cost accounting has been introduced on 1 January 19X6 and the current cost index for the stock in question (all numbers stated at month end) was as follows:

19X6	October	105.2
	November	107.4
	December	109.7
19X7	November	123.3
	December	124.2

The base index at 1 January 19X6 was 100.

Required:

Calculate the cost of sales adjustment for current cost accounting purposes for the year ended 31 December 19X7 and state the current cost of the stock shown on the balance sheet as at that date. What accounting entries would be required to deal with any adjustments which would be needed for the purposes of current cost accounting?

3. The balance sheet of the Denworth Company as at 31 December 19X6 and as at 31 December 19X7 showed the following items:

	31 December 19X6 £	31 December 19X7 £
Trade creditors	2,354,000	3,002,100
Trade debtors	800,200	1,200,250

Included in trade creditors and trade debtors were all the items falling to be considered in the net working capital adjustment for the purposes of current cost accounting. The relevant index number at month end for the MWCA items were as follows:

Opening MWCA items	19X6 November	104.7
	December	106.4
Closing MWCA items	19X7 November	118.8
	December	120.1

The average age of all items included in trade creditors and trade debtors was one month.

Required:

Calculate the monetary working capital adjustment for the purpose of determining the current cost profit for the year ended 31 December 19X7.

4. The balance sheet of the Austin Brewery Company as at 31 December 19X6 and 19X7 showed the following information:

	31 December 19X6 £	31 December 19X7 £
Share capital and reserves	2,305,792	2,505,898
Proposed dividends	10,000	12,500
Total shareholders interest	2,315,792	2,518,398
Net borrowings:		
Debentures	200,000	200,000
Deferred taxation	17,000	19,900
Bank overdraft	25,000	30,000
Taxation	2,200	3,152
	244,200	253,052

The balance sheets shown above are on a current cost basis. The current cost adjustments made were as follows:

	£
Depreciation	2,000
COSA	3,500
MWCA	4,750

The net profit, calculated on a historical cost basis for the year ended 31 December 19X7, was £30,000 before payment of interest amounting to £20,000.

Required:

Calculate the gearing adjustment to be applied to the current cost profit for the year ended 31 December 19X7. Show the current cost profit before taxation for that year in your answer.

5. The current assets and current liabilities of a high class retail company at the beginning and end of the year to 31 December 1980 are summarised below.

	Opening		Closing	
	£000s	£000s	£000s	£000s
Current assets				
Stock	54		75	
Debtors	40		50	
Cash	21		15	
	—	115	—	140
Less: Current liabilities				
Trade creditors	50		60	
Bank overdraft	30		50	
	—	80	—	110
Net current assets		35		30

The bank overdraft is considered a permanent source of finance. Stock at the end of each year represents purchases made equally during the preceding three months. Debtors represent sales in the preceding two months.

The monthly Index of Stock Prices and the General Price Index was:

	Stock Price Index	General Price Index
1979		
October	115	162
November	117	164
December	118	167
1980		
January	120	170
February	124	174
March	126	178
April	129	175
May	132	176
June	132	177
July	134	179
August	134	180
September	135	181
October	138	182
November	140	184
December	141	186
Average for year	132	177

Required:

(*a*) Explain the purpose of the monetary working capital adjustment.

(*b*) Calculate the monetary working capital adjustment in accordance with SSAP 16 by reference to the data given above (work to the nearest £100).

6. The five-year financial record of a company as presented in the published accounts prepared on the historical cost basis is shown below.

	Year ended 31 December (£m)				
	1980	1979	1978	1977	1976
Capital employed					
Capital and reserves	631	499	421	377	323
Loans	149	29	34	33	35
	780	528	455	410	358
Fixed assets	764	460	326	297	268
Net current assets					
—stock	10	15	25	24	26
—net monetary assets	6	53	104	89	64
	780	528	455	410	358
Profit after taxation	152	78	44	54	37

The indices which represent the price changes appropriate to the particular assets held by the company and the General Price Index over the years were:

	Year ended 31 December				
	1980	1979	1978	1977	1976
Beginning of year					
General prices	188	168	146	117	100
Fixed assets	165	144	121	110	100
Stocks, other current assets and current liabilities	180	160	140	120	100
Average during year					
General prices	197	182	157	135	108
Fixed assets	172	154	133	116	105
Stocks, other current assets and current liabilities	190	170	150	130	110
End of year					
General prices	204	188	168	146	117
Fixed assets	180	165	144	121	110
Stocks, other current assets and current liabilities	200	180	160	140	120

Required:

Present a revised five-year financial record which reflects the application of inflation or current cost accounting principles in so far as the data provided permits, explaining any calculations you made.

7. The recently issued consolidated balance sheet and profit and loss account of a public company, prepared on an historical cost basis, are summarised below.

Consolidated balance sheet	30 September	
	1980	1979
	£m	£m
Capital and reserves	631	499
Loans	149	29
	780	528
Fixed assets		
Cost	1,016	590
Depreciation	232	130
Net	784	460
Current assets		
Stocks	502	304
Debtors	332	211
Liquid funds for day to day use	25	23
	859	538
Current liabilities		
Creditors	405	208
Taxation	20	15
Overdraft	418	234
Dividends	20	13
	863	470
Net current assets/(liabilities)	(4)	68
	780	528

Consolidated profit and loss account for year to 30 September 1980	£m
Turnover—Home	1,246
Turnover—Export	532
	1,778
Trading profit	303
Depreciation (the same rate on all fixed assets)	102
Profit before interest	201
Interest	13
	188
Taxation	30
Profit after taxation	158
Ordinary dividends	26
Retained profit	132

The directors have asked you to prepare current cost accounts in accordance with SSAP 16.

A loan of £120,000 was raised halfway through the year.

The cost of sales adjustment for 1980 has been calculated as £21m and the monetary working capital adjustment as £9m.

There have been no sales of fixed assets during the last five years and those held at the beginning of the year represent purchases of £100m, 130m, 150m, 210m in 1976, 1977, 1978 and 1979 respectively, spread equally throughout each year. They have been depreciated at 10% p.a. including the year of purchase.

The stocks at the year end represent purchases made at the year end (50%) and equally over the year (50%), and similarly for trade creditors. The age analysis for debtors showed that 75% represented year end sales and 25% equally over the year.

The indices which represent the price changes experienced by the particular assets held by the company and the general price index over the years were:

	Year ended 30 September				
	1980	1979	1978	1977	1976
Beginning of year					
Fixed assets	165	144	121	110	100
Stocks	180	160	140	120	100
Other current assets					
and liabilities	180	160	140	120	100
General prices	188	168	146	117	100
Average during year					
Fixed assets	172	154	133	116	105
Stocks	190	170	150	130	110
Other current assets					
and liabilities	190	170	150	130	110
General prices	197	182	157	135	108
End of year					
Fixed assets	180	165	144	121	110
Stocks	200	180	160	140	120
Other current assets					
and liabilities	200	180	160	140	120
General prices	204	188	168	146	117

Required:
(a) Calculate the depreciation adjustment for 1980.
(b) Calculate the gearing adjustment for 1980.
(c) Present the current cost reserve account.

Index